THE RED EXECUTIVE

Well-known for his work on Russian economics, David Granick has taught at Fisk University and the Carnegie Institute of Technology. He has held research fellowships from the Guggenheim Foundation and the Social Science Research Council, and, in 1959–60, he was at the University of Glasgow on a Fulbright grant. He is now Associate Professor of Economics at the University of Wisconsin. His previous works include *Management of the Industrial Firm in the USSR: A Study in Soviet Economic Planning* and many articles for reviews and journals.

THE RED EXECUTIVE

A Study of the Organization Man in Russian Industry

BY DAVID GRANICK

Anchor Books
Doubleday & Company, Inc.
Garden City, New York
1961

The author and Doubleday & Company, Inc., herewith render thanks to Harvard University Press for permission to use an excerpt from *Factory and Manager in the USSR*, by Joseph S. Berliner.

TO THE RUSSIAN AND AMERICAN MANAGERS,
TEACHERS, AND RESEARCHERS
WHO HAVE PATIENTLY PUT UP
WITH MY QUESTIONS

acknowledgments

This book began as a gleam in the eye of my friend, Professor John Attlee, who has been urging me to write it ever since I completed a study of Soviet factory management of the 1930's. It would, however, have gone no further except for a trip to the Soviet Union in the summer of 1958 which was generously financed by the Inter-University Committee on Travel Grants. The writing of this book was supported by the Research Committee of the Graduate School of Industrial Administration, Carnegie Institute of Technology, out of the School's research funds.

My colleagues at Carnegie Institute of Technology have been most helpful in criticizing my comments concerning American industry. Professors Melvin L. Anshen, Myron L. Joseph, Allan Meltzer, Peter Winters, and Harrison White have been particularly generous with their time in criticizing different portions of the manuscript. However, in no sense do they share responsibility either for errors of fact which I may have committed or for my interpretations.

A good deal is owed to three imaginative and painstaking student assistants: Jack W. Walker, Thomas P. O'Mara, and Timothy W. McGuire.

Richard K. Winslow, my editor at Doubleday & Company, Inc., has done yeoman service in seeing the book through. My father has also given helpful editorial assistance.

Most of all, I am indebted to my wife Kaete. Not only did she put up with all the customary but highly frustrating travails of a writer's wife, but she has been my regular, day-by-day critic who helped bring the manuscript into shape.

contents

PART ONE: THE SETTING   1

ONE: BROTHERS UNDER THE SKIN?   3
TWO: TRUTHS AND CANARDS   11

PART TWO: MANAGERS IN THEIR
FORMATIVE YEARS   33

THREE: ANCESTORS   35
FOUR: COLLEGE EDUCATION   46
    How Much?
    What Kind?
    How Is It Learned?
    The Student Himself
FIVE: THE FIRST JOB   74
SIX: WHAT IT ALL MEANS   80

PART THREE: THE MANAGER'S WAY
OF LIFE   87

SEVEN: THE STANDARD OF LIVING   89
EIGHT: THE MANAGERIAL GAME   107
    Ulcers
    Bonuses
    Job Security
    Upward Mobility

PART FOUR: BREAKING UP THE
BUREAUCRACY   117

NINE: THE NATURE OF THE BEAST   119

TEN: BUREAUCRACY AND HOW TO LIVE WITH IT   129
    How We Do It
    Pre-Khrushchev Russia
    The New Russian Organization Chart
ELEVEN: TWO WORLDS   141
    Size of the Bureaucracy
    Organizational Personality
    Communication Upward
    Role of the Market

PART FIVE: WHO RUNS THE BUSINESS?   157

TWELVE: STOCKHOLDERS AND THE COMMUNIST PARTY   159
    American Managerial Revolution
    Clash of the Commissar and Party Secretary
THIRTEEN: LABOR   178
    Informal Groups at Work
    Trade Unions: Immature and Overripe
    Suggestions and the Boss's Ego
FOURTEEN: THE CIRCLE OF CONTROL   201

PART SIX: INSIDE THE FACTORY   205

FIFTEEN: FACTORIES EAST AND WEST   207
    Size
    Materials Handling
    Quality Control
    Maintenance
    The Product and Plant Changeovers
    Shift Work
    Women
    The Worker Goes to School
    Research, Development, and Design
SIXTEEN: RUNNING THE FACTORY   227
    Shop Management
    Budgeting and Production Targets
    Storming
    Maintenance Organization
    Quality-Control Organization
    Flexibility and Size

The Foreman
*Economic and Organizational Pressures in the
  Soviet Plant*

PART SEVEN: RUSSIAN INDUSTRY AND
THE WORLD 249

SEVENTEEN: ECONOMIC COMPETITION 251
  The Rate of Growth
  The Underdeveloped Countries
EIGHTEEN: BUSINESS HANDS ACROSS THE IRON CURTAIN 266
  Trade Makes Friends—and Enemies
  The "Managerial Class"
EPILOGUE 279
SOURCES 283
INDEX 287

part one

THE SETTING

1. BROTHERS UNDER THE SKIN?

Some years ago I finished writing a book about Soviet managerial practice. In the reading of Soviet industrial daily newspapers and the Russian trade magazines, I had discovered a world of management behavior which varied radically from the formal structure described in Soviet textbooks. I was excited. Here, I felt, was the straight story concerning a system of administration completely different from American practice. Certainly this picture bore little relation to generalizations about American business in books I had read on economic theory and on formal organizational procedure.

Then I began talking to people much more knowledgeable than I about American business practice. They also were astonished at my picture of Soviet management. But the reason for their surprise was just the opposite of mine. Why, the Russian managers use the same gimmicks as we do! they said. The Russians have the same organizational problems, and the same ways of handling them. Their managers get around the formal rules of their firms in the same ways as we. I had rediscovered the American world of management, they said.

I was reminded of this experience of mine the other day in reading of an interview with Anastas Mikoyan, the Russian trade czar. The American reporter felt that if Mikoyan were in an American business, he would soon end up owning it. At first glance, this speculation seemed improbable; but when one thought about it, it became quite reasonable. For Mikoyan is a man who has risen high, and has long remained a kingpin in a bitterly competitive managerial system. If Soviet informal management structure is rather like American, one would expect fairly similar types of men to be top executives in both countries.

An American scientist-administrator, back from a Geneva conference on nuclear energy, recently told me that the Russian delegates acted like capitalists. They worried about the cost of producing power by atomic energy versus the use of coal and water power, and their talk was all in rubles and kopecks.

In the summer of 1958, while visiting Russia, I asked a regional industrial administrator how plant managers were persuaded to change their behavior in line with shifts in administrative rules. He spoke of a variety of devices, but a key one was that of closely tying the bonus system for managers to their adherence to the new rules.

I talked with the director of a Moscow manufacturing plant about how he elicited worker suggestions for production improvements. He said that a method used in his plant was to give a bonus not only to the worker making a suggestion, but also to the worker's foreman. The director was here trying to wrestle with one of the real problems found in American industry in operating worker-suggestion systems: the foreman may look at any suggestions coming from his men as a reflection on him for not having thought of the idea first. The Russian management was trying at least to neutralize the antagonism of the foremen, and was using a device which American firms might well consider.

That same summer, Soviet colleges were preparing for a drastic shift in their admission procedures. Where formerly almost all freshmen came directly from high school, now the vast majority were to enter only after an intervening two years at work or in the Army.

I spoke about this change to the administrative officer of a major economic institute, comparable to one of our business schools. His institute had partly shifted over in the previous academic year. Candidates who had worked since graduation from high school were admitted if they passed the entrance exams with a "C" average. But those coming directly from high school had to enter into a competition in which there were twenty applicants for each opening in the freshman class.

Noting this difference in entrance standards, and being heavily under the influence of American magazine articles which had lauded the high and serious purpose of Soviet students, I assumed that students with work experience would drift toward the bottom of the class. No indeed! I was assured. The institute's experience was that students with a background of work were indeed academically below the others during the first semester, having entered under vastly lower standards of admission, but that they were already ahead by the second semester. The reason I was given was one which would sound familiar to any American college teacher: freshmen directly out of high school were not attuned to serious study, were vague as to their future career interests, and in general were not prepared to settle down to working. In short, business-school freshmen in the Soviet Union were—in this respect—like business-school freshmen in the United States.

A last example. On the same trip, I chatted in his Moscow office with one of the country's leading academic authorities on managerial organization. He described an important administrative simplification in the procedure of control over plant managements by higher authorities, and said that it had already been generally put into effect. Yet, when I inquired in administrative rather than academic channels, I learned that this simplification was not in use in any of Moscow's industry, and I received the distinct impression that it was not widely used elsewhere. Russian academic authorities seem to be quite as hazy about Russian management practice as our own people are with regard to American practice. One hears the same complaint from researchers on both sides of the Iron Curtain as to the difficulties of really studying factory structures in depth. In institutions where it is claimed that this has never been a real problem—as in the topflight Leningrad Engineering Economic Institute—research opportunities seem to be a result of close personal contacts between school and plant personnel, with continual consultant arrangements acting as an important sweetener to the relationship. The issue of whether an industry is governmentally planned, or is run as a private enterprise, seems to be rather beside the point in many management areas.

When one thinks of the underlying constraints common to both the American and Russian industrial systems, it is not really so surprising to find similarities between management practices and environments. In both countries, a rapidly growing, modern industrial structure has been built. Both nations have been dominated by frontier aspirations, with a worship of size, speed, and material success. Both share the common traditions of a European-dominated culture.

I am, of course, not saying that Russia and the United States are spitting images of one another. While both are "democratic," Soviet democracy refers essentially to the right of all Soviet citizens to espouse and work for the current line of the Communist Party hierarchy. The constitutions of both countries guarantee freedom of speech, press, and assembly. But the Soviet Constitution explicitly guarantees these freedoms "in order to strengthen the socialist system," and it is the Communist Party Praesidium which decides what will strengthen or weaken the socialist system. Although both countries have trade unions, strikes—the American union's ultimate weapon—are virtually unknown in Russia; the only strike heard of in recent years was within the forced-labor camps shortly after Stalin's death. In both countries, consumers receive money income which they can spend, or not, as they please. Yet in Russia it is the government that decides which goods will be available for them to choose from.

The list of fundamental differences between the American and Russian ways of life is a long one, and there is little need to spell it out here. But there are also similarities, and one finds them in particular when looking at the ways of administration and business management.

In going to any foreign country for a period of time, or even when moving into an unfamiliar social environment within the United States, I have generally noted three stages in my own reactions. My first impression is of strangeness and difference. But once I pierce the surface dissimilarities, my reaction shifts to the opposite extreme. Everything now appears fundamentally the same. All that I can see are the underlying identities, although it is true that these take different forms in different settings. It is only in the third stage, I would suggest, that real knowledge begins. For now I search anew for differences, but this time for those subtleties which are important in structuring the environment and the personalities of people rather than for the obvious elements which first hit the eye of the tourist.

In this book, we must try to operate on the third level of reaction. Let me offer an example.

Soviet managers have been trained in technical institutes narrowly geared to a single industry. They have lived their lives in a tightly planned economic structure, constantly responding to bureaucratic pressures. They are Communist Party members, operating in a world whose lodestone is "Party activity and belief—above all and before all!" What a difference between the Soviet and American manager!

But let us press deeper. Take the director of the Moscow Electric Meter Plant. A man of about forty-five, he was educated as a mechanical engineer—presumably in an institute attached to the optical industry. He worked as assistant foreman, superintendent of a machining shop, and finally as chief engineer in a Moscow optical plant. His career opportunity came when it was decided to convert a toy plant into one producing electric meters; it was he who was chosen to take over the enterprise and build it up. When I met him, eight years later, a fairly progressive plant organization had been developed under his leadership.

Here was a man starting out in one industry, working his way up within it, and then switching to another for major advancement. His technical training was in mechanical engineering, but his current work is in electrical engineering. Narrow specialization? Or not too dissimilar from American managerial experience?

Consider the planning environment within which our director works. Is this so different from the milieu of a plant superintendent, or even of a division head, in a large American corporation? Is it clear that the Russian director's degree of autonomy, within the rules of his organization, is so much less as to put him into the category of "bureaucrat" as compared to the American plant superintendent who plays the completely different role of "independent decision-maker"?

Or consider the Moscovite's Communist Party membership. Does this really matter? Do his views on surplus value and

Communist China affect the way he produces electric meters? Clearly he is not primarily a politician who just happens to be running a plant. Does the political issue have any relevance at all?

Yet . . . yet. We must push further. Given the similarities between the Russian and the American manager, what are the differences?

The college training of the Russian is that of an engineer. He has had to pick up his accounting, some statistics, and his ideas as to organization and administration mostly while on the job. His American counterpart would more likely be a business-school graduate. Both may have ended up with the same background, but they have got it in reverse order.

Will this different ordering in the learning process, this difference in formal education, affect what the Russian and American managers think is important? Will it influence the choice of long-run problems which get to the top of their desks instead of remaining buried in the papers? It is hard to dismiss these differences as irrelevant.

Will it matter that the prototype of the previous generation of top management was radically different? For the American, it was the "cut-and-try" businessman, scornful of theory and eggheads, interested in his own operation and caring little for society as a whole. For the Russian, it was the dedicated professional revolutionary, moving into whatever line of endeavor the Communist Party sent him, knowing little about the technical details of his industry, convinced that proper theory —both in social events and in the natural sciences—is the salvation of mankind. Are these differences as to the history of management in the two countries unimportant? Will they not affect the behavior of current managers, whether by their acceptance or rejection of the earlier traditions?

Let us return to the planning environment within which the Russian manager functions. Marketing is not a problem; he can sell everything he produces. Salesmanship, advertising, product design to meet the competition and make obsolete last year's model: all of these major American problems disappear. But procurement! The placing of unscheduled orders for materials in the middle of the year! Here is a genuine Soviet problem area.

Is it really evident that we can ignore the Communist Party membership of the Soviet director? But then, how about indoctrination in large American corporations? Are the differing emphases as between American firms irrelevant to their operational behavior? Can we dismiss the question of whether a firm's policy is to strive for safety through high cash reserves or for expansion and commitment of funds? Whether its major concern is for immediate or long-run problems? What its attitude is toward labor relations, or toward the proper degree of centralization of management? In the continuing process of striving for conflicting subgoals—subordinate only to an often nebulous "profit" objective—can we disregard the differences in subgoals which are stressed by the various firms?

If American firms are deeply concerned with having a policy for their management teams, and if these differences in policy really matter, would we not expect the factor of indoctrination to be at least as vital a source of contrast between the United States and Russia as between individual American firms? Particularly since the Russian indoctrination goes back in the manager's life to adolescence and even to childhood?

In this book, we shall concentrate on two aspects of the managerial problem. Who are the managers? What is their education, their politics, the base point from which they view the world? Secondly, what are the pressures and incentives which circumscribe their world? What do the managers have to accomplish, and how do they do it? How do Russian managers and their environment differ from what we see in America?

At this point, I must frankly confess to being opinionated. The management world in all countries is heterogeneous. Which are the dominant trends, which the minor ones? Often no one knows, even about American industry. Definitive research has not been done. The observer has impressions; doubtless they are often biased or simply wrong. But in comparing countries, it is precisely the dominant trends in each which are of key importance; the overlap of individual cases around these trends will be wide indeed. So I feel no need to apologize for the fact that it will often be debatable whether my "dominant trends" are truly the most important, or even whether they are trends. I am aware of the problem, and I hope that the reader will remain aware of it also. One comforting thought: it is probably no more difficult to pick out the dominant trends in the field of Soviet management than in that of American management.

2. TRUTHS AND CANARDS

It is usually considered sound administrative procedure to avoid, wherever possible, asking permission for dubious activities. In the Soviet Union, visits by tourists to research institutes fall into this category. Thus, when I wished to visit the Research Institute attached to the State Planning Commission, I simply went there without any by-your-leave.

When I arrived, I was greeted with rather more formality than I had experienced during the preceding two weeks in the Soviet Union. A young, efficient-looking guard at the entrance stopped me with a military salute. This reception was a far cry from the sweet old lady doorkeeper at most Soviet buildings, who will generally ignore you if you walk by resolutely, acting as though you belonged there and knew exactly where you were going. The guard wanted to know my business; I gave it. He telephoned the office, and a young economist came to escort me upstairs to the office of the assistant director of the institute.

From here on, all proceeded normally. I spoke briefly to the assistant director, told him that I wished to talk with some of the institute's economists, and gave him a list of the problems I wished to ask about. He said that he would make arrangements. (A week later I had a three-hour interview.)

These formalities over, my guide and I chatted. He was a bright economist, in his mid-twenties, and surprisingly familiar with American economic writing about the Soviet Union. He asked what various American scholars were now doing, and who was now teaching what at the different American universities. Except for the fact that we were talking in Russian, the whole visit was much like one I might have had at an American institution housing classified documents.

It was only when we turned to a discussion of American industry that the tone changed. I pointed out to him that there was no good factual evidence for a substantial increase in the degree of monopoly during the past half century and that, if anything, the weight of the evidence pointed toward a mild decline. He in turn pointed out to me that Marxian economic theory proved the inevitability of an increase in monopoly, and he gave me a quick rundown of the relevant sections of a course in Political Economy I. I was willing to give him points for theory, but appealed back to the facts. "The facts be damned," was obviously his feeling; he *knew* the truth of the matter. Finally, he cited some data which was clearly beside the point. We left it at that.

I have thought of this conversation many times since. This young Soviet economist had a fairly simple view of America. He accepted a theory which predicted trends of development, and if facts conflicted with it—then the worse for the facts.

Now this intellectual position is not quite as nonsensical as it sounds. "Facts" often have the discomforting characteristic of later turning out to be not true at all. The history of the natural sciences and of invention is full of cases of men who ignored the "facts"—followed their theories or hunches—and proved to be right. All the same, it would seem that the odds are against you when you ignore whatever weak collection of "facts" do exist.

Soviet social science has certainly suffered from its certitude in *a priori* knowledge of America. But Russian Marxists are not the only ones to accept a simple image of a foreign society, drawn from a theoretic concept of what seems reasonable. Americans also have been known, on occasion, to suffer from the same disease.

Soviet society is a complex one. Russia is a big country. One can find evidence for "the things everyone knows" about Russia—and plenty of counterexamples also. In this chapter, I shall try to show some of the variety.

"Everyone knows that Russian managers have no authority, and all decisions are made at the top."

For the American tourist, it is a major undertaking to get

into a Russian factory. The Soviet agency Intourist—which is supposed to handle all of the official contacts between the tourist and Soviet institutions—is primarily organized for arranging museum visits, buying theater tickets, etc., and in most towns is quite at a loss in going beyond this.

When I had been in Moscow for several days and had not received any answer to my request to see factories, I decided that direct action was in order. Moscow is full of kiosks where, for a price varying between three and seven cents, one can get addresses, telephone numbers, and directions. I asked for the address of a well-known machine-tool plant, took an Intourist car to the plant gate, and told the driver not to wait. He drove off readily, and I was on my own.

"Red Proletariat," an old Moscow plant, is a collection of fairly small multistory buildings. The main building faced on the street, and I walked in. From the entranceway, I could see some of the shop operators working; but in between was a guard checking passes. I decided to try to bull my way through and got in line behind a couple of Russians who seemed to be new workers.

When I reached the guard, I asked for the chief engineer of the plant—a man comparable to an American plant superintendent. The guard treated my question as routine, and sent me around to the office which provides passes. This was in a separate building located further within the plant grounds, but apparently there was no objection to a stranger walking around alone in the factory area.

The office for distributing passes was a crowded one. There were some women, who seemed to be new workers, and several men, apparently agents from other plants or organizations, who were waiting to carry on their business in the plant. The phone in the waiting room was in frequent use for intraplant calls.

When my turn in line came, I told who I was and whom I wanted to see. Consternation. Did I want a job? Was I sent there on business by some other Russian organization? Where were my papers? Sure enough, just as I had claimed, I had a foreign passport.

At this point the clerk called over a guard who seemed in

charge, and with relief turned my case over to him. The guard retired with my passport into a far corner of the room and examined it with suspicion. When he reached the point of carefully examining all visa stamps from countries other than Russia, it was clear that he was simply stalling until he could think of something to do with me.

Meanwhile, some of my fellow benchwarmers in the waiting room joined in. If I wanted to see the chief engineer, why didn't I call him? Here was the phone; they knew his extension and supplied it. It seemed a better idea than depending on the guard, but I felt committed to the ways of officialdom.

Finally, the guard came back with a new address for me. He couldn't give me a pass; but if I'd go to the Regional Economic Council, they could supply one. The Council had a special Sector for Foreign Relations, and I was their problem.

This was a new angle for getting into plants, one which Intourist had never mentioned, so back I went to the center of town. At the Sector for Foreign Relations I was greeted with open arms. What would I like to see? I named four plants. Were those the only ones? Weren't there any more? I gave ten more names. I asked to see one of the officials in the Regional Economic Council. Fine! They would arrange things. I should call back in two days.

I called back. Embarrassment. Yes, I could see the official in the Council (I did), but the factories were a different proposition. They had called each of the plants I had mentioned, and in each case were turned down. The managers were busy, and none could spare the three to four hours which would normally be involved. There was nothing to be done; the plant managers had the last word.

Later, I tried again through another, and presumably more impressive, staff organization. Again promises, and again a veto from the plant level.

Here, apparently, was a normal line-staff relationship. The staff sectors of higher bodies could intercede, but the decision was a line one on the local level.

In another situation, however, plant managers were much less independent. In the Moscow City Council organization, I talked with the man in charge of all industry under the City

Council. After our interview, he too promised to arrange a plant visit.

This time, when I called back, the appointment was on. I was to come to the Moscow City Council and go out from there to the plant. When I arrived, the director of the factory I was to visit was waiting for me. Apparently, he had been unceremoniously summoned to meet me downtown and personally escort me to his plant. It was quite clear that in this case, with a line official making the arrangements, the plant director was not asked for his consent.

"Everyone knows that Russia is a land of secrecy and watchfulness, where security-consciousness-plus reigns supreme."

Buildings which house institutions of any type—universities, courts, administrative bodies—all have doorkeepers whose job it is to learn your business before you may enter. No one, Russian or foreigner, is allowed to enter even such an innocuous institution as a university without a special pass. This is bad enough, but for the foreigner there are further provisions. If you order a car through Intourist, you must say where you are going, and the information is entered into a bound volume as a semi-permanent record. The theory as to security is rigid indeed.

The practice, however, is a good bit more pliant. Only once was I ever kept from entering a building for lack of a pass; this was at the New Moscow University, a tourist haven. Yet when I told this fact to my Moscow guide, she seemed honestly surprised that I had never been stopped before. At the University of Kiev, the university president is apparently a stickler for regulations. Three or four times a year, according to a student there, he personally stands at the university entrance to check on student passes. But since half of the students will have left their passes in their rooms, classwork is pretty thoroughly disrupted on these mornings.

In Moscow, Leningrad, and Kiev I wandered freely through buildings housing the City and Regional Economic administrative bodies. When I had appointments there, my hosts would sometimes escort me part way out of the building when we were through, but usually they were quite happy to return to work when I protested that I could find my own way out.

Even the regulation requiring Intourist to know where you are going by car is only loosely enforced. It is quite acceptable to say that you'll be "driving around the city." Furthermore, Intourist is only interested in your first stop; they have no record of any additional ones. Finally, there is nothing to prevent the foreigner from walking or taking a bus, streetcar, or cab and completely ignoring Intourist.

Communist Party buildings and meetings are said to have far stricter security provisions than those I encountered. Even here, however, theory and practice seem widely separate. A Ukrainian secretary of a Young Communist League student group claimed she never carries her membership card, even to show at large meetings where she is not personally known, and yet has never been kept out of a meeting for this reason.

"Everyone knows that the standard of living of the Russian man on the street is practically nonexistent."

Housing is the strongest case for this. In Kiev, where new apartment houses were still going up at great speed in 1958, space per family even in the new buildings was extremely tight. Apartments were being built with one to three rooms, plus bathroom and small kitchen. It was just as well that few refrigerators are available in the Soviet Union, for a family which owned one could never fit it into one of these "compact" kitchens. But the most striking feature to an American is the size of family required to qualify for one of these apartments. An apartment of three rooms is intended for seven to eight people, two rooms for five or six people, and any smaller family is expected to fit into one room. These rooms seemed medium-sized—about 165 square feet apiece.

Soviet official statistics for 1956 show that Kiev was just average for Soviet cities, with 83 square feet of housing space per capita—including halls, kitchens, bathrooms, and closets.

A Moscow court case which I attended illustrated in comic form the consequent situations. It was a civil case, brought by a woman against her former husband who was still officially registered as living in her apartment. He had actually not been there for several years, for he was living elsewhere in Moscow with a second wife. But since he was still officially registered in his first wife's apartment, he had the legal right to return whenever he wished. The woman wanted his name expunged from the register.

The husband put forth a fascinating defense. His second wife's apartment was crowded, he said. It was a single room of 130 square feet and he, his wife, their baby, and his mother-in-law were all living there. His second wife refused to allow him to be registered as officially living in this apartment, for who knew what might happen in the future? They might separate, or—apparently a greater risk—he might bring into the apartment his child by his first wife; for this child was still registered on his passport. But, the husband insisted to the court, he had to be registered as living somewhere. It was the law. Where should he go? To the moon?

The court granted the first wife's request for removing his name from the apartment's register. Although the judge and the spectators found the case a bit on the farcical side, I felt a sneaking sympathy for the second wife, who wished to be absolutely certain that a fifth person would not legally be jammed into her single room.

This is one side of the Russian living standard. But there is the other side, symbolized by the mystery which bothered me all through my stay in Russia: the case of the missing children.

Walk down the streets of the big cities in the summertime; look in the parks; go to the housing developments: no kids. Only a handful can be seen of all those between infancy and fourteen to sixteen years old. Where are the children?

Off at camp, was the answer I was given for the older ones. For the younger ones, their nurseries and kindergartens simply moved lock, stock, and barrel out to the country. The kids were on vacation.

A Moscow factory operated a Pioneer camp for the children of its own workers. The factory had a total labor force of 400, and the camp had room for 360 school-age children at a time. The director said that children went either for one month or for the entire summer, depending on the parents' wishes. According to the director, most parents were not charged any-

thing for the camp. The maximum charge is 90 rubles per
month per child ($9 at the tourist exchange rate) compared
to a cost of operation of 600 rubles per month per child; the
subsidy was contributed equally from factory and trade union
funds.

I could not believe that most of Russia's children really got
away from the big cities during the summer. But if not, where
were they? I was forced to conclude that the story I was told
seemed to be borne out. Later, I checked official Soviet statistics for the entire urban population of the country. Estimates
from the data for 1955 (the latest year available) showed
that 60 per cent of all the seven- to thirteen-year-olds went
away during the summer in some organized group fashion,
and over one fourth of the total went to camp. The 60-per-cent
figure does not include those many children who simply went
to the country with their families.

This is the difficulty with comparing living standards in different countries. Minimum housing by American standards is
the height of luxury in Russia. But summer camp, a major
expense for those American parents who can afford it, is commonplace and virtually free of charge for Russian urban
dwellers.

*"Everyone knows that Soviet working conditions are terrible
—a throwback to the nineteenth century."*

At the Moscow airport, waiting for the plane to Kharkov,
I chatted with two American engineers. They had recently
visited the Kharkov Tractor Plant, which was first built in the
early 1930's and is still one of the major factories in the Soviet
Union. Their main impression was one of dismay at the lack
of safety precautions. Dangerous conditions extended even to
such matters as slippery floors in the work areas.

In the various plants I visited, slippery floors were not a
problem. But one could not help being impressed by the relative absence of safety devices on presses and cutting-machine
tools. This was despite the fact that, in each town, I was clearly
taken to see one of the more efficient plants.

The American iron and steel delegation, also visiting Russia
that summer, was told that there were about 720 lost-time

accidents during 1957 in the Magnitogorsk steel works. These accidents included four fatalities and six cases of severe disability. This accident rate is about twenty-three times as high as that of the American steel industry.

The "Hammer and Sickle" combine motor plant in Kharkov is an old plant in name only, for it was almost completely destroyed during the war. I was shown around the machine shop, the foundry, the forging-pressing shop, and the main assembly building, all of which have been built since the war. It is a plant with new buildings, an old reputation, and a skilled work force, and thus should be highly favored as industrial factories go.

Despite these advantages, there seemed to be only one toilet for each large building. Water fountains existed, but they were so scarce that I noticed only one on my tour. Nothing resembling Coke machines existed; there was no traveling canteen; the coffee break was an unknown institution. In the "workers' state," worker amenities seemed to have a low priority indeed.

At present, instead of a coffee break, a physical-training break is being tried. In early 1959, Moscow News reported that over 400,000 workers in Moscow factories were involved in this organized exercise. Salutary results for industrial safety have been claimed.

Yet, to show the other side of things, I spoke to an American who had sold agricultural equipment to the Russians, and he recalled a discussion of a particular machine. The Russians agreed that his machine was both cheaper and more efficient than a competitor's—but still it was unacceptable. It was too noisy and made the operator too dirty; better to have a less efficient machine which provided superior working conditions.

The chief engineer of a Leningrad plant, discussing mechanization which he had introduced, insisted that one important criterion for judging a given mechanization proposal was its effect on the amount of worker strain in plant operations. Now it may or may not be true that this criterion has been operationally important, but certainly worker conditions are *thought of* by Russian managements when they are planning changes—whether they actually do much about them or not. Even this is more than was true of some mineteenth-century managements.

"Everyone knows that the Russian economy is operated as a tightly co-ordinated, planned system."

All major decisions are made within the State Planning Commission, the nerve center of the economy. Investment programs are decided upon—and decisions as to these are linked with plans for output growth in each of the main sectors of manufacturing, trade, and agriculture. Plans are laid as to the number of workers to be employed by each sector. Schedules are worked out for the use of materials. In 1958, the State Planning Commission itself approved the allocation to users of 760 different types of materials, fuels, and equipment.

These decisions, in turn, get siphoned down to the level of the individual plant. A director receives a yearly program for his factory which tells him how much he is to produce, what his product-mix is to be, how many workers he can hire and how much he should pay them. He receives allocation orders for the materials and fuels he needs, and there is little he can buy without these orders. Management's job is to produce the planned output—and more if possible—with the inputs given to it.

Moreover, the factory's inputs and outputs are stated both in physical terms (X tons of steel as inputs, and Y number of trucks as output) and in rubles. The director buys and sells at prices set by the government. He is expected to earn a profit, and even has a "plan" for how much this is to be. (The government, as owner, then absorbs virtually all of this profit into the state budget.) Here is a system of planning with a vengeance.

Under these circumstances, industry should be little concerned with the marketing of goods or the buying of materials, for these activities are programmed ahead of time. The Moscow City Council, for example, has roughly 250,000 industrial employees under its control. In this large operation, only about 2 per cent of the total number is involved in buying and selling goods for the various industrial plants. (This 2-per-cent figure, of course, excludes both warehousing workers and all retail salesmen.) This ratio seems quite low by American standards.

At the same time, the Soviet planning system leaves plenty of room for bargaining on the local level. Let us take, for example, the management of a shoe plant. The factory director will be told the total number of shoes to produce, and this total will be broken down into three subgroups for men, women, and children. In addition, he will be given a single ruble figure for the value of his total planned shoe output. But it will be up to him to negotiate with a wholesaling organization as to the particular types of shoes he is to produce.

This arrangement leaves the director a good deal more leeway than appears on the surface. He is given a certain labor force, a specific amount of equipment, and a fixed volume of materials with which to work. It is up to him to try to negotiate the sort of product-mix of shoes which will be easiest to produce with his resources. True, he cannot produce only cheap shoes; for while this would make it easy to fulfill his quota for the number of shoes, their total value would be less than called for by his plan. But there are other, slightly more subtle, methods of juggling his production.

If the director can get away with producing only a few styles of shoes, he will have long production runs and be able to cut costs. If he can bias his production toward small-size shoes and away from large ones, he can save on leather inputs. Finally, although the state sets the prices for his shoes, different styles will yield him different profit markups. The director can try to specialize in those styles which offer the highest profit.

How far the director can go in all this depends on his bargaining position. In the past, this position has been good, indeed. Always less has been produced than the customers would buy. Thus, wholesalers have been fairly easy to deal with; since they could sell anything, why antagonize the producer in a sellers' market? Only the final customer complained bitterly about the results of this system.

In recent years the sellers' market has eased off somewhat. Much greater stocks of goods seem available now than in the past, particularly of items like shoes which are sold to individual consumers. The wholesalers or retail stores which con-

tinue to buy "shoes," without worrying about sizes and styles,
are likely to find too many shoes remaining on their shelves—
and their own sales plans will remain unfulfilled. As the sellers'
market has eased, the wholesalers' backs have stiffened. The
bargaining position has changed. But the bargaining remains;
the "plans" only set the framework within which it occurs.

Where negotiations are important, where state organizations can shop around, the man with the salesman's personality
comes into his own. But in the Soviet Union's sellers' market,
he does not gravitate into sales but rather into purchasing. It
is here that he operates with his expense account, his personal
contacts, his joviality. His bonuses are a substitute for com-
missions. He has even been known to operate as a "five-per-
center."

*"Everyone knows that Soviet managerial recruitment is a
highly organized affair."*

Recruitment begins on the educational level. Generally
speaking, the starting line for the race to Soviet industrial management ranks is today located squarely at the point of graduation from an engineering or business administration institute.
But the number of freshmen entering these institutes is considerably below the number of applicants. It is the schools
which choose their students—although it is true that their
choice is limited to those who voluntarily apply to them.

When the student graduates, the American West Point system applies. The top student chooses his job out of those openings available to graduates; then the next chooses; and so forth
down to the low men on the totem pole, who take what is left.
But all must accept the jobs offered, and stay there for two to
three years. Recruitment of new candidates for the management team is organized in this fashion.

What happens after the three years? In a formal sense, the
man is free to go where he chooses. But all industry is state-
owned, and working one's way ahead within it is like trying
to advance inside a single American company. The young
manager cannot go off and join the competition.

Although there are a few exceptions, managers generally
cannot move up even to the plant-director level without first

becoming Communist Party members. In joining the Party, however, a new and fundamental obligation is undertaken. The Party member must take any position to which he is sent; his services are exclusively at the service of the Party. This tradition is a carry-over of the pre-Revolutionary concept of the Russian Communist Party: that only professional revolutionaries are fit for membership. The Communist Party maintains various personnel bureaus to determine the slots into which its members should be placed.

Thus the ambitious manager joins the Communist Party, but in doing so loses all freedom of movement. He may even be sent into some entirely different field of activity. During a campaign to improve agriculture, the Moscow shop superintendent of a machine-tool plant may suddenly learn that he is now to become a Ukrainian collective farm chairman.

This is the over-all view. But let us look at the recruitment picture as it appears from interviews with Soviet managers.

I asked the director of the Moscow Electric Meter Plant how he came to be appointed. He said that he was asked in and offered the job by the representatives of the organization which owned the plant; namely, the Moscow City Council. Thereupon he resigned his post as chief engineer of a factory under the control of an industrial ministry which was quite unconnected with the Moscow City Council. Although he was a member of the Communist Party, he claimed that the Party played no active role in this change of job. It was effected only by the decision of the Moscow City Council organization to offer him a post, and by his own decision to accept this chance for advancement. Here was a type of recruitment which seems quite unorganized—one organization simply pirating away the best management men from wherever it could find them.

The chief engineer of this plant, also a Party member, was hired four years ago when his predecessor went elsewhere to take a better job. He also had been hired away from an industrial ministry, and the director told me the story of how it was decided to make him an offer.

The Moscow Council's industrial staff first nominated the

winning candidate, and then asked the director for his opinion. Since the chief engineer's former plant was in the same part of town as the electric meter plant, the director knew the candidate and okayed his selection. According to the director, he would have been allowed a veto power in this choice of his chief assistant. After the director had approved, the job offer was made.

How does managerial recruitment look from the viewpoint of the man in charge of industry at the Moscow City Council? Recruitment of recent college graduates is completely organized, he said. The Council sends its requests to the Ministry of Higher Education, and recent graduates are sent to it for a two- to three-year period. Here the Council has little choice.

For higher posts, an effort is first made to recruit from inside the organizations under the Council. "Promotion from within" is the policy. But when no good candidate is available here, the personnel department looks elsewhere. How does it go about looking? I asked. Informally, was the answer. It may advertise in the popular newspaper *Evening Moscow;* those who know of the opening will tell their friends elsewhere, and these can apply directly. No formal channels exist for such recruitment.

I asked whether management people feel free to accept an offer, since this means leaving their existing organization. This is no problem, I was assured. An offer of a better position elsewhere is considered a valid reason for resigning a post; nor is the resignation a blot on a man's record. Managerial mobility between plants and even between organizational jurisdictions is common enough; a man is expected to take the best position available.

In all this, no word about the Communist Party. Does this really mean that the Party plays no role in the changing of jobs of Party members? My guess is that, where the Party has no special plans for a particular member, his job can be left to negotiations between him and the hiring organization. Why should the Party interfere in most cases? The Party cannot take an active role in everything. But when the Party organization does care to take a hand, its word is decisive.

"Everyone knows that Russian managers are competitors for power with the Communist Party officials."

Everywhere in Soviet society there stands the Communist Party: the counterpart of the holder of legitimate power. At the topmost rung of society there is the Council of Ministers—and opposite it is the Praesidium of the Central Committee of the Communist Party. In the plant there is the director—and the secretary of the plant committee of the Party.

To quote Stalin, in words which still remain the very heart of Soviet orthodoxy: "The Party is the core of power. The Party directive has the force of law." But the Party directive does not by itself create law; it only defines its direction and purpose. "Party directives are only the kernel of law, just as the Party is the kernel of state power."

This orthodoxy is a solid foundation for permanent built-in conflict. The director of a factory is "responsible" for its operations. But while the words of authority are the director's, the spirit is that of the plant committee of the Party. Among its other duties, the Party plant committee must assure itself that the factory administration makes the proper decisions and carries them out correctly. Moreover, the plant committee means in particular one man: the secretary of the Party committee.

The conflict would be resolved if the Party secretary really ran the plant, with the director taking his orders. But things are not that simple. When a director follows the instructions of his Party committee, and his actions later prove to be wrong in the eyes of the government representatives supervising the plant, the director is personally held at fault. He cannot slough off responsibility. At the same time, if things go badly in the plant, the higher Party authorities will hold the Party secretary to account. Thus, willy-nilly, the two must form a team.

Here, then, we have a problem in small-group behavior. There may be co-operation with equality, but clearly a simpler—if often less satisfactory—relationship is for either the director or the Party secretary to dominate. But if the relationship is to be that of domination and subordination, who will dominate? The answer is not given by the situation, which is unstructured; generally speaking, it will be the stronger personality with the greater personal prestige. But if they cannot work together in any fashion, one or both will be removed by higher-ups.

This structure builds competition for power directly into the management systems. But still, we can ask, is this competition really between Party and management, or just between individuals? After all, the managers normally are also Party members.

One way of getting at this issue is to ask whether individuals almost always remain within the ranks of either Party or management officialdom without crossing over to the other camp. If they do cross over, if this year's manager may well be a Party official next year, then it is difficult to interpret the conflict as Party-management struggle.

I have tried to query Soviet managers about this. Do people switch back and forth between the management and Communist Party hierarchy, I asked, or do they tend to stay in one or the other? When I put the question directly, all agreed that there was little crossing over. But it was clear from the answers of these same people to other questions that they wished to emphasize the tendency of people to remain in the same job. This desire certainly may have biased their answers.

There is another way to get at this same question. Who are the Party secretaries and organizers, the functionaries on the plant level? I tried this form of the question on one high official in a regional economic council who had just been insisting to me that the industrial and Party hierarchies did not intermingle. Oh, he said, a Party organizer in a factory *must* be an engineer! How else could he know what technical problems to look out for in the work of the factory? By "engineer," he elaborated, he did not mean a recent graduate; he meant someone who had not only a degree, but also experience as an engineer in one or more plants.

In interpreting this answer—which, it is fairly clear, represents some degree of exaggeration—one must remember the role of the engineer in Soviet plants. A typical starting job for him is as assistant foreman. Management ranks above the foreman level seem mainly staffed with engineers. A man chosen as Party secretary in an important plant would be moving into a tough administrative post, and he would be expected to have had responsible administrative experience. It seems a fair guess that engineers chosen for Party posts have not served their apprenticeships in design or in methods departments, but rather in management positions.

Clearly, movement also sometimes runs from Party to management ranks. Thus, the United States iron and steel delegation in 1958 reported that the director of the major steel plant in Chelyabinsk had a few years earlier been Party secretary of that area.

Furthermore, when we think of the Party secretaries, we must remember that many hold these posts as leisure-time activities. In smaller plants, the secretary will be a full-time factory employee, just like the president of a small union local in American industry.

In one such plant with a labor force of four hundred, I was told that the current Communist Party secretary was in charge of planning and scheduling for the factory and had a business-school education. Moreover, he had not come to the plant as Party secretary, but had originally been hired in the dispatching office. Some time after he became head of planning—a key management post within the plant—he was also elected Party secretary. It is hard to believe that when he and the plant director differ, whether it occurs when both are wearing their management hats or in the evening when they are acting as members of the Communist Party plant committee, either interprets the clash as a management vs. Party fight.

"Everyone knows that since there is no free enterprise in Russian industry, incentives for management are very weak."

The Soviet Union is a country in which the manager has no possibility of starting his own business and gaining future financial independence in this way. He cannot share in his firm's profits through becoming a partner or by stock options. He has no path to wealth through capital gains and stock purchases of growth companies.

Even when he has plenty of money, there are things he would badly like to have but which are simply not for sale. He cannot rent a larger or better-built apartment by looking in higher-rent areas; there are no free-enterprise builders ready to put up luxury apartments to meet the rental market. He can build his own house, and then own it outright. But he cannot build on the scale he wishes and can afford; building materials are scarce, and allocation orders are required for them. Thus, money cannot be transformed into better housing —for the profit incentive of the builders is missing.

It is not so easy for the manager to pass on his advantages to his children. Think, for example, of education. Tuition is free for all—right through postgraduate training. But partly as a result of this, there is a tremendous press of students at the college level. The father's ability to meet a high tuition bill offers his children no advantage in the severe competition for entrance into the freshman class. The major work incentive of being able to pass on his advantages to his children is lost to the Soviet manager. The children must stand on their own feet.

But, of course, the Soviet manager has financial incentives of his own. These are far from negligible.

Take salary and bonuses. In one Leningrad plant of the food industry which I visited, earnings of average workers were 700–800 rubles monthly. At the same time, the monthly salary of the plant director was 3000 rubles, and he earned monthly bonuses averaging 1500–1600 rubles. In Moscow, the head of all construction work under the City Council, building twelve million square feet of housing a year, receives a monthly salary of 4000 rubles. He was singled out to me as a man who regularly earns "high bonuses"; in construction, the top bonus permissible is equal to the basic salary. So here was a man with an income of probably 7000–8000 rubles. This is perhaps nine to ten times the monthly earnings of the average worker in his organization.

It seems reasonable to think of directors of plants with a total labor force of 500–1500 employees as receiving something in the order of five to six times the earnings of the average worker. To see this in American terms, the average wage earned by an American worker employed all year in manufacturing in 1957 was $4300. An American plant director would have to earn $22,000 a year in order to attain the same position relative to the average American worker as the Russian director holds compared with the Russian worker. One small-scale 1957 study of American firms showed that, in actual fact, the top policy-making executive in firms of under 1000 employees earned an annual average of $28,000 in salary and bonus.

Moreover, we have not considered the tax angles. The top income tax rate in the Soviet Union is only 13 per cent. Take a Russian director with three children: his tax will be about 12 per cent of his income. Our American manager earning $22,000 a year, also with three children, would pay some 17 to 19 per cent in tax.

Yet, before we go overboard, let us remember what the Soviet manager earns in absolute terms. Our Leningrad director, earning 4500 rubles a month, is still only receiving an annual gross of $5400 at the tourist exchange rate of 10 rubles to 1 dollar. This is just 25 per cent more than the wages of the average American factory worker.

Let us come back to the manager's problem in educating his children. Have we really painted the whole picture when we said that his money and position give him no advantge here?

One obvious consideration comes to mind. Personal favors play their role in any society. A plant manager is more likely to be able to exercise some influence—especially in marginal cases—than is a loom operator. It is, of course, impossible to know how important a role is played by influence. We hear or read the occasional complaint about it. But, by and large, college admissions officers do not discuss the matter.

Another consideration, curiously enough, is purely financial. Soviet college students receive free tuition, but the problem of living expenses is still a real one. Where do they get the money for this?

The regular day student does not work on the side during the academic year. It is unclear whether school authorities would forbid him to do so if the situation arose, but apparently no student tries. Studying is considered a full-time occupation.

Soviet colleges do, however, give cash stipends to their students. But to qualify, one needs about a "B" average. Higher stipends are given to those with all "A's." The pressure is on.

Now this means that the academic standard set for stipends is about that equivalent to Dean's List in an American college. True, since admissions standards are much higher than in most American colleges, only about 20 per cent of Soviet college students fall below this level. But this marginal group must get financial help from home if it is to study. It is here that a manager's income can be a real help to his children—a mixed satisfaction.

"Everyone knows that a Russian manager's job is a risky one. The pay may be good, but life expectancy is short."

The Russian manager works within a fine mesh of rules, procedures, and detailed targets for all aspects of his operations. If he breaks these rules, he is not simply violating company policy. He is committing a criminal offense under Soviet law; for it is sacred Soviet dogma that "The Plan is law!" Yet, if the manager is to operate at all, he must cut red tape. It seems a fair generalization that all Soviet managers are, *ipso facto*, criminals according to Soviet law.

Clearly, this does not mean that they are all regularly hailed into court. Yet the past record in this regard has not been good.

Many Soviet managers of the 1920's and early 1930's were people who had gained their experience before the Revolution. This meant that, in Communist Party eyes, they were tainted by their bourgeois past. Always they were suspect of desiring a return to the old regime, and the accusation of sabotage came easily to the fore. Machinery breakdowns—common in a period of vast industrial expansion with an unskilled labor force—were likely to be followed by court proceedings or, even worse, by secret police hearings.

By the mid-thirties, these managers had largely disappeared. A new generation of long-time Communists had taken their places. But the great purges of 1936–38 cleared out this group as well. Their jobs made them centers of attention, antagonism, and envy—and this was dangerous indeed in this period of storm.

There were possibilities of this purge re-occurring during the years at the end of Stalin's life, and during the political infighting among his successors. But the fact is that it did not take place. It seems clear that the labor camps were virtually emptied of political prisoners and have not been refilled. There are no indications that changes of top personalities in the Soviet Union have strongly affected the fate of managements at the plant level or even at somewhat higher strata. Soviet managerial life has not again been caught up in the turmoil of the thirties. Even the legal situation has eased somewhat, with managers recently being freed from criminal responsibility for some of their production failures. The unsuccessful manager today is not likely to be faced with anything worse than demotion.

All the same, it cannot be comfortable for the Soviet manager to have constantly to pursue—in the normal course of duty—activities which are criminally punishable. Yet at this point, it is worth glancing at the American scene for perspective.

Back in 1949, Professor Edwin H. Sutherland in his book *White Collar Crime* examined the legal history of seventy of our two hundred largest nonfinancial and nonutility corporations. He traced the records for the number of convictions of these corporations and their subsidiaries during the corporate lifetime—which averaged forty-five years. Most convictions seem to have occurred during the fifteen-year period after 1934.

Of the seventy corporations examined, 60 per cent had convictions entered against them in criminal court. For this 60 per cent, the average number of convictions was four apiece.

This record would seem to indicate that Russian managers are not alone in finding that one cost of doing business is the violation of some laws. Moreover, just as the American business community generally looks upon these as "technical" rather than "real" crimes, the same seems to be true of the Soviet business community.

Thus, one Russian manager boldly stated—and not just in private conversation but in a signed article in a newspaper with national coverage—that the zealous plant director must be willing to juggle his books so as to cover necessary expenditures from grants made for other purposes. It was clear that he considered complete obedience to the rules and laws governing Soviet industry as the sure sign of a ne'er-do-well manager.

part two

MANAGERS IN THEIR FORMATIVE YEARS

3.   ANCESTORS

Men are a product of their history as well as of their environment. A man's history begins before he is born: in his family background. Presumably, a nation whose managers are all Back Bay Boston Cabots should function differently from one whose managers come from the wrong side of the tracks.

An example of the importance of family origin can be seen in France. One acute observer of the French scene, David Landes, describes the typical French business as a family firm. The manager is not a professional, but rather is the representative of his family—and views his business in terms of the continuity of the family over the centuries. His overriding goal is not profits, expansion, or efficiency—but rather security for the firm and unchallenged control over it by the family. Growth and increased profits, when they can be achieved only through borrowing or by diluting ownership, are viewed as baubles for which the sensible manager will not strive. In Landes' words, "The French family firm, when successful, is as solid as a rock precisely because it is almost drowned in its own liquidity."

Although one may dispute Landes' characterization of French business, it illustrates well the role in management which family background can play. Still, we should be cautious in theorizing as to precisely what its importance normally is. One might expect, for example, that those who have risen out of poverty will be better disposed to their fellow men. Yet Edgar Lee Masters reminds us that this is a dangerous generalization, and warns us to

> Beware of the man who rises to power
> from one suspender.

Studies of American business leaders show a considerable tendency for these executives to have come from business or professional homes. There is dispute as to whether this trend has become stronger or weaker over the last century, but it seems clear that it has always been and still is strong.

Mabel Newcomer examined the records of the men who were president or board chairman of the largest American corporations in 1900, 1925, and 1950. She found the following:

OCCUPATION OF FATHER	PERCENTAGE OF THOSE EXECUTIVES SERVING IN		
	1900	1925	1950
Business owner or high corporation official	72	66	69
Professional	22	23	18
Salesman, clerk, or minor administrator	4	4	6
Manual worker	1	6	8

In an independent study done at about the same time, W. Lloyd Warner and James C. Abegglen questioned 8000 business leaders who represented all levels of top management in substantial companies in 1952. It should not surprise us that Warner and Abegglen found a higher degree of mobility between father and son than did Newcomer, for they included executives at a somewhat lower level of the corporation hierarchy. But even they found that 49 per cent of the executives had fathers who were independent nonfarm businessmen or were executives, and that an additional 14 per cent of the fathers were professional men. (See graph on page 37.)

Warner and Abegglen made an interesting additional calculation. They compared the percentage of fathers in a given occupation with the percentage of all adult American males who were engaged in that occupation during the same period. The son of a businessman had seventeen times as good a chance of becoming a member of American top management as did the son of an average blue-collar worker. (See graph on page 38.)

This degree of class stability between the generations in the

UNITED · STATES

CHANCE OF A MAN IN A GIVEN OCCUPATION HAVING A SON WHO IS A TOP MANAGEMENT EXECUTIVE IN THE UNITED STATES

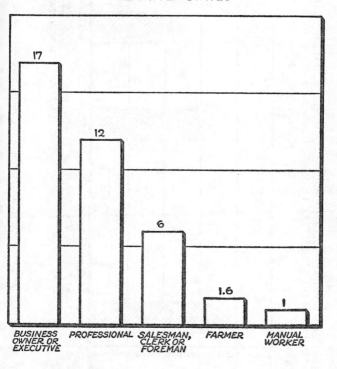

17	12	6	1.6	1
BUSINESS OWNER OR EXECUTIVE	PROFESSIONAL	SALESMAN, CLERK OR FOREMAN	FARMER	MANUAL WORKER

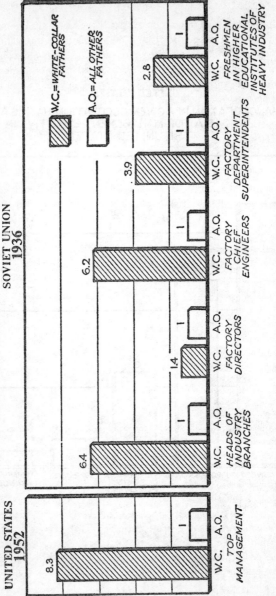

RELATIVE CHANCE OF A WHITE-COLLAR EMPLOYEE, PROFESSIONAL, OR BUSINESSMAN BECOMING A MANAGER OR POTENTIAL MANAGER (CHANCE FOR SONS OF ALL OTHER GROUPS=1).

UNITED STATES 1952

SOVIET UNION 1936

W.C. = WHITE-COLLAR FATHERS
A.O. = ALL OTHER FATHERS

W.C. A.O.
TOP MANAGEMENT
8.3 1

W.C. A.O.
HEADS OF INDUSTRY BRANCHES
6.4 1

W.C. A.O.
FACTORY DIRECTORS
1.4 1

W.C. A.O.
FACTORY CHIEF ENGINEERS
6.2 1

W.C. A.O.
FACTORY DEPARTMENT SUPERINTENDENTS
3.9 1

W.C. A.O.
FRESHMEN IN HIGHER EDUCATIONAL INSTITUTES OF HEAVY INDUSTRY
2.8 1

WHITE-COLLAR INCLUDES OWNERS, MANAGERS, PROFESSIONALS, AND CLERKS

American economy may be explained on fairly simple grounds. One can talk of the direct business influence of the fathers, the financial obstacles to higher education for lower-class children, the prejudice by business executives in favor of juniors with similar background, and the role of social contacts and the old school tie.

But if this is the entire explanation, then we should expect the opposite results to prevail in the Soviet economy. The Revolution of 1917 turned upside down the existing class structure. The entrepreneurs, managers, and professionals who were the top groups before the Revolution now found themselves at the bottom. A person's "social origin"—i.e., the economic class of his father—was written into his internal passport and followed him for life. Children of the bourgeoisie were automatically suspect, and were discriminated against consciously and even legally. If we apply to the Soviet Union the above arguments explaining American class rigidity, then we should expect a simple reversal of the tendency for children of the Russian former upper classes to float to the top of society, and would predict that they now moved automatically to the bottom.

Statistics on this subject unfortunately end in the 1930's. Moreover, the data as to occupation of parents is broken down into only a threefold classification: worker, farmer, and white-collar. Still, even this data is reasonably strong. It shows that the son of a white-collar employee, professional or business owner, had eight times as good a chance of reaching top-management rank in the United States as did the sons of manual workers and farmers, and that he had six times as good a chance in the Soviet Union.

In all Soviet management groups in 1936, children of executives and professionals did much better than did children of farmers and manual workers. Despite the open Soviet bias in favor of those with worker and farmer parentage, the American pattern was repeated—although, of course, the Soviet pattern was somewhat weaker. It is worth noting, as further accentuating the Soviet pattern, that the sons of men who had entered white-collar positions only after the Revolution—the new Soviet middle class—were in 1936 usually listed as of worker or peasant origin rather than as coming from a white-collar family.

Two questions about the Soviet figures immediately come to mind. The first is the question of why there are such large differences between the various Soviet management groups. Are not these differences highly suspicious, suggesting that the underlying data is worthless? Second, what is the family origin of the management of 1959? A lot of blood has flowed under the bridge since 1936, and patterns might have changed sharply.

The extreme differences among our 1936 management groups seem fairly easy to explain. Only the factory director group displays relatively little advantage for the children of white-collar men. But these directors were chosen to a large extent as political figures, entrusted with the task of ensuring that the Communist Party's will was followed in the plants. Forty per cent had barely a primary education. By and large, these men disappeared in the great purges of 1936–38, and were replaced by professional engineers.

The other differences among Soviet management groups fall into a regular pattern of either no change or of gains for white-collar children the higher the management post. But this is precisely the same picture which we find in American business both in 1928 and in 1950–52.

How about the present? What can we learn about today's pattern from looking at these 1936 figures?

The department superintendents in factories were the lower and middle management of the 1930's. It is they who must be supplying much or most of today's top management, for in 1936 two thirds of them were under forty, and 80 per cent were graduate engineers. Note that 45 per cent of this group had fathers in white-collar occupations.

The youngest category was that of the engineering students of the period. Despite open discrimination, 30 per cent of the entrants into the high-priority engineering schools in 1935 were children of white-collar people. The proportion was lower in earlier years; but these preceding classes had low educational standards, and their graduates were saddled for life with an inferior education. During the next few years after 1935, the proportion of white-collar freshmen rose still further. Some of this group of former students, now in their early forties, have doubtless already entered Soviet top industrial management; and Soviet top management of the next decade should to a large extent be recruited from among them.

It is mathematically possible that few or even none of the former department superintendents and engineering students with white-collar parents have reached today's middle and top industrial management. Today's top management may have been recruited solely from those whose parents were manual workers or farmers. But there is no evidence pointing in this direction.

To the contrary. We have seen that the Russian 1936 data fell directly into the American pattern of greater social stratification with movement up the management ranks. If anything, this tendency has probably increased in present-day Russia simply because of the lesser amount of hostility toward the children of white-collar parents.

Now this picture is an astounding one. Our expectations as to Russian class mobility, which we derived from simple explanations of American class rigidity, have failed completely. Occupational mobility seems much the same in the Soviet Union as in the United States. The same social groups dominate the paths of advancement. Prejudices and hostility appear to have little effect. The Russian October Revolution itself could not break the traditional pattern.

This relative success of Soviet white-collar children cannot easily be explained on the basis of their greater influence and social contacts; for theirs is precisely the group which has had to prove itself against prejudices. Nor can we explain their success on the basis of educational opportunity; colleges have been free and generally have even paid scholarships to cover living expenses. How, then, can their success be explained?

I would suggest that the answer lies in the importance of the kind of training which occurs within the family. Children stand a better chance of learning the skills needed for success in abstract fields such as engineering if they come from homes where abstract thinking is valued and used. Their efforts will be stronger if the family motivates them. They are more likely to develop managerial social skills if their parents are practitioners of what would otherwise appear as these "black arts."

Not only is this true within the American family, but it seems to be the case even in the Soviet home, where family influence has probably been much weaker. The Russian family is split apart by the child's being away in the six-day school or in organized leisure activities. Moreover, since apartments are so crowded, the child is likely to remain outside the home even when he has a choice. Yet despite all this, family influence on the child still remains strong enough to outweigh social biases against white-collar children and to leave these youngsters with a strong net advantage.

Thus social stability is strong in both societies, although probably somewhat stronger in the United States. But along with the actual social stability which we have noted, both societies share a common myth: the myth of social mobility. In both countries, unlike those of Western Europe, we find the belief to be dominant that a man gets ahead on his own merits and not on those of his ancestors.

The existence of this mutually shared myth is important. For one thing, the myth actually holds true to a somewhat greater degree than our figures have shown. This is so, in that we have considered only the immediate family backgrounds of top executives. But if we were to go back another generation, and talk of the occupations of grandfathers instead of fathers, then we would see a good deal more movement from class to class.

But more important, the myth tends to be a partially self-fulfilling prophecy. The youngster coming from a laborer's home believes that he has a decent chance for success in management; he therefore gears his actions, his education, his thinking in this direction. His superiors, also, believe that he has a chance; they do not automatically write him off when thinking of candidates for promotion. The myth of equality of opportunity is a strong force pushing in the direction of this equality. The myth probably helps to keep alive a dynamic management team in both nations; more than in other countries where there is no such myth, all segments of the population can feed into the managerial group.

There is still another way of looking at this problem of mobility. One may well ask: Are the various professions viewed in different countries as lying in the same hierarchy? Do the best youth in all countries see a high business management post as a desirable career goal, or do some nations' youth treat it as a bad second choice? Social mobility may mean nothing more than that businessmen's sons reject business, and so leave open vacancies which must be filled from families lower in the social scale.

Such rejection is clear in many non-industrial countries of the world where any type of business is considered distasteful and not an occupation for a gentleman. But even in Western Europe there are complaints that the better minds go into other fields, sheering away from the mundane problems of industry. One hears statements that the real management problem in Western Europe is to persuade the best people to become managers.

It seems safe to say that the United States does not face this problem. Financial rewards from business, combined with an abiding interest in money on the part of most Americans, are sufficient to attract a fair share of our best talent into management. Nor is our businessman exactly a social outcast.

The Russians seem to be in the same position as we are. It is true that the Russian executive is not quite as financially favored as is his American counterpart. The military do as well as he. Scientific research is equally well paid. Work within the Communist Party hierarchy may be as financially rewarding. Nevertheless, the Russian manager is very well off by national standards in a land where money is highly valued. Moreover, the engineer is the national hero, and the goal of most engineers is management. Financial rewards combine with social prestige to draw into management a good proportion of the best Soviet raw material.

In the light of all these similarities, we may speculate as to one important area of difference between American and Soviet managers which relates to social mobility. This difference seems to emerge directly from the common myth of equality of opportunity.

In the United States, two thirds of top management personnel have fathers who were business owners, executives, or professionals. Youngsters coming into business from these family backgrounds can feel comfortable functioning as "organization men." For the cards are stacked somewhat in their favor. If they do only as well as their competitors in the organization, and no better, they should advance upwards in the company. They are not men who must make their way over all obstacles.

The relatively relaxed attitude of American junior managers which stems from this social structure would seem to lay a psychological underpinning for the coming into being of the "organization man." Clearly, this psychological atmosphere alone is insufficient. National prosperity and expansion seem to be essential preconditions for the birth of the organization man; a dog-eat-dog business world could hardly support him. Large monopolistic firms—rather than a host of small and bitterly competitive companies—may be a necessary feature of his economic environment. But, presumably, it is not solely the objective surroundings which are important for the existence of this sort of management. The view of the world held by junior managers will help determine whether their response is competitive or co-operative, individualistic or group-angled, aggressive or placid.

Soviet junior managers have a different problem. As so often happens in the Soviet Union: everyone is equal, but some are more equal than others. Side by side with the myth of equal opportunity stands a countermyth: The U.S.S.R. is a workers' state, or at most a state belonging to the workers and peasants. The Soviet Union is still the land of "the dictatorship of the proletariat."

Now it is true that the term "proletariat" has been gradually expanded to include artists and managers; by now, virtually everyone in the country comes under the folds of this verbal cloak of approval. Yet despite all the fancy-Dan Marxist gymnastics, it seems certain that the pick-and-shovel coal miner is viewed as a better proletarian than is the bookkeeper in the mining office.

As a result of this national social attitude, the Russian youngster from a white-collar home is psychologically at a disadvantage. It is not enough for him to be as good as his competitor in order to succeed in management; he must be better. Yet, apparently, a plurality or even a majority of top-management executives are recruited from precisely this group. These executives are likely to be highly competitive, "tough-minded" people. For we have the curious situation of heavy recruitment coming from the very social group against which there is discrimination.

It is certainly true that such discrimination was much more real for the present group of managers than it is for the following generation now still in college or just entering industry. Even for this new group, however, it still seems to exist. Khrushchev's emphasis on manual labor as a proper prelude and even accompaniment to college is simply one reflection of this continued bias. When and if the time comes that this discrimination should end completely, we may still expect a lag reaction to its previous existence; traditions live on beyond the reality they once reflected.

How about those managers who come from worker or peasant homes? True, they have had the advantage of being from the "proper" social class. But they have generally suffered from poorer training within the family in terms of what is needed to become a successful manager. They too are men who have faced disadvantages, who have had to fight against serious obstacles.

The above argument, while clearly speculative, would seem to indicate that there are elements in the American pattern of mobility between social classes which tend to favor the development of "organization men." But the identical mobility pattern in Russia, when interpreted in terms of a slightly different myth both as to what is proper and as to what actually occurs, acts to stunt the growth of the "organization man" personality. It is an interesting example of the power of ideas.

4. COLLEGE EDUCATION

Now that we have begun our managerial biographies and have seen our future executives born and safely ensconced in the family bosom, let us skip over the years of childhood and adolescence. Let us press on to the period of training for management. How does such training differ as between the United States and Russia?

How Much?

The educational level of American management has been rising rapidly—in fact, although for different reasons, almost as rapidly as did the proportion of college graduates among fountain clerks during the depths of the Great Depression. But while we still have a long way to go before management is made up solely of college graduates, the Russians have already almost reached the saturation point.

Warner and Abegglen's study showed that 57 per cent of American top managers in 1952 had college degrees. This is an impressive figure when compared with the 32 per cent which was found in a similar study of business leaders in 1928. It is even more impressive when we remember that in 1950 only 7 per cent of American adult men had degrees.

Yet, the Russian picture is even more striking. Although we have no current general statistics, I received the impression from conversations in the Soviet Union that a college education is virtually an absolute requirement for a candidate for an industrial management post. For example, I was told that at least 80 per cent of the entire staff of the Leningrad Regional Economic Council had college degrees, and that all plant directors were college graduates.

Statistics of the 1930's for heavy industry tend to confirm my impression. Back in 1936, 65 per cent of the heads of industry branches had engineering degrees; 90 per cent of the chief engineers of factories had engineering diplomas; and 80 per cent of department superintendents were in this category. Only plant directors had a lower educational level, with less than one third having regular degrees; but by 1939, the proportion in this group had been raised to 85 per cent in the industries of defense and ferrous metallurgy. Moreover, it seems certain that since the mid-1930's—in the Soviet Union as in the United States—the proportion of management men with college degrees has been growing.

Some recent data, available for entire industries in the Soviet Union, offer general support for this view, although they do show that there are still a significant number of holdouts in management who have not had a college education. Of all plant directors in the Ministry of Machinebuilding on December 1, 1956, 89 per cent had a specialized high school or college education; in the Ministry of Heavy Machinebuilding, the proportion was 94 per cent. But in the Ministry of the Oil Industry, the figure fell to 78 per cent; and in the low-priority and low-salaried Ministry of Light Industry, only 45 per cent had this education. While some of the college-trained directors did not have the appropriate "specialized" education, and some of those with a specialized education were not college graduates, these groups probably cancel each other out reasonably well. The percentage of directors with college diplomas in these industries was presumably roughly at the levels indicated by the percentages.

Thus our first difference between the countries is that there is a much larger group of managers with formal college training in Russian industry than in American. This is quite surprising, when we consider that mass college education has a far older tradition in the United States. The total number of college graduates in the 1929–40 period was only 54 per cent as high in the Soviet Union as in the United States, despite the larger Russian population. This figure falls further to 39 per cent when we eliminate graduates of teachers' colleges. If we were to examine an earlier period, the ratio would drop off catastrophically. In view of the contrasting sizes of the pools of college graduates of managerial age which the two countries have been able to call upon, we can appreciate the tremendous emphasis given by the Russians to college training as a management requirement.

What Kind?

How about national differences as to what the student studies in college? Are these important?

Coming back to the Warner and Abegglen study of American managers, 40 per cent of those managers who were college graduates had Bachelor of Arts degrees. Another study showed that only one quarter of college graduate top managers in industry have majored in engineering.

These figures illustrate the strength of the "general education" tradition in American management. The man with the "rounded" background in college is quite prominent. The data for today's top managers seem to back the viewpoint of those business leaders who stress the value of a liberal arts education, and who assure the aspiring businessman that he is not cutting his throat by majoring in English.

Russian education has taken the opposite tack. Almost all Russian managers have engineering degrees. Their work is in the "hard" fields. A small scattering of them have business-school degrees. But only a few who have changed fields wildly can possibly have a liberal arts background. American "rounding" plays no role in the philosophy of Russian higher education.

How can we explain these differences? Partly, although perhaps of least significance, we may suggest that liberal arts programs in the United States have represented a "gentlemanly" type of education for the sons of professionals and business executives. These programs have played the same role as did the study of Confucianism in passing examinations for government posts in the pre-1912 Chinese Empire: They provide the mark of a "gentleman." It has not really been expected that they would offer any relevant training for actual administration. This explanation is suggested by the fact that, although

68 per cent of those American top managers in 1952 who were sons of laborers had some formal business training, only 50 per cent of the sons of major executives had bothered to get even a modicum of this sort of education. In Russia, the "gentlemanly" consideration was washed out of education with the Revolution.

Of more significance is the issue of how students choose their major subjects in college. In the United States, the student decides this question for himself; only the mildest constraints are put upon him by "advice" from the various academic departments in his college. By and large, he does not have to choose his major subject on the basis of which department deigns to admit him; furthermore, students still pick schools rather than schools picking students.

The Soviet college system is fundamentally different. The state pays the piper, and so it picks the tune in deciding how many majors there will be within each department in each college. The Soviet student goes to the department where he can find an opening, and it is the government which decides how many students will major in each field within any given year.

Given this situation, it is not surprising that there is a tremendous emphasis upon the professional courses. These are the ones with immediate payoff to the country as soon as the student graduates. Suppose that a federal agency in the United States, operating under the political pressures implicit in the need for budgetary allotments, were to decide on the number of college freshmen to admit into each field. Would it be out of the question that the number of engineers might rise sharply at the expense of liberal arts students?

The third main factor, and perhaps the most fundamental of all, is a straightforward difference of opinion as to the nature of "general education." What is the task of general education, and what sort of training best carries out this purpose?

Let us begin with a negative definition: general education is not training to perform a specific job or group of jobs in some particular fashion known today. This is trade-school education, whether the school is teaching students how to make brooms or how to perform surgical operations.

Professional training may be thought of as the next arbitrary stage on a continuum moving away from the trade school. It is training in how to fulfill particular functions, but with the emphasis upon the methods of tomorrow. Professional training recognizes that our knowledge in a given area changes, and that the student of today will spend much of his life operating with tools not now available. The objective of this training is to prepare him to utilize these as-yet-undiscovered tools and, if possible, to contribute to their development.

General education pushes still further along this same path. It begins from the premise that widely differing professional avenues can be conceived as all branching out from a common area. All professions share the requirements of clear thinking among their practitioners; of creativity and open-mindedness to strange ideas; of an ability to communicate freely and simply; of some common knowledge of the social and physical underpinnings of society and of the individual. Not only is this required for each profession individually, but the lessons learned in one cannot be transmitted to other fields unless they share some common base.

Note that this concept of "general education" uses a narrow criterion: that of helping the educated person to *do* something. We could employ a different criterion: that of helping him to *be* a particular type of person. Here, a change in the person himself would be the final objective. This latter concept of general education on the college level is doubtless important in the United States, but it does not seem to be so in the Soviet Union. There, the criterion is utilitarian.

Employing the utilitarian concept of general education, what should be taught in a college-level general education program? Here, it seems to me, there is legitimate ground for disagreement. Certainly one meets intelligent Americans, as well as Russians, who argue that an engineering major is better suited for this purpose than is a major in philosophy. These people claim that engineering provides a better foundation in modern clear thinking, grounded as it is in quantitative data and exposed to the tests of clearly perceptible failure. They even argue for it as a solid training in clear and precise communication, the engineering report being better suited for this purpose than the general essay. When we consider the best examples of engineering education in both American and Russian colleges, rooted in mathematics and the physical sciences and yet also giving some attention to communication in the student's native language, to a foreign language, and to the social world, this sort of claim seems far from absurd.

Thus it appears to me that one reason for the heavy emphasis upon engineering education as the appropriate one for prospective managers in the Soviet Union is a commitment by Russian educators to precisely this sort of education as a valuable model of "general education." Here we have Leibnitz's "best of all possible worlds": the needs of both general and professional education are viewed as best served by the same program.

Even American professional training for management has taken on a different pattern than has Russian professional training. I am thinking of the great development of the business administration schools in this country, both undergraduate and graduate. It is still too early for them to have made a major quantitative contribution to the present top management of American industry, but there seems no question that at least the graduate business administration schools will soon be making their mark.

Soviet business institutes seem much less important today in their quantitative contribution to future middle and top management than do the American business administration schools. The engineer is still the Soviet ideal of the properly educated industrial administrator. The stronger business administration courses make sure to provide a substantial amount of straight engineering work.

At the same time, these institutes do serve a recognized function in Soviet industry. When I discussed this matter in Russia, one administrator argued that the typical engineering graduate, when he first enters factory work, is still illiterate in business matters. This is a major handicap to him in junior management posts, and he faces a major task of further learning on the job. The business-school graduate has a major edge on the engineer in this regard. Nevertheless, there is no indication that a Soviet student interested in management is better advised to go to a business administration rather than to an engineering school. Each type of education is viewed as having its own advantages and similar prestige.

American business administration schools and departments today appear under a proliferation of titles. They may be called industrial management or industrial engineering departments. Not long ago, many were still operated under the aegis of economics departments. But, generally speaking, one can categorize their professional offerings as follows:

Many undergraduate programs offer a general engineering prelude to the study of business courses. They provide their graduates with a broad smattering of engineering subjects and of the physical sciences underlying them. The industrial engineering program at Columbia and the industrial management major at Carnegie Institute of Technology are representative of this group. The graduate business administration programs which follow this philosophy do not themselves offer engineering work, but they recruit a major portion of their students from the graduates of engineering colleges.

A second feature of American business administration programs consists of technical courses in tools and in particular subject matters of management. Courses in the tool areas of accounting, statistics, and economic analysis and in the subject areas of marketing, production, and finance are common. Some programs give more of an emphasis to tools, some to subject areas. Some programs proliferate their courses; others offer only a few basic ones. But all present these technical business subjects under one guise or another.

The third feature of American professional business education is for our purposes the most interesting. It is education in human relations, in how to work with and manage people. It is the *administrative* part of business administration education. This is an aspect which has become ever more important and intriguing to the student. Its development seems to be the counterpart of the great expansion of psychology within the liberal arts and teachers'-college programs, presumably as a result of the widespread interest of students in the arts of Madison Avenue manipulation.

Russian business administration schools can be separated

into three types. The first of these is typified by the Moscow State Economic Institute. According to its assistant director in charge of administration, most of the institute's graduates go into economic planning work on a regional level.

All students in the institute take the same courses for the first two or two and a half years. Perhaps two fifths of this program consists of engineering subjects, and the rest is made up of basic sciences, economic geography, blueprint drawing, accounting, and such non-technical subjects as a foreign language and political economy.

The remaining two years of the undergraduate teaching program call for specialization according to the student's major. He may major in the Department of General Economics, specializing in national planning, price setting, and personnel planning. Or he may go into the Departments of Industry, of Agriculture, of Finance, or of Purchasing. In all of these departments, courses are intended to provide the technical basis for professional work. But nowhere is there any training in problems of administration itself. Only formal organizational patterns are covered; the student will emerge with a sound picture of the formal organizational structure of firms, industries, and regions; of chains of command; of the particular pieces of paper which move up and down the hierarchy. But college courses are not considered the proper setting in which to raise the issue of what lives behind the façade.

Financial and marketing institutes are a more specialized type of business administration school. They train bankers, accountants, comptrollers, and store managers. They provide a technical education, just as does the Moscow Economic Institute, although probably with much less attention to engineering training.

The third type of business school is the engineering-economic institute. There are only three of these in the country, but each has a first-class reputation. Their stature in Soviet education is shown by the fact that each school has its own *Journal*, something fairly rare for Soviet institutions. The graduates of these institutes go mainly into junior executive posts on a factory level.

The Leningrad Engineering-Economic Institute provides its

students with a strong engineering background. In addition, students are given work in economic geography, economics of the firm, economics of industry, and statistics. Problems within the firm such as production scheduling and inventory control are considered of major importance. There is even some of the American "Operations Research" flavor. But, again, no attention is given to management problems as such.

It seems to me that the key difference between the American and Russian business administration schools lies in their attitude toward management administrative techniques. The Russian colleges ignore the entire human relations area; psychology is reserved primarily for the teachers' colleges.

Clearly this does not represent a difference of opinion between Americans and Russians as to whether the human element in business is worth considering. Both groups are convinced of its importance. But it does seem to represent a fundamental difference of opinion as to what can be taught within a classroom situation. The Russian business schools operate on the principle that some men are born good administrators, some ripen on the vine through the process of living, but none can be manufactured in a classroom. American business administrators feel that a catalyst can be introduced into the ripening process through formal instruction and through exposure to business cases which simulate real-life problems. It is necessary to point out that the Russian schools do employ a substitute device for simulating the management world. This device is the creation of a tight organizational world of their own for the students.

The out-of-class life of the Russian student is highly organized, filled with meetings and activities. This is particularly true for the Comsomol (Young Communist League) members, and virtually all of the future managers gravitate to this organization. The Comsomol body within the school, just like the Party unit later in adult life, is expected to guide and direct activities of all other popular bodies. Thus a Comsomol member, and particularly an elected officer, gets a good deal of organizational and managerial experience. The Comsomol member, in trying to influence other student organizations, has the managerial problem of achieving leadership partly through authority but primarily by gaining the co-operation of the general membership.

Extracurricular training in leadership is also, of course, widespread on the American campus. Furthermore, it is a device used by junior business executives for their own self-training; work in charities and churches offers solid opportunities for exercising managerial functions and learning by doing.

But the importance of this experience seems to be considerably greater in Soviet than in American practice. The Russian individual—student or otherwise—spends much more of his time in organized groups than does the American. Qualitatively, the opportunity for leadership training in student organizations is the same in both countries. But quantitatively, it seems more important in Russia.

There is a final question worth pursuing here concerning the subject matter of managerial education. Within the bounds of professional training, does the Russian program seem to be narrower and more specialized than the American? Russian management education, as I pointed out earlier, has mainly been in engineering. It is difficult to make comparisons as to breadth between this type of training and an American business management program. But let us juxtapose it against the usual American engineering program; this comparison seems particularly reasonable since a fair proportion of American industrial managers have engineering degrees.

There is no doubt but that greater narrowness did exist in Soviet education at the time when present top management personnel were in college. Until quite recently, Soviet engineering institutes were each under the jurisdiction of the administrative body for a specific industry; and each institute gave degrees in specialties specifically geared to the needs of its own industry. Contrast this practice with the usual American pattern of covering a fairly wide area, such as all mechanical engineering, within the compass of a single degree.

This Soviet policy of specialization can be viewed as having been an effort to provide trained manpower to industry as quickly as possible, for such educational specialization made a

Russian graduate engineer much more useful in his first few years on the job than an American engineer would be.

Nevertheless, specialization has proved expensive, and by and large has been given up. The Russian objections to this policy are the same as those voiced in the United States when specialization here tends to get out of hand. First of all, the narrow specialist is bound to be lacking in general scientific background. As the technology of his chosen specialty changes, he is poorly prepared to change along with it. Equally serious is his inability to incorporate ideas from other specialties into his own field; for he knows nothing of these other specialties. The second objection to such specialization is that there is no guarantee that an engineer will remain at work in the specialty he studied at college. The relative need for engineers shifts in unforeseen ways over the years; an individual's own interests change; he may hear of better opportunities in a different specialty. Thus a narrow specialist often turns out to have zeroed in on the wrong target.

All of this boils down to the proposition that the training of engineers with narrow specialties may have a high payoff in the first few years after graduation, but that it is poor strategy for the long pull. As the Russians have ground out more and more engineers, they have increasingly turned their sights on the graduate's level of competence at age forty instead of age twenty-five. In this respect, Russian and American education have pulled considerably closer together.

But there is one important respect in which Russian formal engineering education is still more specialized than is American. The Russian program leans much more heavily on training within industry.

The Russian engineering student spends roughly an extra year in college. This additional period allows him to specialize somewhat more deeply without losing breadth in the earlier years; in particular, it permits him to spend most of his last year working on some specific engineering diploma project. This diploma project is normally done at an individual plant, and the student will often return there to work after graduation.

This sort of specialization seems rather like the type of company training program which has swept much of American industry during the last ten years. The Russian gets this training while still called a student; the American gets it after he has graduated. The real difference does not seem very great. It is interesting that in this respect the American engineering training has changed, growing more like the Russian, while the Russian training has shifted toward the American pattern in giving up narrow specialization during the first four years.

How Is It Learned?

America is widely known as the land of "cut-and-try." It is the country of the inventor rather than the scientist; the experimenter as opposed to the theoretician. It is perhaps the only nation where a man can be chosen to head up research in an area precisely because he knows nothing about the subject, and where the definition given for the word "authority" is "someone who knows all the ways *not* to solve the problem." Nowhere else is it expected that the successful problem-solver should have the "fresh look" approach of trying everything, and should cross out of his dictionary the words "theoretically impossible."

The above seems to be a widely held European stereotype of the United States, and one which has long been accepted in the Soviet Union. Certainly there is a large amount of truth to the stereotype, and there was even more before the great immigration of European intellectuals which began in the mid-1930's. But while most West Europeans have reacted wholly negatively to this American research pattern, viewing it as the cult of barbarians, Soviet scientists and engineers have had a sneaking sympathy for it.

It is true that Russian methodologists have scoffed at the American brute-force technique of trying all ideas, sensible or not. But they have also rejected the German concept of struggling for the single best solution with test tube and slide rule, rather than giving a trial in the field to a whole variety of promising ideas. They have viewed proper Soviet research as cutting a swath midway between the extremes of American empiricism and German trial-by-theory.

These national differences in research design can be viewed as having economic roots. In contrast to Western Europe, America grew into maturity at a time when it had few scientists with a first-rate theoretical background. On the other hand, there were plenty of capital funds available for financing bright ideas. When practical discoveries were made, profit potentials were great; for there was a whole continent in which to market the resulting products. Keen competition prevailed among American producers in the race to bring out a marketable item in a new product area. European industry has been much less competitive.

Thus, in America, good theoreticians were scarce; capital for trying out ideas was plentiful; the prospective market was big enough to make good all the wastes of cut-and-try methods. As important as all the other factors taken together, speed of invention was of the essence in this competitive society. Better to undertake expensive experiments, build many variant models of the same design, and come out with a marketable product in two years—rather than use pencil, paper, and test tube only and take ten years to achieve a result. Time was less urgent in Western Europe.

Soviet science inherited the West European tradition from Tsarist Russia. But Russia of the thirties, forties, and fifties had developed some of the American characteristics: the prospective area of application was immense and, most important of all, time was of the essence. Still, Soviet Russia has not had our abundance of capital available for experiments on a pilot scale—and this was particularly true before the 1950's. As a result, Soviet research has tended to be more theoretic than American, although more empirical than West European.

One would expect these differences in tradition to affect education and, in fact, they have done so. Soviet technical education is solidly rooted in study of the basic physical sciences and mathematics, with the foundation in theory reaching back to the high-school level. Social science teaching, in its turn, is totally based on a single theoretic approach: Marxism.

Normally, one would expect an emphasis in the schools upon theory to stimulate the student's mind. For where there is such an emphasis, the "why" problem becomes the key one.

Moreover, not just any verifiable answer is satisfactory; rather, there is a search for that solution which is most general, which answers the largest number of "whys" at the same time.

Perhaps this theoretic emphasis is stimulating to the Soviet student in the physical sciences. But certainly its effect in the social sciences seems to be the reverse. Here, all problems are treated in terms of Marxism. There is no clash of ideas in the classroom, but only the learning of a single concept. "Theory" seems to become the simple memorization of a point of view.

This was brought home to me sharply in conversation with a straight-"A" student who was preparing for his exam in Marxism-Leninism—the Soviet version of philosophy, and considered the "queen of the sciences."

The material he was studying consisted of basic documents from the various congresses of the Soviet Union's Communist Party. During the 1920's, these congresses were scenes of hot clashes among the Bolshevik leaders. The period bristled with controversy. But the student's assigned reading consisted only of reports approved by the Stalinist majority along with speeches by Lenin, Stalin, and Stalin's chief supporters. His task was to memorize the gist of their arguments.

I became curious as to whether it would be possible for him to read the other side of the argument. So I went to the excellent card catalogue in one of the best Soviet libraries. I had been told by the librarian that this catalogue was complete (with the exception of some specified material kept in separate catalogues), and indeed it seemed as large as our own Library of Congress' main catalogue. But no entries were recorded under the names of the major Communist opponents of Stalin.

I then queried the student as to whether he thought that his official reading list was a proper one. Did he feel that he could get a proper grasp of the points at issue?

The student seemed puzzled and somewhat shocked at my questions. He was reading the "true" views of the situation from the original documents, and achieving a "true" insight into the Opposition ideas. Why should he possibly be interested in reading the Opposition documents themselves?

In fact, as the student thought about the question, he

seemed to feel that I was violating our unspoken agreement not to raise issues of international politics. Would you read Marx in your college courses in the United States? he retorted. When I replied that the *Communist Manifesto* is widely assigned to undergraduates as an historical and political document with which they should be familiar, he was only more bewildered. These crazy Americans! he clearly was thinking. Don't they know that they're undermining their own system?

For him, theory was something that one memorized just as one learned facts. In the social sciences at the undergraduate level, there are no theoretic conflicts; rather, there is truth and falsity, and one learns the truth. There is nothing in such an approach to theory which can stimulate the mind.

Even when we leave the area of politics and Soviet dogma, we find a sharp difference between American and Soviet educational practice with regard to the clash of ideas. At least in the better American schools, courses are often problem-oriented and the student is faced with the need to offer solutions to questions for which there is no single best answer. Alternative approaches are expected, and the student is forced to think rather than simply to disgorge memorized data. This does not seem to be true in the Soviet classroom.

I visited Leningrad University at the time of the final examinations for the 1957–58 academic year. Since Soviet examinations are oral, instead of being written as ours are, I asked to be allowed to attend one. This required not only the permission of the professor giving the examination, but also of the university president's office. It took a couple of days to get official permission, but "professional courtesies" were extended once I reached the right people.

The examination which I attended was in a fourth-semester course in "Socialist Industry." I had taught a somewhat comparable course dealing with private industry that same year at Carnegie Institute of Technology, and I was interested in comparing notes on the two courses. My own course, since it was entitled "The Business Enterprise," would presumably be narrower. My students were in their fifth semester, and so would be at a roughly comparable level of development with the Soviet examinees.

A Soviet final examination is a real backbreaker for the instructor. Each student in the class is examined individually and orally, and most of June is set aside for these exams. In this particular class, each student was examined for between twenty and thirty minutes. The teacher was the sole examiner.

The procedure is to prepare ahead of time a series of "tickets," each of which contains three examination questions. These tickets are placed face down on the examiner's desk, and each student chooses one at random when he enters the room. The student then sits down with his ticket and prepares his answers, making as full notes as he wishes. When his turn comes to be examined, he recites his three answers to the instructor. After receiving a grade, he puts his "ticket" back among those on the examiner's desk and leaves the examination room.

One result of this "ticket" system is that the best students are the first to come in for their examinations. I discovered this fact when I expressed my surprise that, of the five students whose examination I attended, four received "A's." The examiner looked upon this result as normal; the "D" students would be in later that afternoon and on successive days, once they had been able to pump the first students for the questions. This cramming did not seem to worry the teacher at all. There were enough "tickets" so that the student getting the questions ahead of time really learned no more than that he should know the work covered in the course. It seemed to me to be a quite normal case of radically different student-teacher perceptions of an exam.

Here are the questions given on two of the "tickets" of students whose answers I heard.

FIRST TICKET:

1. Organizational planning in industry of the U.S.S.R. Communist Party measures for improving planning in industry.

2. Fixed capital of socialist industry and its composition.

3. The main divisions and indices of the Plan of capital construction.

SECOND TICKET:

1. Perspectives of development of the industry of the Soviet Union according to materials of the Khrushchev report "Forty years of the Great October Socialist Revolution."

2. Profitability of socialist industry and its significance for the development of the national economy.

3. The meaning of the term "productive capacity" of the industrial enterprise. Indices of capacity.

The most striking feature of these questions is that they are extremely open-ended and have no sharp focus. They are not really questions so much as they are topics.

When the first student came up to the examiner's desk to be tested, I expected the teacher to push him in some set direction with additional questions on the topic. But no! The examiner's additional questions were few, and these called only for more detailed factual information. By and large, the students recited from their notes without interruption and at a speed which was astounding. It seemed as though they had memorized the answers from their textbook or from the lectures. Seldom have I heard papers read at the speed with which these youngsters recited.

Listening to these students, I could not help but be impressed. None of our own "A" students would have the detailed factual command of the subject matter which all of these "A" students showed. At the same time, I wondered how much of this detail they would remember five years later. Not much, I would suspect!

But while I was surprised by their exhaustive knowledge of facts, I was even more struck by the total absence of personal opinion in their answers. It appeared as if no application of thought was required. In contrast, our own examinations emphasize the need for problem-solving. Let me illustrate this by two recent questions from the Carnegie Tech "Business Enterprise" exams for juniors.

1. Discuss the possible strategies in pricing a new product,

the factors that must be considered, and the ways in which the relevant information can be gotten.

2. Discuss the concept of cost-push inflation, with emphasis upon:
   a. The assumptions as to behavior and motivation of firms.
   b. The role of these assumptions in the theory.
   c. Your own view as to the accuracy of these assumptions with regard to the current American scene.

It seemed as though one could contrast Soviet and American college education in the better schools by saying that one emphasized a sound command of the factual material, while the other stressed an ability to apply to the solution of problems whatever factual data happened to be remembered.

By the time I had heard three students recite, and still had not heard a single one offer an idea of his own, I was growing impatient. With the fourth student, I decided to interpose myself into the examination situation once she had received her grade.

One of the examination questions asked this student was: "Directives of the 20th Communist Party Congress for the Sixth Plan in the fields of the energy and fuel industries." The girl quoted statistics showing the proportion of Soviet energy coming from various sources; she indicated that the proportion coming from oil, natural gas, and hydroelectric power had increased and was to increase further. She said that this tendency to diminish the relative importance of coal, peat, and firewood was "progressive." The examiner then asked how the Soviet proportions compared with the American—and he grinned at me. Indeed, it was one up for him; for the girl came through with American statistics which sounded reasonable enough, although I had no idea as to whether they were precisely accurate. Presumably in the interests of international friendship, she added that the American proportions were more "progressive" than the Russian.

She then passed on to the next questions, and finally got her "A." Once she had received her grade, and it was entered upon her official record, I broached the general atmosphere of good will by requesting permission to ask her a question of my own. "Of course," I was told, and I received the instant and complete attention of all the students sitting around, waiting to be examined.

"Why," I asked, "do the Soviet Union and the United States have different patterns of fuel consumption? Why are oil and gas more prominent in the United States, while coal and peat are more heavily used in the Soviet Union?"

It was an absolutely basic question. Clearly the reasons for the national differences were economic, and this was an economics examination. If the girl knew why the Soviet leadership was interested in changing the proportion of different types of fuels utilized, other than because such a change was "progressive," certainly she would know the answer to my question.

Unfortunately, I drew a complete blank. The girl did not have the faintest idea of what to say. After an embarrassing few minutes, the examiner "rephrased" my question into one asking what were the differences between the two countries. The girl repeated her original answer and then she left the room, to the quite evident relief of all three of us.

During my stay in the Soviet Union, I talked over this experience with a number of recent graduates of Soviet colleges. They had majored in a variety of fields, and I wondered if their experience corroborated my impressions as to emphasis in the examinations upon facts rather than upon thought. Yes, they agreed, this did seem to be the emphasis. As a teacher, I was gratified that most of them felt that such an emphasis was a mistake.

Since returning to the States, I have often thought of this difference in teaching techniques. If we follow standard American educational philosophy, we would expect the Soviet professional to be much less self-reliant and creative as a result of this sort of training. Yet American scientists have generally come away favorably impressed with Russian scientists, even with the younger group. American managers who have toured Russia have been impressed with Russian managers. The Russian record of accomplishment certainly seems to show that initiative and creativity have been displayed at many levels.

It is possible that once again we have here a difference of concept as to what can profitably be taught in school. Certainly the Russians are aware of the need for creative problem-solving. But the problem-solving approach, they may well feel, is something best learned either on the job or, for those going beyond their diploma, in graduate school.

After all, Russian educators may argue, the recent graduate will not be doing much on his own when he first starts work. He will be a minor part of a team. Therefore, let his college teach him the skills he will need to perform his team functions, and let it provide him with the factual "building blocks" for creativity and analysis. Once he is on the job, facing actual problems, he will learn to solve these problems effectively. If he does not learn, then he will never be promoted to a position where it much matters whether or not he has this analytic skill. This is one type of sink-or-swim philosophy, and it leaves the techniques of problem-solving for on-the-job training.

American college education also, of course, leaves part of the training process for learning on the job. But it tends to be more the factual, rather than the analytic, elements of learning which are thus postponed. There is no difference between the two educational systems as to what the fully trained man should know. But there is a reasonably sharp difference of timing as to when the various parts of the training should be received.

Counteracting this apparent policy of memorization in Soviet higher education is one major piece of individual student effort: the diploma thesis. Engineering students, for example, spend most of their fifth year writing individual theses.

These theses are taken quite seriously, as is shown by the arrangements made for their defense. Normal course examinations, for example, are graded only by the instructor in the course. Moreover, an order of the Ministry of Higher Education prohibits attendance of anyone except the students being examined and the faculty of that department. Exceptions are made only for those receiving permission from the dean of the faculty or the president of the university (as I did).

But the thesis defense is open to the general public, and anyone in the audience has the right to question the student being examined. Moreover, there is an examining committee with members from outside the student's own university. The decision of the examiners is made by *secret ballot*. All this is a necessary prelude to the granting of a diploma which in standing is no more than comparable to our own Bachelor's degree.

I attended one such diploma defense at the Leningrad Engineering-Economic Institute. The defense was held in a hall with a seating capacity of one hundred people. Seated on the rostrum were four examiners and the student's advisor. Of the four examiners, only two were from the institute; the other two were representatives of the industrial plant at which the student had done his research and of the Ministry of Higher Education. In the audience there was an official Opponent, a few older people who were probably faculty members, and a horde of students who were there to see the show.

The thesis had been circulated earlier among the examiners. Now the student gave a formal twenty-five-minute report. He was held strictly to schedule; the chairman calling time on him in the middle of a sentence, and then giving him another fifteen seconds to finish up. The Opponent, clearly not a student, read his criticism; this was then answered by the student. The examiners asked questions, and the student answered them all together. The proceedings ended with the chief examiner requesting questions from the audience, and with the student's advisor saying a few words about the project and the student. The whole affair had now taken forty-five minutes. The student was dismissed, and the next student began his report. The examiners would vote later, after hearing all the thesis reports for that afternoon.

It is always difficult to know how seriously an examination is really taken by the people concerned. I can only say that this one had all the external aspects of being more than a formality. Furthermore, the administrative secretary of the department assured me that it is quite common for the examining board to require the rewrite of a project, or even to fail the thesis completely. The secret ballot, combined with keeping the advisor off the examining committee, was clearly a device to prevent the results of the examination from being entirely predictable. In this respect, the Soviet diploma defense goes further than do our own Ph.D. defenses of dissertations in assuring that the occasion is a genuine test of the candidate.

The thesis project is thus a major individual effort by the student—one which requires at least a minimum of individual initiative and organization. There is nothing comparable in American undergraduate education, except for Honors programs in a few schools. Yet one may still question how much genuine problem-solving is generated by this technique.

The thesis which I heard defended, for example, was an extremely careful study of the administrative organization of a small Leningrad plant. One of the institute's staff commented to me afterwards on its being an excellent job. Yet it was neither analytic nor critical. It was simply a first-rate description. To me, its content was symbolized by the fact that the student had memorized his talk. At one point, the student stopped short—his memory failing him. After a moment, his advisor supplied the next few words—also, curiously, from memory. With this prompting, the student went on to complete his report with utter self-assurance.

The Student Himself

The student who works for a "Gentleman's C" is a much commoner feature of the American college landscape than of the Russian. The reasons for this are fairly clear.

First of all, the Russian schools exercise a much more rigid pre-selection. No Russian colleges, for example, operate under the rules of some of our major state universities which must, by law, accept all high school graduates from the area. There are few American schools, even today when the wartime baby boom is beginning to hit the colleges, which have such a crush of applicants that they accept only one out of twenty, as does the Moscow State Economic Institute. The student who has coasted along in high school and who expects to do the same in college is much less likely to have the opportunity of making a nuisance of himself in a Russian freshman class than in an American one.

Secondly, the college student in Russia is likely to be better motivated than his American counterpart. For the Russian, a college degree is a necessary prelude to any of the professions or to management positions. The student who flunks out has the entire range of most desirable future careers cut off to him forever.

It is true that something of the same situation exists in the United States. During the depression of the 1930's, it was said that one needed a college degree to sell ties in Macy's. But the high proportion of successful American businessmen without college diplomas shows conclusively that the degree is still far from an essential ingredient in the American success story.

Thus the penalty for the student who aims for a "C" and just misses getting it, is a good deal more severe in the Soviet Union than in the United States.

Thirdly, an American student is quite likely to be working on the side. A recent U.S. government survey showed that 60 per cent of full-time undergraduates work during the school year, and these earn an average of eleven dollars a week. In one large, metropolitan university, a sample survey of the students showed that fully one seventh of upper-class full-time students held forty-hour-a-week jobs. Such students are doing well when they earn honest "C's."

While this heavy combination of work and study is certainly an extreme, part-time work is accepted as a commonplace even in our best colleges. Students quite normally contribute to their own support. Sometimes work is a necessity for staying in college; often it is a means of earning money for such "frills" as dating. It is treated as normal by all hands and is, in fact, frequently considered desirable for its own sake.

The Soviet day student, on the other hand, does not work during the school year. In Russia I asked what would happen to a student who did take a part-time job. The answers ranged from an indignant comment that he would be thrown out of school, to the more official statement that he would be permitted to work—but that few or no students do, in fact, have jobs. The occupation of "student" is a full-time one.

Postwar data as to the drop-out rate in American and Russian colleges clearly reflects these differences in admissions policy, motivation, and availability of time. Let us compare the number of freshmen entering college between 1945 and 1950 with the total of college graduates between 1949–50 and 1954–55. (The earlier years are taken for the United States, since the college program normally requires four years. The Russian course takes five years as a rule.) This comparison is a pretty accurate measure of the proportion of entering students who actually finish college, whether or not they have transferred from one school to another.

The Soviet completion-rate in this period was 84 per cent. Only 16 per cent of the students had dropped out. In the engineering schools, the same picture held; a bare 15 per cent of the 1950 freshman class failed to graduate in 1955.

In the United States, on the other hand, 26 per cent of all college students dropped out. Even these figures are an underestimate of the drop-out rate; for I am not counting junior college students as entering freshmen, although they are included as graduates if they later complete a four-year college. If junior college entrants are counted as freshmen, then the proportion of drop-outs rises to 40 per cent.

It is hard to believe that many of the American drop-outs are a direct result of the private expense of education in the United States compared to the Soviet Union. It is true that there are no tuition fees in the U.S.S.R. But tuition in our own state universities, at least for residents of the state, is so low as to be negligible. Any student holding a part-time job can easily finance it even without a scholarship.

Much more serious is the fact that the American student is generally on his own with regard to finding the funds for living expenses. If his family cannot help him, he must earn the money himself. The average Soviet student, on the other hand, is subsidized by the government.

Yet even this factor has probably not accounted for many American drop-outs in the prosperous postwar years. An American student may well have to leave a particular college for lack of funds, but certainly he can find some college in the country where he can earn his way while studying. The large number of students who do pay their own way shows that it can be done. The student who quits for lack of funds seems either to lack the motivation to accept the hard work involved, or to lack the ability to work while studying full time. In either case, we are thrown back upon our earlier factors of motivation and time available for study.

The full-time student with family obligations is no better off in the Soviet Union than he is in the United States. In neither country is he likely to be able to stick it out. For the best such students, special scholarships play the same role in both societies.

Consider the normal student in the Moscow State Economic Institute. As a freshman, he will receive 300 rubles a month; this will increase to a peak of 400 rubles in his fifth year. If he is a straight-"A" student, he will get 25 per cent more.

According to the assistant director of this institute, the student pays nothing for his dormitory space. His medical care is also free. He must spend an average of two and a half to five rubles for lunch, and three to five rubles for dinner. If we take the minimum figures given by the assistant director, and add two rubles for breakfast, then the student will be spending 225 rubles monthly on food alone. If he is an upperclassman, perhaps he will have the equivalent of $18 a month left for all his other expenses. Even by Russian standards, this is scarcely enough to support a family.

When we put to one side the question of graduation, the emphasis on grades is still quite disparate in Russia and the United States.

The Soviet student's grades are the key factor in determining his first job. This is because graduates are assigned to jobs for three years, with the best students having their choice among the available openings. Of course, company recruiters who come to an engineering school in the United States are also interested in grades. But the stress on them seems to be considerably less than it is in the Soviet Union. "Personality" with all its intangibles plays a larger role in the United States.

Naturally a Soviet "big man on campus" will have an easier time than will the wallflower in getting a desired job. The student playboy, leaning on family influence for the future, is a type written up in many sketches in the Soviet press. All comparisons between societies are a matter of degree. But taking it all in all, the "grind" is a more respectable and common-place character in Russian than in American life.

Of most immediate import to the Russian undergraduate is the relationship between his grades and his living standard. The size of the American undergraduate's meal ticket, on the other hand, is more likely to depend on his football prowess.

In all the Soviet Union, 82 per cent of students receive cash stipends. Yet roughly a "B" average is required to qualify. The reward for doing better, for breaking into the "excellent" group, is a bonus of 25 per cent or more.

Two features in this system are worth noting. The first is that cash stipends are sufficiently common so as to be within the reach of virtually all who are admitted into the colleges. No one need give up the hope for a scholarship as representing a level of work clearly beyond his abilities. At the same time, a high grade average is required.

A modified form of this system is commonly used in Amer-ican graduate schools. A "B" average, or even a "B" in all courses, is set as a requirement for a Master's degree. As doubt-less also happens in Russia, this often leads to a depreciation in the standards used to define a "B"; but the net academic effect still seems better than if only a "C" average were re-quired. Students appear more motivated by the need to get this higher grade. A small amount of inflation can have quite as helpful an effect on student motivation as Lord Keynes claimed that it has on worker motivation in industry.

The definition of a "B" grade seems to differ with the indi-vidual school in Russia. Thus, the Minister of Higher Educa-tion declared in 1958 that 82 per cent of all university stu-dents receive money scholarships. I was told that over 90 per cent of the students in the excellent Leningrad Engineering-Economic Institute receive them. In this case, a high-priority and first-rate institute is more generous with its scholarships than is the average Soviet college. But opposite instances can also be observed. Leningrad University, which certainly has a better-than-average student body, gives scholarships to only about 80 per cent of its students. Moreover, the proportion is lower—I was told by one of the teachers—in the natural sciences than it is in the social sciences; this is because the natural science departments are more demanding.

The second feature to note is that the "A" student is well rewarded. A bonus of 25 per cent (Moscow Economic Institute) to 65 per cent (Leningrad Engineering-Economic Institute) is worth working for, particularly in view of the meager living conditions of the average student. Perhaps this is one reason that some Soviet educators with whom I talked resisted suggestions that student scholarships might be a bit too low. A student has no right to live high on the hog, they insisted. But doubtless, in addition both to the incentive and morality issues, they also wish to require at least some sacrifices from students as a way of weeding out those lacking in motivation.

Nevertheless, with all these prods working on the student, Russian colleges still do not have things all their own way. Let us not forget the administrator from the Moscow Economic Institute who thought that the policy of having students work before entering college would provide his institute with a more serious student body. Obviously, like teachers the world over, he felt that there was a lot of room left for improvement.

Up to this point, we have talked only of the full-time day student. The justification is that this group completely dominates management education in both countries.

The Soviet Union has a widespread system of extension courses, run rather like the American Army extension program. Students study at home, and only come to their colleges for exams. But while one quarter of Soviet graduates from all types of courses came out of these extension programs in 1955, only 6 per cent of the engineers came from this group. Since the war, between one fifth and one third of all engineering freshmen were extension students; but they have run no more than 2 to 6 per cent of the graduating classes. Thus we can dismiss the extension program as a source of Soviet management personnel.

Evening classes are slightly more important. In both countries, they provide an education for a fair number of people holding down engineer-type posts. But it seems quite safe to say that the quality of the education is sharply below the day-session level in both countries. In neither the United States nor the Soviet Union do they seem to be a major source of engineering graduates. In Russia in 1955, for example, only 4 per cent of the engineering graduates came from these inferior evening programs.

5. THE FIRST JOB

We have traced the birth and schooling of our young heroes, the future executives. Now it is time to put them to work.

Let us look at their early job experience. Certainly the manager's first impressions of business should play a powerful role in shaping his future approach to it.

Warner and Abegglen, in their study of American top managers in 1952, give us data as to the types of jobs held by business leaders when they first became self-supporting, as well as five years afterwards. We have data for those who graduated from college on the one hand, and for all other business leaders on the other. If a man's position is an executive one, it is considered as such in the following chart even if one of its requirements is professional competence. Thus a man who enters business with a law or engineering degree will not necessarily be included in the "professional" category.

The data is striking in what it shows of the paths to American top management. Only one seventh of all the business leaders ever did manual work on a full-time, regular basis. Moreover, only a tiny fraction even of the manual workers passed through the foreman's position on the way up. Manual workers who found the road to business success have carefully skirted this dead-end post. (Data for posts after fifteen years in business bear out this conclusion.)

The only really meaningful difference between college-trained men and those without degrees is that the first group was more likely to start out with a professional job, while the second had a better chance of beginning as a clerk or salesman. But if we put these types of positions together and call them both "functional" posts, then two thirds of each group started

UNITED STATES — PROPORTION OF BUSINESS LEADERS

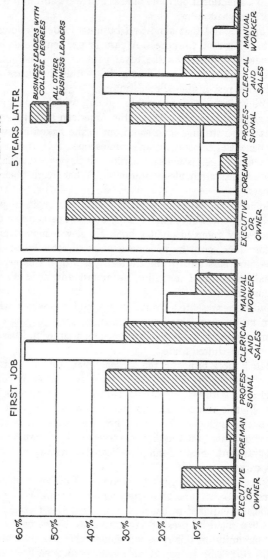

out in a functional post and almost half were still in functional work five years later.

Thus we find that almost all business leaders followed the white-collar road to success. A bare 12 per cent were able immediately to begin on the royal path of administrator; two thirds took the functional detour. But within five years, almost half were responsible administrators.

The Russians have not published data which is comparable. But some differences between the American and Russian patterns are so striking as to stand out to the naked eye without the benefit of the statistician's microscope.

By and large, as we said earlier, all Soviet industrial managers today are college graduates. What were their early careers?

Some of the older generation resemble a regional planner I met who had worked in a factory and had earned two college degrees by going to night school. He slowly moved up on a factory level until he became a plant director when he was fifty-four years old. In the thirteen years of his career which remained before I met him, he at last advanced above the factory level.

But he represented a small group, and one which will now soon be retiring. This body of men, whose first jobs were in manual work, is today perhaps not much larger in Russia than it is in the United States.

Much more typical is the Moscow plant director who came out of engineering school to start work as an assistant foreman. Beginning with his first job, he had administrative responsibilities. In this respect, he was like a bare 12 per cent of our American managers. But more than that, his career started on the shop floor and was linked there to his success in getting out the work. Few of our American top managers have had this experience.

Since even the current generation of Russian managers, let alone the next, are graduates of engineering and business schools, I inquired rather widely in Russia as to the types of jobs first filled by present-day graduates. There was a degree of unanimity on this question among the experts which was quite surprising to me, since I had learned early in my trip that Russian authorities are no more likely to agree with each other than are their counterparts in other countries.

First as to engineers, the backbone of the managerial staff. The emphasis is upon getting them into production work immediately. An engineer may be appointed as a foreman directly when he comes out of school. Probably more common, and certainly more sensible, is the practice within the organizations under the Moscow City Council of giving the young engineer an assistant foreman's job. This practice, as it was explained to me, is intended to provide the young graduate with production and administrative experience without jeopardizing output. After he gains experience here, the engineer may move up in the line organization to, for example, assistant shop superintendent. Alternatively, and much more commonly, he may be shunted into one of the functional organs of the plant such as design or methods study.

In the past, there have been many engineers who have gone directly into design or methods work on the plant level. Many, in fact, have been hired straight into organizations which coordinate or service a number of factories.

But those who have taken this early path are probably not the ones who have later advanced to top management. For such engineers immediately have one strike against them for the remainder of their careers. The proper, "patriotic" path for the engineer has always been set forth as that of working directly in production. The engineer who begins this way is conforming to the proletariat image; however far he may later get from the shop floor, he still falls within the picture of the work-oriented specialist. But the engineer who starts out in a functional post and, worst of all, within an organization above the plant level, is by definition a chairwarmer and a bureaucrat. Clearly he is looking for the easy job, preferably one which will keep him in the "big city."

Furthermore, the Soviet managerial function is much more heavily production-oriented than is the American. The Russian manager, at any level, is likely to be spending more of his time worrying about the sheer quantity of work turned out. Since this will be the orientation of his future jobs, the fledgling Soviet manager can learn a lot on the shop floor which he will never get later if he misses this opportunity.

Business-school graduates have a different start. Even those coming from the engineering-technical institutes tend to begin with a functional post.

The Leningrad Engineering-Economic Institute normally sends its graduates out either as shop dispatchers or as shop economists. But both jobs, while functional, are closely linked to production processes. The shop economist's task, for example, is to work out the various needs (for materials, labor, etc.) and production targets of his shop within the over-all plan set by the factory administration. Equally or even more important, he must check as to how things are going and must make planning changes in line with events.

While the recent graduate of the Institute thus begins in a functional post, he may soon switch to a minor executive position. One chap with whom I talked had graduated from the Institute in 1946. Between then and 1953, when he left industry to take up graduate studies, he had worked as shop economist in a plant in the Urals, and then as assistant shop superintendent in a Leningrad plant.

Graduates of general business schools such as the Moscow State Economic Institute have the title of "economist." They are most likely to be hired directly into planning work in a regional organization, a collective farm, or a very large firm. They are "planners," and can advance to major functional positions in Soviet management.

Nevertheless, their chances of getting into top management seem relatively limited. The magic title of "engineer" does not include them, although it does cover the "engineer-economists." Never do they have the chance to get their hands dirty. They are normally not in line for the supervisory jobs. It seems indicative that when the Leningrad Economic Council needed a chief "planner," it took a man with an engineering degree who had been a plant manager earlier. The general business-school graduate seems to be off the main trunkroad to management roles.

Russian education now appears to be on the way back toward an earlier Soviet tradition. In the early 1930's, large numbers of students had had a long period of factory work before they entered college. Under the current system, Russian high school graduates are again supposed to get their feet wet in the "real world" before getting on with their formal education.

This new development in Soviet education will once more sharply raise the proportion of managers whose first job was that of manual worker. But this is a trend for the future. Moreover, it seems fairly safe to predict that these future managers will be men who, from the start, looked upon manual labor as only a two- to three-year jumping-off place for higher education. Nevertheless, this development should further reinforce the present grounding of Soviet management in industry problems on the shop level.

In comparing the early careers of American and Soviet managers, two distinctions stand out most clearly. First, the Soviet manager has probably had close contact with production problems on a shop level. If he himself has not been a manual worker, he has been in intimate contact with such workers at an early stage in his work life. The American manager, on the other hand, is quite unlikely to have had this experience. Instead, he generally began in a white-collar job, working with other white-collar people.

Secondly, the main road to management in the Soviet Union is through production and "line" operations. This is where the future manager starts. He may move off into staff jobs for a while, but the line is the mainstay of his experience. The American manager, in comparison, usually begins in "staff" work and is divorced from direct contact with production.

6. WHAT IT ALL MEANS

We have written the biography of our young executives from their birth through their education and their first immersion into the waters of business life. Now it is time to ask what the tale signifies.

First, let us summarize the key distinctions which we have found between Soviet and American managers in the formative period of their careers.

1. Both groups come from reasonably similar social classes; namely, from predominantly white-collar families. But the Soviet myth as to the superior virtues of the proletariat leads to considerable psychological pressure on the successful management candidates, and breeds a tough-mindedness which is not easily malleable into an "organization man" type of management. This conclusion, it should be noted, seems to be the most speculative of all the distinctions I have made.

2. There is a considerably higher proportion of college graduates among Soviet than among American managers.

3. Of the college graduates, a much larger percentage of the Russians have engineering degrees.

4. Soviet college education provides a firmer factual base than does American, but a weaker analytic training.

5. At the same time, the total Russian tradition is more theoretic. The Soviet manager, after his school years, is more prone to do general reading than is the American manager.

6. The Soviet manager is much less likely than is the American to have received any formal training in human relations. On the other hand, because of his Young Communist League activities he will probably have had a good deal more practical experience in this during his years in school.

7. The Russian's first major practical experience in business is during his last college year, and thus it occurs while he is still under academic tutelage. This year serves as a strong bridge between college and the "real world." Such a bridge is generally missing in the American manager's experience.

8. Russian managers have an early, heavy dose of work directly in production. By and large, this is not true of American managers.

9. Early jobs held by Russian managers are most often those of minor executives. American managers are much more likely to begin with staff or other technical roles.

One implication which might be drawn from these distinctions is that Russia today is one up on American industry, in that a higher proportion of its managers are college-trained. American business has been rapidly moving in the direction of demanding college training from its managers. Of American business leaders studied in 1928, only one third had graduated from college. By 1952, over one half were graduates. But Russia has moved considerably faster and further in this direction than we have.

Normally, one assumes that a college education should tend to improve a man's business skills. This assumption may lead to the conclusion that Russian management is, in this respect, better off than American.

But, indeed, we need not conclude this. Certainly there are other features besides education which make for managerial success. Perhaps these others are vastly more important. If a college education is set up as a first requirement for a management post, as it practically is in the Soviet Union, this rule may cut off from consideration a whole host of men who would in fact make first-rate managers. Although there is no fee for education in the Soviet Union, many Russian country boys must be cut off from college simply because of the poorer quality of primary and secondary education in rural areas as compared to the cities. Moreover, many boys who might become fine managers in time may have no interest in academic studies. It must be true, in Russia as in the United States, that narrowing the field of candidates to those with college degrees eliminates many men with excellent potential. It may even result in an actual lowering of the average ability of those managers who are chosen in this competition.

In short, the quality of Russian management may suffer, rather than gain, from the fact that a diploma is a requirement for a manager's post in the Soviet Union. As we in this country tend to move in the same direction, the same deterioration may occur here.

Turning again to Warner and Abegglen's study of American business leaders in 1952, we find some helpful information relating to this issue.

Warner and Abegglen grouped their business leaders according to whether they were associated with firms which had been either stagnating or only slowly expanding, had been expanding moderately, or had been expanding rapidly during the period in which the business leader had been with the company. They found that the most rapidly growing companies had the lowest proportion of college graduates as their top managers, and that the stagnating firms had the highest proportion.

Then they grouped the managers according to whether they worked in slowly, moderately, or rapidly expanding industries. The same results held: those industries did worst which had the highest proportion of college graduates. Finally, within each type of industry, individual companies did worst which had the largest percentage of graduates.

A last test was made to see whether, perhaps, these results were due primarily to the social classes from which these managers came. But no! Regardless of the occupation of the manager's father, the college graduates were grouped in the least successful organizations.

Warner and Abegglen did not try to explain these results, and I shall also beg off. But certainly the results lend no support to the view that college graduates necessarily make the best managers.

It *may* be that the less successful American firms and industries gave great weight to the mere fact that a man had a degree. As a result, they may have bypassed people with first-rate management possibilities, and have been left with many second-raters. Russian industry may be doing the same thing and, indeed, suffering from it.

I do not wish to draw the positive implication that American business has an advantage over Russian in that fewer of our managers are college-trained. I do not wish to conclude that, as we approach the Russians in this regard, we can expect a deterioration in the quality of our management. But the Warner and Abegglen material is worth pondering. The evidence is not conclusive that we and the Russians are both on the right road, and that they are further along it than we are. The road may be going in the wrong direction.

There is a second implication from the different backgrounds of Russian and American management which I would support. This is an implication with regard to the types of new ideas which will most easily spread in the two countries.

Since Russian top management is completely dominated by graduate engineers, and since Soviet society tends to have more of a bias toward the value of theory than does the American public, I would expect Soviet industry to be more receptive to new technological ideas than are American firms. This Russian receptivity is heavily reinforced by the fact that the early work experience of managers is in production, and that their first study of technology in the factory is under the guidance of professors who are professionally most concerned with what is novel. The quicker Russian absorption of new technological schemes should apply particularly to those schemes aimed at better performance in existing jobs.

This is not to suggest that we should necessarily expect Russian industry to be more inventive than American. But it is to say that technical innovations should spread faster throughout the Russian economy. While clearly other factors are important, the interests and training of top managers will be a vital factor in determining this rate of adoption.

No one has done a real study to see whether in fact innovations usually do spread faster in Russian industry than in our own. But certainly we have examples of this. *Business Week* in October 1958 reported on the all-basic brick open-hearth furnace. Ten years ago, experiments by U. S. Steel demonstrated the feasibility of this sort of furnace. Russian engineers read American accounts of the experiment, and began building such furnaces with minor modifications which were needed in order to justify them economically. But in the United States, these furnaces did not begin spreading until American steel men visited Russian plants and saw what the Russians were doing.

If we leave the field of technology and turn to other aspects of business, I would expect precisely the reverse pattern. The Russian engineer-type manager, whose first mistress was production, will tend to treat everything except technology as frosting on the cake. Changes in accounting, procurement and marketing, and finance should all have tough sledding in gaining acceptance in Russian business.

This bias, coming from the education and early work experience of the individual manager, is reinforced by the prejudices of the society. It was not so long ago that Russia was a peasant country, with all of the peasantry's traditional and frequently justified suspicion of the bookkeeper, the merchant, and the financier. "Business" activity was considered a blood brother of outright theft.

Marxism simply reinforced this traditional attitude. Marx himself spoke of capitalism as having "created more massive and more colossal productive forces than have all preceding generations together." But twentieth-century Bolsheviks looked upon this as a description of the distant past. Their attitude was much closer to that of America's early technocrat Thorstein Veblen, who viewed the main function of the businessman as being that of holding back the engineers, slowing down the advances of technology, and thus preserving markets from being swamped by a cheap and endless supply of goods. The businessman was viewed as a capitalist saboteur of production.

The necessary tasks of administration, the things which deserve doing in a socialist society, were, as late as 1917, viewed on occasion by Lenin as being so simple that any literate person could perform them.

Doubtless all this has changed. Today the peasant attitude would be rejected with scorn. Any educated Russian would agree that Lenin's statement represented great naïveté. Nevertheless, the attitudes remain as hidden background prejudices, rejected by all hands and yet exerting their powerful influence.

A third implication which may be drawn from the distinctions between Russian and American managers relates to the relative importance of their first years on the job.

Russian engineers generally move into junior executive posts soon after leaving college. Here, so far as a future managerial career is concerned, they seem to be in a "sink or swim" position. With no formal training in human relations, organization theory, or any other aspect of "working with people," they are now thrown into a position where this aspect of their behavior is critical. Their only previous training has been activity within organizations while still at school.

The odds are heavily against the success of any single engineer. For most of these engineers will soon move on into design or methods-study work. Only a relatively few will remain in "line" operations. But it is probably from these few that future managers are primarily chosen. This system of narrowing down the field is quite in line with the concept that "good administrators are born, not made."

No doubt, their first work years are also vitally important for American managers. But the stress seems less. In particular, since most American top managers begin in functional rather than in executive positions, the process of separating executives from others is one of selection rather than rejection. Future managers are generally moved into minor executive posts; if this does not occur at one point in a man's career, it can still occur later. But the decision in the Soviet case is more final; for here, many start on the executive path and most are weeded out. It is less difficult for an ever-hopeful candidate to get onto the executive road further along if he remains still untested than if he has once been ejected from it.

part three

THE MANAGER'S WAY OF LIFE

7. THE STANDARD OF LIVING

A story, supposedly true, which I heard in Moscow tells of the Minister who, during Stalin's reign, built himself a large and expensive home outside of Moscow. Shortly after it was completed, the Minister was called into Stalin's office. "Do you like children?" Stalin asked him. "I love them," the Minister enthusiastically assured him. "Good," said Stalin. "I wish to thank you in the name of the Soviet Government for the beautiful home you have just presented to the state as a children's club." The story was told to me approvingly; "gracious living" rings no bells of approval against the backdrop of the Soviet housing shortage.

When Russians who use their money to build the sort of home they can afford are thought fortunate to remain unpunished and simply to be allowed to present the home as a "gift" to the state, then it is difficult to make a meaningful comparison of the money incomes received by Russians and Americans. When, in addition, we must remember that Russians have different tastes and customs than our own, and thus have their own ideas as to the proper ways of spending money; when the sorts of goods available in Russia free of charge or at nominal cost are not the same as here; when there are variations as to size of family and thus as to the demands on the family budget; when there are differences as to whether the man is the sole family breadwinner: when all these conditions hold, as they in fact do, then direct money income comparisons between Russia and the United States are senseless indeed.

We can only compare what people do with their incomes. Thus, I shall try to describe the Russian executive's "way of life." I shall quote Russian salaries and prices in rubles instead of in dollars, since it is difficult to find a single sensible exchange rate in which to express all purchases. But, if one wishes to transpose mentally into dollars, ten rubles to one dollar is about as realistic a ratio as any other.

To begin with, the Russian urban family today is a rather small one. Two children seem to be the magic number, with many back-sliding parents having only one. When I told Russians that my wife and I had three children, they all looked upon ours as a large family. Three children, I was told, comprise the ideal—but seldom realized—Soviet family: two children to reproduce the parents, and "one for Khrushchev."

While the Russians have the reputation of a puritanical people, they are quite modern in their approach to birth control. I have seen contraceptive devices openly displayed for sale. In addition, abortion, which had been illegal since 1936, was again legalized in 1955 so as to eliminate the hazards to the patient of contraband practice.

While the Russian urban family has shrunk in the postwar period, the American family has grown larger. The two-child, middle-class family of the depressed 1930's has turned into the three- and four-child family of the prosperous 1950's.

Along with the difference in family size in the two countries, there is a sharp difference in the role of the wife. In Russia, 45 per cent of the city labor force is made up of women, compared to 33 per cent in the United States. Roughly 80 per cent of all urban Russian able-bodied women work at full-time jobs, while the American figure is 28 per cent, with an additional 10 per cent working part time.

Moreover, mothers of young children in all Russian social classes hold down jobs. It is the socially accepted pattern. The woman who does not work is simply out of things. In the United States, on the other hand, income differences sharply affect the proportion of working wives. Of those wives whose husbands earned between $3000 and $4000 in 1956, 28 per cent worked full time in 1957. Of those whose husbands earned above $10,000, only 8 per cent worked full time.

One Russian teacher in her early twenties with whom I spoke was eager to get married; she wanted children—or, rather, one child. But she expressed horror at the idea of staying at home with a child, even for a few years. How dull it would be! How awful to stay within the home all day, instead of being out on the job in contact with other adults!

It is certainly true that we can find the identical attitude among young American intellectuals. The difference lies in the fact that it is only the exceptional American girl who feels this way—while I would guess that it is a widespread Russian feeling. Russian management wives to a large extent come from this group of people who find their stimulation outside the family circle.

Thus the American family budget is drained by more children than is the Russian budget. At the same time, there is only one breadwinner in the American manager's home—at least when the children are young—while there are two in the Russian's. These differences in family patterns make slightly ridiculous comparisons of living standards which rest solely on the average earnings of *individuals* in the two nations. For most people in all countries dip into the family till, rather than spending as a lone individual, and so it is the family earnings and needs which count.

Why is it that these Russian-American differences exist? Partly, no doubt, it is due to the poorer economic conditions in the Soviet Union. The American family has expanded with prosperity. The Russian budget is sufficiently strained with only two children; the apartment is crowded enough without additional kids. The American wife can afford to stay home and take care of the children; the Russian cannot.

This is part of the answer, but only the most dogmatic of economic determinists would say that it is the full explanation. It was not many years ago that population experts were all agreed that families grew smaller as families and countries grew wealthier. We are hardly now in a position to assert that the relationship is invariably the reverse. The Russian mother has cheap and good nurseries available for her youngsters once they are two months old. The American mother has no such ready opportunity for returning to work, and she may find it impossible to leave young children with anyone; taxes plus the cost of child care may be greater than her total earnings. But most important of all, there is the social expectation. Two children are the "right number" for the conforming Soviet family. The young wife is expected to work until her seventh month of pregnancy, and return to the job when her child is two months old. If she should not do so, what would the neighbors think?

Let us, then, take these differences in family size and number of breadwinners as differences in national "ways of life." Given these, what is the income of a Russian managerial family and how is it used?

A Leningrad director of a food plant, managing an organization of eleven hundred employees, earned in 1958 an average of 4500 rubles monthly. In plants under the Moscow City Council, directors normally earn between 1900 and 4500 rubles monthly for managing factories with two hundred to one thousand workers. In major steel plants, directors earn 6000 to 7500 rubles. In this key industry a department superintendent, who could well be in charge of a group as large as the entire Leningrad food factory, might earn 4500 rubles monthly, and a senior foreman 4000 rubles. All of these earnings figures include the substantial Soviet bonuses.

In the family of one of these managers, the wife's contribution to the family larder will probably not be too important. The minimum Soviet wage is 300 rubles monthly. An average wage is in the neighborhood of 800–900 rubles. A woman translator in Moscow, who had no college degree but knew two foreign languages, received 900 rubles a month in 1958. Let us put the total managerial family income at, say, 5500 rubles monthly. An American executive at the level of our Russian would be earning $20,000 to $30,000 annually.

Of the Russian income, perhaps 13 per cent will go for income tax, and another 3 per cent for Communist Party and trade union dues. (Managers belong to the same industrial union as do their workers.) Four thousand six hundred and twenty rubles are left.

Rent in the Soviet Union is a low budget item, and is related both to the amount of space in the apartment and to the family income level. Including utilities, 1½ to 4 per cent of income is a fairly representative figure. Thus 175 rubles will go for this item.

The quality of the housing will probably be as low as the rental figure itself. With a family of four, our manager by rights is entitled to only one room. But since his family size is on the borderline of qualifying for more space, it seems reasonable to expect that a man of his position can wangle two rooms out of the housing authorities.

If he should live in one of the new apartment houses, similar to the mass of buildings being erected in Moscow behind the New Moscow University, his apartment will be located in a four- or six-story building grouped together with others around an open lawn and play area. A six-story building will probably have a self-service elevator. Judging from the statistics I saw at one development for a planned street of thirteen houses, the four-story buildings have sixty-four apartments each.

If our manager is lucky, his flat will be in one of the houses erected during the last two years; these have a fairly airy and light architectural feeling rather than the heavy pomposity which characterized the construction of even five years ago. Also, to this architectural layman these newer houses seem a good deal better built. They are conceived as garden apartments with trees and play areas alongside, although the open space enclosed by each block of houses is tiny indeed by American standards. With regard to this, however, there are regional differences. New housing in Kiev has a great deal more open space and trees than has that of Moscow, for Kiev is proud of its natural beauty and strives to maintain it.

Our manager's apartment will have two medium-sized rooms, a small kitchen, a toilet, and a separate bathroom. Wall closets are a rarity; the family will be lucky if there is a single small one in the apartment. The kitchen will have a two-burner stove, a small sink, some built-in work space next to the sink, and a good bit of overhead storage space. But there will barely be room for the smallest model refrigerator.

There is another tack which our manager may take in the hunt for satisfactory housing. Instead of living in an apartment, he may build his own house. In fact, in the six years of 1951–56, 27 per cent of all the urban housing space erected in the Soviet Union was put up for private individuals. These houses can be financed through long-term bank loans, and labor can be hired to help build them. But this is far from a solution to our manager's housing problem. Suburban gracious living is not within his grasp. For he requires allocations of land, materials, and labor from the town's housing authority. The sort of house he will be allowed to build will probably be poorer than the apartment he could rent. Building one's own house seems to be an expedient worth investigating only by those who cannot get the comparatively good Soviet housing I have just described.

A third alternative exists for the manager as a result of the peculiar Soviet institutional arrangements for housing construction and operation. Something like two thirds of all city housing is built and operated by the various city councils, but the remaining third is run by factories and other economic organizations for the use of their own employees. I was told that during the two years 1957–58, the Moscow City Council was building the equivalent of 1260 buildings of 64 apartments each, while institutions were putting up the equivalent of 1535 such apartment houses within the city limits.

Factories and higher bodies erect and operate their own housing as an important fringe benefit for employees. In a country where the housing shortage is perennial, management often cannot hire workers unless it is able to offer them at least as good a place to live as their present quarters. No Russian is allowed to move to Moscow, for example, without first finding an apartment. In practice, this means that a Moscow factory can hardly hire an out-of-town skilled worker or engineer without giving him at least part of a room in a factory-operated apartment house, for there is no other way of getting him into Moscow.

In theory, factories allocate apartments among their employees according to family size and to length of time on the waiting list. In practice, of course, good housing is used both as a bonus and as a means of attracting skilled workers and other employees to the plant. This creates the opportunity for management to build and allocate to itself first-class housing, which is the third method managers may use to solve their personal housing problems.

No doubt this alternative is sometimes taken by managers. One can read of such "scandals" in the Soviet press. But this is risky business, for it is somewhat difficult to hide a house. Dangerous animosities are bound to be created by such open diversion of materials which could otherwise have been used for mass housing. Normally, the manager will satisfy himself with housing which barely provides family privacy and a modicum of space.

Of the managerial family's remaining 4445 rubles, a substantial portion will go for food. A reasonable figure for a month's expenditures on food eaten at home is perhaps 1500 rubles. Figuring at a ruble-dollar ratio appropriate to the relative prices of food in Russia and in the United States, the 1500 rubles should have the purchasing power of some $100. To this, let us add another 500 rubles for meals eaten out by husband and wife. These additional 500 rubles should cover about 60 meals in the low-cost institutional restaurants where Soviet workers and professionals eat on the job.

The total family food budget of our mythical manager thus comprises about 43 per cent of his net income left after taxes and Party and union dues. In purchasing power, it may be close to $220 a month. This purchasing power figure is so high primarily because of the large number of full restaurant meals bought at very low ruble prices. A second reason is the Russian love for food. When I entered Russia by train from Helsinki, the conductor on the Russian car was quite defensive about the state of Russian clothing as compared to Finnish. "The Finn likes to put his money on his back," he told me in explanation, "while the Russian puts it into his belly." A final reason for the Russian's high food expenditures is the long Soviet history of unavailability of manufactured consumer goods. In contrast, food has more generally been ready to hand, provided one had the money.

Two features of the Soviet economy keep the ruble food budget from rising still higher. One of these features is the low price of meals in factories and other places of work. Most eating-out is done in such dining halls, and this seems to be at least as cheap as eating at home. Thus in Russian colleges, students and faculty normally eat a main meal for three to five rubles. Even in a railroad station restaurant, I bought two large meat sandwiches and a bottle of beer for four rubles, while an American friend had a plate of steak and three vegetables for five rubles. Although fifteen rubles to a dollar seems a proper conversion rate to use for food eaten at home, four rubles for one dollar is more appropriate for restaurant meals.

The second relevant feature of the economy is the fact that, during much of the year, fresh fruits and vegetables are simply unavailable. In seasons when they are for sale, often they can only be purchased at farmers' markets where the various collective farms sell their produce for what the market will bear. But the Russian housewife, like most Europeans, is accustomed to daily shopping. Since no farmers' market may be convenient to her home or place of work, she is likely to do most of her shopping in stores where the selection is quite poor. Thus the manager's wife may fail to buy food luxuries simply because she cannot conveniently shop for them daily.

Turning to clothing, our manager's family may spend some 800 rubles monthly. This would have the purchasing power of some $60.

Ready-made clothing now seems to be generally available in the Russian stores. Even imported items can be bought, and some curious anomalies arise from this. In the huge central department store at Moscow, I looked over a number of men's suits which hung on open racks. Russian-made suits were selling for 670 rubles apiece. But alongside them were imported suits—the only one with a recognizable label was Czech—which seemed to me to be of much better quality and cut, but which sold for only 470 rubles. At the moment when I was there, although it was in the evening when most men would be off from work, I was the only one even window-shopping at this particular suit counter. Thus these imports would not seem to be rarities to be instantly snatched up.

Custom-made clothing is also available. But this is really expensive, as is the making of clothing oneself. Material which did not seem of particularly good quality sold for 100 to 200 rubles a square yard. If our manager wishes custom-made clothing, his clothing budget will shoot up sharply. But, judging from the rather tasteless cuts of clothing seen on people in the expensive hotels and in the first rows of the theater, I would judge that ready-made clothing is the rule.

A major item in American household budgets is transportation. For the Russian family, on the other hand, 50 rubles can cover the month's needs. Public transportation is cheap; the Leningrad and Moscow subways charge half a ruble, and bus and streetcar charges are proportional. Moreover, this transportation was absolutely first-rate in all the cities I visited. Even in the outskirts of town, a five-minute wait is unusual and a case for indignation at bureaucratic inefficiency. This seems to hold right up until 2 A.M., when public transport stops for the night.

It is possible that our manager will own a private car, particularly if he lives near Moscow, where private automobiles seem concentrated. But his chances are not too good. Between 1945 and the end of 1956, only 642,000 passenger cars had been produced in the entire Soviet Union; of this total, substantially less than half was sold to private individuals.

While our manager probably does not own his own car, the chances are high that he can have the use of one belonging to his factory. It may even be assigned, along with a chauffeur, for his own exclusive use. Nevertheless, while he may use this car for his wife's shopping trips and for Sunday excursions, he is unlikely to feel completely free in doing so. The office car represents the same sort of problem to the manager as does allocation to himself of unusually good factory housing, and its use for personal purposes is increasingly frowned upon as more automobiles are put on the market for sale.

It is difficult to evaluate the importance of this absence of a car. The automobile plays a crucial role in American suburban living; but the Russian manager does not live in the suburbs, and in any case his wife is at work all day. Russian public transportation within cities seems vastly superior to American, and thus the car is hardly necessary there. The lack of an auto is an important limiting factor when on Sunday jaunts and on vacations; on the other hand, there is a substantial network of rapid streetcars and trains going from the cities to the villages and nearby country spots. Certainly the absence of a parking problem is, under the circumstances, an important counterweight to the absence of a car. Due to good public transportation, the Russian manager generally has an easier time getting downtown or to work than does the American with his car.

At this point, we have accounted for 65 per cent of the Russian manager's net income as going for rent and utilities, food, clothing, and transport. After making allowance for tobacco, laundry, haircuts, books, and other miscellaneous items, he still has some 1225 rubles left.

Medical care is free, and nothing except minor amounts for medicines need be allocated for this. Nevertheless, there is some private practice of medicine, and our manager may choose to spend a little money here. One Russian told me of going to a private dentist, and he complained bitterly as to the results. The private practitioner couldn't get rid of the toothache, although the problem was later taken care of at the regular free clinic. But other Russians have had the reverse experience, and so some minor fees are paid to private doctors.

Since education at all levels is free of charge, and more than 80 per cent of college students receive stipends for living expenses, our manager will not be putting anything aside for his children's education. If his children are of preschool age, a charge for their care in a nursery or kindergarten may be made. But even though this charge is scaled to income, it would hardly exceed 150 rubles monthly.

Vacations are another item which represent negligible cost. Camp for the youngsters is almost free. A month's trip to a vacation spot such as the Crimea for a manager living in Moscow—five hundred and fifty miles away—could be handled economically on 1800 to 2000 rubles for the manager and his wife. The expenditures of such a trip could be increased substantially without exceeding the amount normally spent at home during a month. It is therefore no added drain on the family exchequer.

If we set aside 50 rubles a month for all the above items —medical care, education, and vacations—we would seem fully to cover our manager's needs.

A large amount to set aside for entertainment would be

600 rubles monthly. Top prices for tickets to the legitimate theater are 20 rubles; at the ballet and at musicals, they may run to 30 rubles. Movies are a good deal cheaper. If our manager and his wife go out three times a month, 200 rubles should easily cover the cost of the best seats in the house plus refreshments between the acts. Entertainment of friends at home, plus occasional evenings of eating, drinking, and dancing at the lush hotels, might add at most another 400 rubles.

This leaves 575 rubles a month for purchases of consumer durables and for savings for old age and emergencies. In purchasing power for buying consumer durables, this would represent some $45 a month. But opportunities for spending this money are limited. There are long waiting lists for cars. Good furniture is almost unavailable. Only the smallest refrigerators seem to be produced. On the other hand, radios, TV sets, and, recently, tape recorders are readily available in the stores. Moreover, there are some truly expensive items. Country *dachas,* or summer homes, are widespread, particularly around Moscow. True, these *dachas* will normally have outdoor plumbing, and water will be pumped from a well shared by a number of houses. Nevertheless, the *dacha* serves as a welcome escape from the city, at least for summer weekends. In Kiev, the Dnieper River is filled with privately owned boats, among them not only rowboats, outboard motorboats, and sailboats, but also small yachts with cooking and sleeping space below.

How about savings? Will they take up any major portion of this 575 rubles?

Probably the single item most highly advertised in the Soviet Union is "saving." Admonitions to save stare at you from the pages of your newspaper, from posters on the wall, from billboards. Save, the Russian is urged, in order to buy a car, build a house, purchase a refrigerator or a TV set. Installment buying is taboo, except for the case of mortgage payments on housing, and saving is the means by which a Russian goes about buying an expensive durable item. For Soviet man is still economically backward, not yet having caught up with America in learning to apply the lessons of government deficit finance to his own private affairs.

MONTHLY INCOME AND EXPENDITURES

	RUSSIAN MANAGERIAL FAMILY		U.S. URBAN FAMILY HIGH INCOME		U.S. URBAN FAMILY MODERATE INCOME	
	$	%	$	%	$	%
Total Money Income	550		1567		494	
Taxes	71.50		241		40	
Total Expenditures on Current Consumption	460	100	898	100	438	100
Housing and Utilities	18	3.8	121	13.5	61	13.9
Food Prepared at Home	150	32.6 } 43.5	130	14.5 } 22.4	99	22.6 } 28.3
Food Eaten Away from Home	50	10.9	71	7.9	25	5.7
Alcoholic Beverages	20	4.3	19	2.1	8	1.8
Clothing and Clothing Services	90	19.6	127	14.1	54	12.3
Medical Care	—	—	37	4.1	21	4.8
Transportation	5	1.1	115	12.8	68	15.5
SUBTOTAL	333	72.3	620	69.0	336	76.6

With all this promotion of saving, it is interesting that the advertisements do not recommend saving for old age or illness. Presumably, the national pension system is expected to take care of these needs. If this source is insufficient, the family may be expected to help out. The fact that savings are not widely used for these purposes seems confirmed by the fact that total accumulated money savings of the urban population at the end of 1956 were only 599 rubles ($60) per capita.

Our manager will qualify for a pension when he is sixty; this will be the maximum pension of 1200 rubles monthly. We have assumed that his wife was earning 900 rubles monthly; this should give her a pension at fifty-five of 650 rubles. Thus their combined tax-free income from pensions will be 40 per cent of their present income after deduction of taxes and Communist Party and trade union dues. (A 1957 study of fifty American companies showed that some three quarters of them had pension plans for their executives, and that retirement benefits averaged 40 per cent of income at the time of retirement.) In case of accident or sickness, roughly a similar pension will be received.

This is a substantial ruble income by Soviet standards for a couple whose children are grown. Particularly in view of the lesser needs of older people, the couple should be able to live in reasonable comfort. One middle-aged Russian with whom I spoke, a man in the higher-income brackets, assured me that people saved little for emergencies or old age. Considering the steady and rapid inflation which characterized the Soviet economy until 1949, and the unavailability of equity investments to serve as a protection against inflation, it seems reasonable that our manager should do little saving. Nevertheless, he will probably use some of his 575 rubles for this purpose.

Let us sum up this material on expenditure patterns by a comparison with American patterns. For this purpose, let us treat the dollar as equivalent to ten rubles for all types of expenditures. Comparison will be made with two American income groups in 1950: one group had an average annual money income of $18,800 and was comparable in social position to the Soviet managers; the other had an average money income of $6000, which is roughly the dollar amount received by our Russian executive. The American figures are taken from a large-scale United States government survey.

From the table on page 100, we can see that housing, utilities, medical care, and transportation make up one third of the American family budgets; but they comprise only 5 per cent of the Russian manager's budget. On the other hand, food expenditures are 44 per cent of the Russian budget compared to 22 to 28 per cent of the American budgets. These are the differences in expenditure pattern which make it so difficult to meaningfully translate any individual Russian item of spending into American terms. The budgets as a whole are too widely different to allow for any simple comparison.

One reason for the vast variation in budgets is that the Russian manager's wife simply is not free to spend the family money as she sees fit. There is no practical way for her to spend more on housing, for example. Similarly, the selection is limited in many areas of consumer spending, although the choice has been widening over the years.

In this respect, the Russian management family is somewhat in the position of the American upper-class Negro. The parallel is particularly strong as regards housing, with both groups generally being unable to rent or buy improved homes. The Russian manager often feels loaded with money and is quite free in his spending precisely because he has no practical way of purchasing the things he would really like to have. Perhaps it is the presence of this excess cash which makes the Russian engineer, management man, or university professor often shake his head sympathetically, if a bit scornfully, over the economic plight of the American visitor to Russia. The visitor may have a much higher living standard than the Russian, but it cannot be denied that money *is* a problem for the American.

The American manager's spending pattern is, to a considerable extent, built around suburban living. Leisure time and money go into the home and grounds. "Do it yourself" activity is worked into the pattern. The wife's life is rooted in the house. Where keeping-up-with-the-Joneses is important, much of it is based on this type of home life.

By and large, the Russian family has no opportunity for such spending and leisure activity. The wife works all day; there is little beauty and less space in the apartment. Except for summer weekends, where the country *dacha* may be the center of attraction, the home is a good place to stay away from.

The Russian manager is likely to be a sports fan, and spend some of his free time at the ball parks. It may be that he is a man-about-town, but this is unlikely since night club partying in each town is limited to one or a few hotels where there is a band and dancing. As with us, most of the customers in Russia's main cities appear to be out-of-towners on expense accounts.

Thus, with the limitations on other leisure activities, the manager and his wife are likely to spend a fair amount of time at the factory club or in other organized leisure activities. The arts, however, also play a highly important role in Russian social life. The drama, ballet, musicals, concerts, even drawing-room comedy: all have wide audiences in all Soviet cities. The Russian who lives even in one of the smaller cities has opportunities for theater, dance, and music which in our country only the New Yorker can match.

Unquestionably, this tends to make the Russian businessman more broadly based in the arts than is his American counterpart. In this respect, the Russian is part of the general European culture. But he goes even further. Imagine a four-hour dramatic performance in the United States! Only Eugene O'Neill could get away with it. But in Russia, the four-hour five-act play is standard fare.

The Russian executive is also, by American standards, a great reader of books. Perhaps this is partly because he has more leisure for book reading than has the American, since the Russian's newspaper is small—only four pages—and he does not have magazines of the *Life* or *Time* variety. Perhaps he is responding more to old European traditions, well ingrained in Russia, where the term "uncultured" is one of the strongest forms of damnation. In any case, the Russian manager's reading goes considerably further than his daily paper and the trade magazine.

Not only is the demand for technical books in Russia so great that such books are difficult to get hold of, but the same applies to works on administration, accounting, and the like. In the summer of 1958, it was entirely out of the question for me to buy books in Moscow which had been published as far back as 1952 or 1953: they had been sold out long ago. I finally was able to purchase some books, especially recommended to me, which had been published during 1957 and 1958. But these purchases were accomplished only through the good graces of a Russian professor and a friend of his in high bookseller circles; the friend sold me one of the last copies, normally intended for the files. The public demand for these books is so great that one needs luck or influence to buy a desired copy.

The pressure is not so great on non-professional books, but one sees people watching eagerly even for these when clerks shelve books newly arrived in the store. A manager who limited his reading to technical works would certainly be labeled as "uncultured."

But while the Russian manager differs from the American in his leisure-time habits, he completely shares with the American his bewilderment before the age-old "fathers and sons" problem. If the American shakes his head over his eight-year-old girl who has a steady boy friend, the Russian is bewildered at his teen-age son who goes wild over bootleg jazz recorded on X-ray film. Both parents feel equally uncertain as to when they will be called down to the police station to bail out the offspring; juvenile delinquency on the part of the scions of the town's leading lights is today a well-recognized phenomenon of both societies. The hell-raising college boy, with no seeming ambition except to work his way through his father's income, can be met in both societies.

Both Russians and Americans wonder where in the world their children get their habits. True, the Russian youth resembles in mood the "angry young men" of England more than the American "satiated generation," and a father ambitious for his son may at least find more character in the expression of revolt than in simple satiation. But it is difficult for a Russian father, who has lived through collectivization, industrialization, political purges, and war to take seriously as a sign of character the revolt of his son to booze, jazz, and a zoot suit. Both Russian and American managerial fathers doubtless often wonder if it is they themselves who are at fault, in that they are always busy and see their children so little. But both are quite unable to change the pressures of their lives.

There is a further, non-material aspect of consumer well-being which we have not yet considered. This is a comparison with the recent past. For a man's concept of whether he is well off will be strongly shaped by the standard of living to which he is accustomed.

Here, the Russians are in good shape. Real per capita earnings of the urban population are said to have grown by 44 per cent between 1950 and 1956; doubtless they have risen further since then. These official Soviet figures do not seem unreasonable; but even if we take them with a grain of salt, and also remember that it is low-wage groups whose incomes have risen most rapidly, the executives have done very well indeed. In comparison, average personal income in real terms in the United States has risen by 18 per cent between 1950 and 1957. Russian managers thus have much more of the feeling of sharp improvement from year to year in their own welfare.

The other side of this coin is that American executives do not look to any other country as the land of milk and honey. The Russian manager, who knows something of foreign standards of living, is likely to feel unhappy when he makes his comparisons over space instead of over time. However, it seems reasonable to expect that the manager and his family react most strongly to changes which they themselves have experienced and can perceive directly, rather than to those involving sights across the Iron Curtain.

A third side of consumer happiness is involved in Veblen's concept of "conspicuous consumption." To the extent that we strive to keep up with the Joneses, we are best off when the Joneses are poor. Many items of expenditure then become quite unnecessary.

This feature of consumer psychology acts to boost the subjective value of the Russian manager's income much closer to the American level than one might think simply by comparing absolute purchasing power. The Russian manager's income bears somewhat the same proportion to that of the average Russian worker as does the American manager's income vis-à-vis the American worker. As it affects conspicuous consumption, absolute income has no importance; relative income is everything.

The housing shortage itself tends further to accentuate the Russian manager's feeling of comparative well-being. Soviet housing being what it is, people live where they can. Russian districts are far less homogeneous as to the income level of the inhabitants than are American districts, for rent levels are quite unrelated to neighborhood. Living in a homogeneous area, the American executive looks around him and finds that he is not especially well off. His main standard of comparison, after all, is the living standard of his neighbors. The Russian manager surveys the scene, and finds that he is indeed very well heeled compared to his neighbors, since these latter are a fairly typical sample of the entire urban population. His only problem with the Joneses is to live down to them. It is true that this living-down-to-the-Joneses problem may also be faced by the wife of the president of a fair-sized company in an American small town, but it is far from the usual problem of living standard for the American managerial family.

8. THE MANAGERIAL GAME

The previous chapter told how the manager spends his money. Now we shall deal with how he earns it.

Are there any important differences between the American and Russian traditions of the management game? Let us turn to one area of similarity, and to three where varying patterns and expectations have emerged.

Ulcers

In both countries, management is a high-pressure game. Delegation of authority is an ideal on which all can agree, but the forty-hour week for managers still awaits an organizational revolution. In a 1957 survey of 355 company presidents, the American Management Association found that their average workweek ran between fifty-five and eighty-five hours a week. One American business school found that its graduates worked more hours a week the longer they were out of school.

The Russian manager is certainly not far behind the American in all this. Stalin's death, however, liberated Russian executives from one particularly aggravating source of ulcers. Stalin himself was a night owl who believed in having the first long coffee break at midnight. The Kremlin staff, of course, had to establish its work habits around those of the boss. This meant that telephone calls from the Kremlin to ministers and branch chiefs would normally be made long before cockcrow. As this administrative system worked itself down the hierarchy, even plant directors became accustomed to receiving complaints and orders from Moscow at 2 A.M.

One of the reforms after Stalin's death was to put the administrative system back on the day shift. A decree was issued officially ending the night routine. The manager's day was to be somewhat regularized.

While there are occasional American top executives who get their best ideas in the middle of the night, and feel called upon to communicate them immediately, it is a measure of the Russian system that the whole economy should have worked on this plan for a quarter of a century.

Bonuses

The first of the areas of difference between the national management-game patterns is that of incentives for management. Both in Russia and in the United States, managerial incentives are very strong. Since top-management posts are not restricted to candidates qualifying through family or friendship connections, junior executives have opportunities for major advancement. Income differences are sharp, and promotion up the managerial ladder can lead to sharp rises in income. In both countries, there are also strong non-monetary rewards for such advancement: greater power, prestige in the organization, pride in doing a good job.

But while these underlying incentives are similar in the two economies, there is a sharp difference in the bonus system. In the United States, by and large, executives are compensated by means of their salaries. Performance is rewarded primarily through promotion rather than through bonuses. True, American companies do try to give their executives a stake in the firm's future. Stock purchases and stock options play this role. The size of end-of-the-year bonuses depends on the corporation's profit picture during the year. But these bonuses generally are not of major monetary significance, and they are usually only loosely connected with the work of the individual executive. One 1957 study of fifty companies showed that only half of them had executive-bonus plans at all, and even in these firms the bonuses averaged barely 10 to 20 per cent. Thus bonuses normally play a peripheral role in the manager's actual income, although they may seem much more important in anticipation.

Managerial compensation in the Soviet Union is patterned

within quite a different framework. Administrators apply quite literally the official slogan for "socialist" distribution of income: "to each according to his work." (It is an interesting commentary on the ability of people to take themselves seriously that the same principle can simultaneously be put forth in different countries as a unique property of both capitalist and socialist ideology.)

The Soviets have adopted the concept that earnings should be tied closely and immediately to production. For workers, the piece-rate system of payment reigns supreme. For managers, monthly bonuses make up a major part of income and are tied to the operations *during that very same month* of the production unit for which the executive is responsible. Thus, the method used for payment of executives is as close to a piece-rate system as the Soviets can get it.

In one of the largest machine-building plants in the country, the director today receives a 50 per cent bonus each month in which the plant produces its target output. (However, if other aspects of the plant's accounts for the month are bad, this bonus will be reduced or completely eliminated.) For each 1 per cent by which the target output is exceeded, the director receives a further bonus of 6 per cent of his base salary. In a minor plant, the corresponding figures are 22 and 2 per cent.

Top-management personnel in plants under the Moscow City Council, I was told, *normally* earn monthly bonuses of 25 to 50 per cent of their base salaries. In addition, quarterly bonuses are distributed to the three best plants in each industry within the city. The limit to the regular monthly bonus is 100 per cent of the monthly base salary. Management above the plant level is rewarded by similar bonuses.

A Leningrad wine plant which I visited was especially interesting in this regard. Unlike the situation in most Soviet plants, there was no desire to increase output. Thus, although three quarters of all Soviet industrial workers are paid by piece rates, the workers in this particular plant were on straight time wages.

Management, however, was on incentive pay even in this factory. The director's monthly bonus averaged 50 per cent of his base salary; shop superintendents averaged 30 per cent;

and even foremen averaged 40 per cent bonuses. These bonuses, of course, were linked to aspects of their work other than volume of output.

The Soviet system of incentive pay for executives would seem to have two major consequences for managerial behavior. The first of these consequences is to put managers under high pressure. The month's take-home pay is riding on performance during that very month; a bare miss of the production target may cut a man's monthly pay by 30 to 50 per cent. Moreover, missing of the target—at least on an annual basis—is common. Data for all industry in the entire Soviet Union shows that, during the years 1951 through 1954, between 31 and 40 per cent of all firms failed in each year to meet their annual targets.

In comparison, American management seems a low-pressure operation. Bonuses are much less important a part of executive earnings, and even these are generally awarded for a year's operations rather than monthly. Failure in one month can be made up during the next without affecting earnings.

From the Soviet manager's point of view, this atmosphere of continuous strain is further worsened by the types of decisions which he may be forced to take in order to meet his monthly targets. With short-range goals at the forefront of his attention, the manager may well put off activities which do not have an immediate payoff. Maintenance may be postponed; engineers can be taken out of design and put into production functions; the toolroom may be temporarily filled with production work. But the longer-run implications of these decisions are likely to be serious; the manager can only hope that next month he will be able to catch up. The channel between Scylla and Charybdis is a narrow one.

In drawing these comparisons between American and Soviet management behavior, there is some slight danger that we are taking the word for the deed. It is possible that, in practice, Soviet executives are given much the same bonuses each month regardless of performance. The likelihood of this seems remote since figures are available which show a wide variation between plants as to the average bonus of technical personnel in one plant, the 1955 bonus averaged no more than 2 per cent of the basic salary. Nevertheless, if full bonuses are nor mally paid, and if it is in fact highly exceptional for them to be withheld, then bonuses should in reality be treated simply as part of straight salary.

In 1934, a study of a wide range of Russian industries showed that only 24 per cent of shop superintendents and 21 per cent of foremen earned bonuses within a specified month. However, for those who did receive bonuses, these averaged 32 per cent of total earnings for shop superintendents and 27 per cent for foremen. Thus bonuses were granted rather sparingly, but were substantial for those who did get them.

In October 1934, bonuses made up roughly 4 per cent of total earnings of management in the plants studied. By 1940, this share had almost tripled. An explicit postwar policy of raising the portion of bonuses in managerial income had, by 1947, increased the ratio to an amount ranging from 21 per cent in the food industry to 51 per cent in the iron and steel industry. These 1947 figures seem reasonably representative of the current situation.

Clearly, what seems to have occurred is not so much an increase in the amount of bonuses received by individual managers, as a sharp jump in the proportion of managers who receive bonuses at all in any given month. I do not know how far this expansion has gone, but some Polish experience illustrates an extreme form of regular bonus payments.

In one of the major Polish industries, bonuses are paid quarterly and make up 80 per cent of the basic salary of management. During the summer of 1958, I was told that only one or two plant directors—out of the seventy in this industry —fail to receive premiums in any given quarter. In addition, several more receive premiums which are less than the maximum permissible. But over 90 per cent of the directors receive maximum bonuses each quarter. Given these figures, the bonus would seem to be a normal portion of the director's salary, a share which can be withheld only as punishment for major failures. If there are Russian industries or geographic areas where behavior is parallel to this Polish experience, then our earlier implications would not hold for them.

Job Security

Our second area of difference in management patterns is the degree of job security felt by executives.

Soviet management personnel in the 1930's—even before the period of the great purges—generally stayed at the same post for only a few years. During 1934 and 1936, Soviet agencies conducted broad studies of industrial management at various levels, running from shop superintendents to heads of entire industries. Treating each job category and each of the two years separately, the full range for management personnel who had held their posts more than five years was only 1 to 15 per cent. Forty to 65 per cent had been in the given post for a mere one to three years, and one sixth to one third of the total for less than one year. These rates of mobility clearly speeded up during the 1937–38 purge period, and then seem to have returned to the 1934–36 level during the remaining prewar years.

Here, by American standards, was a fabulous executive turnover. One can imagine its negative impact on the feeling of job security among managerial personnel, as well as on their mental balancing of the long-run good of their organization versus short-run goals. True, a study of newspaper accounts of "next jobs" of replaced plant directors showed that only 40 per cent were dismissed or given positions which clearly represented demotion. The others were transferred to posts which may have been only lateral moves or even promotions. But even the 40-per-cent figure, a minimum estimate, represented a fantastically high probability of job failure for Soviet directors. While we have no similar data for other Soviet executives, there is no reason to believe that removal due to failure occurred any less frequently in their case.

It is difficult to know whether the situation has changed in the postwar period. Soviet writers have always been critical of this high executive mobility. Managers and academic people with whom I spoke in the Soviet Union called it a thing of the past; while this may be true, it is also possible that their statements were distorted by the desire to paint a favorable picture.

One professor, who has great authority in Soviet academic and management circles, stated as his impression that conditions are still much the same as they were prewar.

The only recent statistics available are for the coal industry. In 1955, Bulganin complained that the annual turnover rate for directors and chief engineers of pits in the U.S.S.R. as a whole was running 40 to 50 per cent. In the year 1956 there was replacement of 25 per cent of all directors of coal pits in the major Ukrainian center of the Donbass. Here are statistics quite comparable to the prewar figures. Is it true, as I was told, that the coal industry is exceptional in this regard? I do not know.

Whether or not Soviet executive turnover has slowed down compared to the 1930's, it seems reasonable to assume that it is still higher than American turnover. But if it has indeed been reduced, whatever its absolute rate may now be, the result is to make the work environment of the Soviet manager more secure and friendly than that of two decades ago. This period of change is within the experience of many present managers.

Much more important, the penalties for failure as a manager are today much less severe than they once were. At all times, with the possible exception of the worst purge days, most unsuccessful managers were simply demoted or fired. But always the question was there: Did industrial failure occur on purpose? Was the manager a conscious saboteur of the Soviet drive for industrialization or, if not this, was he in any case lax with underlings who themselves were saboteurs? The manager whose production failed to rise at close to the expected rate had to live with the fear of political accusations.

This particular insecurity seems to have lost its *raison d'être* with the last war, and has certainly ceased to be a factor since the death of Stalin. Removal of this danger goes a long way toward eliminating the trauma previously embedded in Soviet executive positions.

Although American managers have never faced these risks of prison and execution, their degree of security has probably also increased in recent years. As companies have become larger and the proportion of managers who are executives in large corporations has grown, the buffeting of managers by the winds of the business cycle has diminished. More and more of them are employed by corporations which do not risk going to the wall or having to sharply slash their managerial staffs. The mild breezes of the 1940's and 1950's have made for a job security unknown in the tempestuous atmosphere of the 1930's. Increasingly, the business corporation has been able to take care of its own, finding a niche even for executives thought incompetent to handle responsibility. In this respect, American managers are like their Soviet counterparts in finding the world kinder than it was in the past. But the dimensions of the change in the two countries are far from the same.

Upward Mobility

The third area of difference between American and Russian managers is the speed of upward mobility within management. Here the traditions are sharply distinguished.

In the middle 1930's in Soviet industry, only 3 to 12 per cent of Soviet top management were over fifty years old. In 1928 in the United States, 57 per cent of top business executives were over fifty according to the authoritative Taussig and Joslyn study. In the Soviet Union, one third to one half were under forty; a bare 15 per cent were under forty in the United States.

The reason for the youth of Soviet industrial management was clear enough. Industry was expanding at a fantastic rate at the same time that the managers inherited from the Tsarist regime were being replaced. Opportunities were unlimited for the able young Soviet engineer with an unblemished Communist Party record. The management game was a game for the youth of the nation.

But Soviet industry of today presents an entirely different picture. True, it continues to grow rapidly—even more rapidly than American industry. But the sharp jump from scratch of the early 1930's cannot again be duplicated. Much more important, a trained managerial group already exists. There is no longer the need for promoting unseasoned executives to top positions. The significance of these facts is that the ambitious

Russian manager of today, comparing his situation with that of the executive twenty years ago, sees his march up the managerial ladder slowed to a crawl. For his standard of comparison is the lightning movement of the thirties. His present prospects are entirely out of line with the management traditions of his country.

American business advancement has also slowed down. In comparison to the 57 per cent of American top managers who were over fifty years old in 1928, Warner and Abegglen found 67 per cent in 1952. Those under forty had fallen from 15 per cent to 5 per cent. But this decline in the promotion rate is of quite a different magnitude from that seen in the Soviet Union.

Thus, even if the average age of Soviet top managers should still be less than that of American management, Soviet junior and middle managers are probably more dissatisfied with promotion possibilities than are their American counterparts. They are quite ready to label a superior as an "old fogey," who is keeping them from their rightful place in the sun, when this official is still a good deal younger than the age which would win this appellation in the United States. Expectations are a product of traditions!

part four

BREAKING UP THE BUREAUCRACY

9. THE NATURE OF THE BEAST

In an Adam Smith world of tiny firms, control took care of itself. The Invisible Hand did the co-ordinating. Man had built and had to maintain those institutions which permitted the Invisible Hand to guide the economy on its path, but no further human intercession was needed. Man might look on aghast as the path led into deep depression, but at least he could rest assured that eventually it would once more wind its way up the roller coaster of high prosperity.

By and large, nineteenth-century America had such an economy. No subtle management controls were needed to co-ordinate activities within any single tiny company, and little government supervision was exercised over business as a whole. But as giant firms sprang up and grew in the last quarter of that century, new forms of guidance became necessary. Many plants were merged within a single corporate structure. The Invisible Hand no longer ran the only faro game in town. Companies such as Standard Oil and U. S. Steel started their own little games.

What this meant for the outside policing of business is a subject we shall not consider here. Not only external supervision, however, but also internal company policing became more necessary. Systems had to be established for formulating company policy and for bringing the lower management levels into line with it.

At first, these organizational structures could be built relatively simply. Either a corporation consisted of little more than a holding company, which owned the stock of separate business firms but left operations to the individual managements, or it tended to be a highly centralized affair. The centralized concern, at least in theory, lodged control in the hands of one man. It was a replica of the village blacksmith shop, multiplied ten thousandfold.

As time passed, however, it became increasingly clear that the modern American corporation had outgrown the organizational form of one-man authority. "Decentralization" became the slogan of the day. In the 1920's, it was already beginning to be the magic password; by the 1950's, it was firmly imbedded in the folkways of management. But while today there is virtually unanimous support for the shibboleth of decentralization, there is still a good deal less agreement as to precisely what is meant by this term.

The Soviet approach to administration is sloganized in the concept of centralized planning combined with decentralized operational decisions. This slogan implants the struggle over centralization, which in any case seems inherent in all large organizations, solidly into the fundamental Soviet "platform." Thus, it is scarcely surprising that this platform should have been subject to radically differing interpretations at various times in Soviet history.

Within Soviet industry of the 1920's, decentralization ran rampant. This was the era of the New Economic Policy, when much of small business, which had been nationalized in the first flush of the Revolution, was restored to private owners or to co-operatives, while large-scale firms remained under government ownership. The country was suffering grievously from the ravages of world war, revolution, and civil war, and nothing more was desired of industry than that it rebuild itself to the prewar level. Central authority had shown itself to be ineffective in these chaotic times as a control center for restoration efforts, and now local industries were thrown back upon their own resources and efforts.

Even government-owned industry was divided up into quite autonomous regional bodies, which soon showed their independence of spirit. Taking advantage of the extreme shortages of goods, these autonomous trusts acted as bad-mannered monopolists and proceeded to charge what the market would bear. In fact, they rather overplayed their hand by setting such high prices that their goods became unsaleable, and inventories of finished goods began accumulating. So long as the government-owned banking system supplied industry with loans on these inventories, the high-price policy was continued despite exhortation by the central government and Communist Party. It was only when the State Bank withdrew its credits, thus forcing the industrial trusts to liquidate their inventories, that prices fell.

Central planning for industry was attempted during this period of the 1920's. But since there was no enforcement of these plans, conflicting national programs were developed within the different operating organizations. The core of agreement between these organizations was little more than a concensus that all national plans except one's own were utter idiocy and should on principle be disregarded.

Surprisingly enough, despite all this confusion the decentralized system performed its task. By the late 1920's, the previous peak level of Soviet industrial production had again been reached. These Adam Smith ways of Soviet industry had succeeded in laying the foundation for the forthcoming surge of growth.

With the commencement of the first Five-Year Plan at the end of the 1920's, and the gathering together of the forces of Soviet society for a great industrial effort, complete centralization came into its own. Government-owned industry was now completely dominant, and regionalization of its administration was sharply reduced; Moscow became the true heart of the country. Equally important, organization along industrial lines was collapsed inward. A bare handful of top administrators, each with his own immense bailiwick, made the decisions for all of industry, construction, and transportation. The days of the individual American capitalist, building an empire under his personal control, were resurrected in socialist Russia.

This centralization played an enormous role in Soviet economic development. It made possible decisions concentrating great resources into key projects. Investment in the iron and steel industry was set at such a scale as to quadruple steel output within eight years. During the same period, there was no investment at all in the textile industry and mighty little in railroads. Capital resources were not to be spread thin, but were to be thrown into those sectors of the economy where they would most contribute to production growth. Economic development was planned as a military campaign and, in fact, military expressions were constantly used by Russian journalists to describe its progress.

Major decisions as to individual factories were made—and unmade. In 1931, the decision was taken to build a huge works which would have an annual capacity for freight-car production of four times the current output of all railroad cars in the entire Soviet Union. Although this investment decision was made in 1931, funds were soon diverted elsewhere. It was 1937 before the projected plant began to produce any cars at all.

Such centralization of decision-making made possible the abrupt transformation of traditional methods of work, without waiting for an evolutionary process of consent. Clearly, however, the system could not last. As Soviet industry grew, it quickly went beyond the administrative grasp of any few men. Some type of decentralization was essential.

By the mid-1930's, this process of decentralization of decision-making began. But it was no return to the 1920's with that decade's regional groupings. Rather it was a breakdown along industry lines; huge industrial bodies were broken into smaller ones which supervised the production of fewer products. Each of the ministries was split, and split again. Yet each splinter maintained its headquarters in Moscow.

Never have the Russians found a satisfactory solution to the problem of organizational centralization. For as the ministries were splintered, central co-ordination of decisions was made more difficult. The new splinters were then combined, only to be once more split asunder. Industrial reorganization in Russia, as in large organizations in our own country, seems to be an endless process. The latest wrinkle is that of the mid-1950's, which we will consider in Chapter Ten: to renounce vertical organization of separate industries, and instead to return to the regional administrative bodies of the 1920's.

The fundamental dilemma of organizational decision-making is that it does not seem possible to make gains in one aspect of efficiency without simultaneously losing ground in other directions. Since the pasture on the far side of the fence always looks greener, the temptation is ever present to reverse direction and regain lost aspects of efficiency.

Centralization of decision-making offers the advantage that relevant information at the disposal of one part of an organization can be brought to bear on the problems of another part. All strings lead to the central decision-maker, and he either has or can get information from all groups. Secondly, the best decision-making and advisory talent in the organization can be mustered at the top; presumably, the resulting decisions will be better than if just "any Joe" had made them.

On the other hand, no central figure at the head of a large organization can hope to keep in touch with nuances of particular, detailed problems. All that he can try to have before him is summary material on which to base a decision. Second, he generally cannot tailor his decisions to individual cases; if he were to attempt to do this, he would soon be completely swamped. As a result, he must make decisions of a "rule" nature, indicating to subordinates how entire classes of problems should be handled. Unfortunately, the very act of classifying cases involves riding roughshod over the individual peculiarities of each, and the classification method as a key ingredient of bureaucracy is inherent in central decision-making.

Centralization of the decision process and of planning has an additional major disadvantage, relating to the execution of the plan or decision. For what is a "good" plan? It is one which, once adopted, leads to actions which in turn result in satisfactory outcomes. However, the *process* used in drawing up a given plan may be quite as important in determining action as the resulting plan itself. This is due to the fact that if subordinates are involved in making the decision as to a particular plan, if they accept the plan as their own rather than treating it as a scheme coming from the distant and clouded heights, they are much more likely to work hard to make the plan succeed. Failure of the plan involves a psychological defeat to themselves, rather than bringing sardonic pleasure at the discomfiture of the "all-wise" figure above.

To add to the complications involved in trying to improve the organization of decision-making, it is necessary to recognize that actual patterns of decision-making seldom coincide precisely with those shown by the tables of organization. Generally, it is rather difficult even for the participants to know who made which decision. It is not easy to pin down authority.

Let me give three examples. A few years ago, a large American corporation was considering a proposal for major investment in a new plant. The president of the corporation opposed the proposal; but by the time he had taken a stand, too many people below him in the company were pushing for the investment. Even the president recognized that the best he could do was to postpone the investment decision; he could not change it. In this case, who had the decision-making authority?

In 1931, the Central Committee of the Communist Party of the Soviet Union resolved that no new factories should be built in Moscow. The object was to hold down the size of the city. Following this "decision" by the second highest policy-making body in the country, the population of the city proceeded to grow by 50 per cent during the next eight years. In 1939, the highest policy-making body, the Party Congress, reiterated the 1931 decision and demanded its enforcement. As of 1956, the Moscow labor force had grown by an additional third.

Who vetoed the resolutions of the top Party bodies? Stalin? It seems unlikely. Despite the limits on executive power shown in the example above, our knowledge of Stalin's personality does not support the hypothesis that he took this particular means of twice circumventing the Communist Party policy bodies. Stalin's method of asserting authority was more direct. No, the final "authority" was held by officials much lower in the chain of command, men who must have felt that there were good reasons for their own pet projects to be treated as minor exceptions to Party policy. Nor could it be said that they hid their decisions from top Party officials. After all, this great construction was in Moscow itself, the very city in which the policy-makers were living.

Soviet postwar investment decisions raise the same decision-making issue. General policy was to move the base of Soviet industry eastward. Expansion of fuel, electricity, and raw material resources followed this policy and was concentrated in the East.

But new manufacturing firms, built to process the materials

and use the fuel, continued to be established in the West and particularly in European Russia. So far did this go, that the National Plan adopted in 1956 had to reverse direction; it called for investment in coal, gas, and electricity in the West in order to service industry which had been constructed there since the war.

How can we account for the fact that this process-manufacturing expansion of 1945–55 occurred primarily in the West? It was due to industrial ministries following their own narrow departmental interests, attracted by the available labor force of the area, said a professor in a lecture prepared under the auspices of the Central Committee of the Soviet Communist Party.

In this case, as in the previous one, top authorities could not maintain control. It is easy to know who set "policy": the Council of Ministers and the Party Central Committee. But it is much harder for anyone to answer the question of who made the major decisions which violated policy.

The pinning down of authority in the organizational maze is only one complication in the pattern of decision-making. An equally important complication is that people who clearly have no authority control much of the flow of information, and so play a major role in determining when decisions are made.

One need not be in a large organization very long before realizing the tremendous influence exercised by the secretary to the top executive. Control of access to the pinnacle of the organization does in fact often resolve an issue, and may even prevent a question from coming up for explicit decision.

Perhaps the most famous instance of control over information is the semi-legendary building of "Potemkin villages" in eighteenth-century Russia. The Empress Catherine was taking a trip of inspection through the Ukraine, and her chief minister Potemkin wished to impress her with the high living standards of the peasantry. This impression was achieved by building stage-set villages along the line of march, and dismantling them for movement up ahead once Catherine had passed through. Catherine saw only these Potemkin villages. The channel of communication—or lack of it—was preserved intact.

The problem of communication upward within organizations is one which lately has been given a great deal of attention. The traditional "open door" policy of chief executives in some small- and medium-sized firms is one way of handling it. If communication is informal, then no roadblocks can be set up on the nonexistent roads. Unfortunately, once a company reaches any size, this policy is practicable only so long as it is largely illusory. For if people really took to bringing all problems into the chief executive's office, formal channels would soon have to be established.

But the fact is that people do tend to communicate through standardized channels, for reprisals may be imposed on those bypassing their immediate superiors. Such reprisals occur regardless of the official policy of the organization toward communication. Of course, standardized channels may include unofficial ones. In the American army, for example, communications are expected to run up and down through the chain of command. But lateral communications, although not provided for officially, are normally treated as consistent with the informal procedures. Two platoon sergeants in different companies may agree as to the hours when each platoon will use a particular piece of training equipment. Skipping of vertical steps in the chain of communication, on the other hand, would certainly be considered as the jumping of channels. Woe to the buck private who tries to see the company commander without permission from the first sergeant.

If communication is viewed as requiring regular channels for ease of movement, then an obvious organizational device for promoting the flow of information upward is to establish alternative paths. The trick is to motivate people toward the use of all of them, and to install *different individuals* as couriers on the various paths. Information as to a given production department's output may reach the factory superintendent directly from the production foreman, or it may reach him through the scheduling department, through the quality control department, or as a report from the accounting office. Thus, any given individual can act as a stopper or biasing agent in only one channel; but the "message to Garcia" can come through along the other lines.

This organizational device, while unquestionably useful, raises two new problems. One is that of organizational rivalry and espionage. Tsar Nicholas I is said to have reconstituted the Russian secret police after 1825 in part so that it should serve as a check on the regular government bureaucracy. The Tsar wished to break through the official wall cutting him off from the mass of his subjects, but in the process of doing this he created an organ which belched forth hatred and fear. Even in a corporation, the creation of any new channel of communication may be viewed as a network for top-management spies and may accordingly affect morale. Harry Bennett's organization at Ford was a notorious example.

There is a second problem which is distinct from this, but is also related to the organizational device of creating alternative channels for the upward flow of information. This problem is that the very process of providing a staff official with a separate line of communication to top management may both prevent him from gaining information himself and may kill off his effectiveness as an aide to lower levels of management.

American managements show an awareness of this dilemma and a concern over it. In a recent study of American industrial relations practice, there was a report on six large firms which periodically send headquarters representatives to the company plants in order to conduct on-the-spot audits of the state of industrial relations. Of these six companies, two forbid the representative to report the results of his audit to anyone except the local plant management, and a third permits communication upward only if the plant manager consents. Thus, half of these American firms deliberately block communication to top management. Apparently they feel that this loss is more than compensated by the gain in plant managements' trust in the headquarters representative, and by its resultant willingness to consult with him rather than try to block his "spying" activities.

The task of combining communication upward with staff advice to lower echelons is a troublesome one for all staff departments. But the staff department which typically finds particular difficulty in juggling these conflicting functions is the financial accounting and auditing department. In the Soviet

Union, for example, factory comptrollers perform a role which embodies all of the traditional dilemmas.

The Soviet factory comptroller is considered a major source of information to higher authorities. In order to preserve his independence and reliability as a communication channel, he is appointed and removed by the higher authorities rather than by the factory directors. But as a result, he has a hard time gaining the confidence of his factory director. Thus, Soviet plant administration suffers from an absence of that pinpointing of problem areas which the comptroller's office is so uniquely capable of providing. All levels of Soviet management recognize the potential value of the comptroller's advice, but the advisory role is hamstrung by enmity and lack of confidence on the part of the plant director. Some directors have even expressed this enmity by such clumsy actions as withdrawing the comptroller's badge which he needs to enter the plant. How could it be otherwise when the man designated as the plant director's "closest aide" is also the spy who may send upstairs the information which gets the director fired?

10. BUREAUCRACY AND HOW TO LIVE WITH IT

How We Do It

With the expansion of the American giant firm, there developed a new scheme for rooting out the cancer of bureaucracy which was growing along with the company. This scheme bore the name of *decentralization*.

In its extreme form, decentralization has meant the creation of what amounts to a group of functionally independent companies which operate under one corporate roof. But decentralization of this type raises in the observer's mind the question of why the corporation should bother to unify into one legal combination these distinct operations.

The answer seems to be that the inclusion of these multitudinous operations into a single corporation serves two purposes. It gives the officers of the corporation the social prestige which goes with a large company. Secondly, it permits the corporation to act as an investment trust. The treasurer of a firm which operates only within a narrow industry class, producing a few closely related products, has no more than two basic alternatives for use of the corporation's profits. He may distribute all the profits to shareholders, or he may reinvest them in corporate expansion within the industry. But investment opportunities in this particular industry do not always seem great. The treasurer has much more opportunity to pick a favorable spot for reinvestment if the corporation is active in a variety of industries.

Thus, a corporation may well choose to grow like an octopus with an arm around each of many industrial pies, even though the head is to do nothing but collect the profits and redistribute them. In American manufacturing in 1954, 82 per cent of those employees who worked for firms which owned more than one factory had bosses whose operations reached into more than one industry. (Here, we are using a Bureau of the Census classification of manufacturing which divides it into eighty-three distinct industries.) Clearly, the attraction of diversification is considerable.

But while complete decentralization can be found in American companies, it is far from normal. The Blaw-Knox Company—manufacturer in ten plants of over two hundred and fifty products ranging from television towers to cement mixers, in addition to being the engineer and builder for food-processing plants and oil refineries—seemed to operate with no genuine central controls by headquarters during the 1930's and 1940's. This type of decentralization, however, has not worked too well. In the 1950's, Blaw-Knox changed its top management so as to reassert central control and begin building a unified organization.

More typically, decentralization has meant giving the power of *final decision* regarding current operations to the various divisions or plants of a company. Each has been permitted to make its own decisions, rather than bucking them upstairs. Such decentralization has generally been along product or geographic lines, rather than by functional divisions such as engineering, finance, and personnel. The reason for this is simple enough: it is extremely difficult to make significant decisions in one functional area such as engineering, without affecting other functional areas such as finance.

This grant of authority, however, has usually been kept within the bounds both of centrally made policy and broad decisions and of central controls. General Motors is often cited as the prototype of decentralization. But the basic G.M. program, which has remained constant since the early 1920's, did not renounce central authority. As an historical fact, it actually represented a strengthening of central policy-making. It was formulated, in part, as a reaction to the inventory losses suffered by the company in 1920–21, when some plant managers rejected the advice of central financial officials of the company. General Motors' decentralization has been firm in placing financial authority in the hands of central management.

In most companies, finance is the most centralized of functions. The American Management Association, studying a number of companies noted for their decentralization policies, found that officers at the level of divisional and departmental vice presidents in the early 1950's were not permitted to spend, without specific authorization, more than $1000 to $25,000 on capital expenditures. For plant managers, the figures were in the $500 to $5000 range. There is little maneuverability here for local managements.

Other functions which are also normally centralized are personnel, accounting, advertising, research, public relations, and even engineering. Important decisions in these areas tend to be treated as more than plant or divisional affairs.

In fact, decentralization of top management decisions may on occasion actually be a device for re-establishing central control. This was true after the death of Judge Gary, who had been the chief executive officer of U. S. Steel from The Corporation's formation in 1901 until his death in 1927. Theoretically, Gary was a dictator in whose hands were concentrated all of The Corporation's central decisions. In actuality, however, the task of control was so huge that no one man could exercise it. When functional departments at headquarters (such as finance) were given some of the chief executive's power, it was possible to assert a working central control over the many U. S. Steel subsidiaries. This type of "decentralization" served to move many decisions to the level of top management, and out of the hands of the local managers who had previously received by default the power which no single chief executive could wield.

With all the limitations as to the practice of decentralization in American firms, it has still meant that the right of final decision in certain matters is relegated to middle-management levels. Its implementation has required that company presidents accept the philosophy that if they strongly disagree with an executive's decision they will not change the decision—although they may, of course, change the executive.

Pre-Khrushchev Russia

If General Motors, with half a million employees, has decentralization problems, think of those faced by the Soviet government, which directly employs fifty million people. Small wonder that the Soviet Union has forever been tinkering with the particular administrative solution which happened to be in force at the moment.

Soviet theory has always called for decentralization of operational decisions to a local level. But the term "decentralization" has never had the meaning in Soviet parlance which is given to it in American business: that middle managers should have the right of final decision in certain areas. Soviet top administrators have, quite explicitly, reserved to themselves the right to meddle directly in the detailed affairs of even the smallest organizations.

A former lawyer for a Soviet bakery, who is now a Russian refugee, tells the story of the bakery needing more flour than its normal allotment during the period shortly before the Second World War. A request for additional flour was put through channels, and in time it was approved. The approval bore the signature of V. M. Molotov, Chairman of the Council of People's Commissars. It was as though the President of the United States were to approve the purchase of oil to heat a New York post-office substation. Let us grant that this was an extreme case, and that probably some fourth secretary of Molotov's actually did the signing. Even so, the case illustrates the extremes to which Russian centralization of decision-making can go.

Until recently, all of the main administrative bodies of the country were located in Moscow. Since decentralization was primarily along the lines of separate industries, detailed decisions concerning a Tashkent textile mill would be made in a Moscow office. Such decisions applied to annual production plans, to procurement and marketing allotments, even to approval of changes in the mill's management organization. The possibilities for red tape were boundless.

When a huge organization is this highly centralized, two possibilities exist. The organization may founder in its own bureaucracy, or it may ignore its own rules. No one can say that Soviet industry has foundered during the last thirty years. The evidence is conclusive that formal decision-making regulations have been constantly violated. Plant managements have had to make their own decisions if they were to produce the results demanded of them. Top authorities in Moscow have had to wink at violations of rules if they wished industrial production to grind ahead. Both groups have recognized necessity.

It would be difficult to assert categorically that this informal decentralization has been an unsuccessful administrative solution. Soviet industry has expanded at too rapid a rate, over too long a time period, to give grounds for a supercritical attitude. In a broad sense, central authorities have been able to make policy and to get it carried out. Similarly, despite all the uncertainties and major exceptions which exist, plant managements have exercised the authority necessary to maintain operations.

But, as perhaps occurs in any administrative system, the participants have found cause for complaint. Middle management has griped at the red tape in the many cases where they do follow the rules. A good example of what may be involved is illustrated in a story told by a Russian refugee and reported by Joseph Berliner. The refugee had been the chief mechanical engineer of a Soviet mining organization, and his story presumably relates to a prewar period when a law had just been passed, with considerable fanfare, to make the violation of quality standards for final products a criminal offense.

As inspector I once arrived at a plant which was supposed to have delivered mining machines, but did not do it. When I entered the plant premises, I saw that the machines were piled up all over the place, but they were all unfinished. I asked what was going on. The director gave evasive answers. Finally, when the big crowd surrounding us had disappeared, he called me to his office.

"Now we can talk," he said.

"Well," I said, "why don't you ship the machines? We are waiting for them."

"Here is the story," he said. "According to the technical specifications the machines must be painted with red oil-resistant varnish. However, I have only red varnish which is

*not oil-resistant and green varnish which is oil-resistant.
Therefore I cannot complete them. You see, if I send the
machines with the wrong kind of varnish I shall not have
fulfilled the technical requirements, and for that I shall get
eight years in prison. But if I don't ship them this will come
under the charge of failure to arrange for transportation.
And what will they do with me then? At worst, they will
expel me from the Party. Well, the hell with my Party card.
So what do you want me to do?"*

*"But listen," I replied, "the mines cannot work, they are wait-
ing for the machines and you are holding them up because
you don't have the right kind of paint."*

*"But I don't want to get eight years. Give me a written note
with your signature and I shall have the machines ready in
nothing flat."*

*"Well, I don't want to get eight years either. So what do I do?
I cable the ministry and ask for permission to use the green
varnish. I should have received an answer at once. But it
took unusually long. Apparently they did not want to take
any chances at the ministry either, and they wanted to cover
themselves. Finally I received permission. I put this cablegram from the ministry in my pocket and kept it for the rest
of my life, and signed the note allowing the use of green
paint, referring to the cablegram. In a short time the machines began to roll from the plant.*

Such management concern for legal provisions is doubtless
unusual in Soviet conditions, if only because a director of the
sort described above would soon lose his job. But certainly the
more common type of director, who would have shipped out
the mining equipment on his own responsibility, would not
have been happy at being forced to engage in such illegal behavior. He would have been well aware that this action might
be held against him sometime in the future.

In actual fact, plant directors have possessed great authority.
But in theory, they have not; and so they have constantly strug-
gled to legitimatize their power. During the course of this perennial battle, they have often felt sufficiently self-confident to

ridicule publicly the laws they were violating. Even at the height of the 1930's purges, there were some plant directors who went out of their way to write signed articles in the national press describing how, in their own work, they had been violating both the law and instructions from superiors, announcing that they considered these violations to be quite proper, and stating flatly that in the future they had every intention of continuing and even extending the violations.

Central authorities have shown growing concern over their own lack of control in certain key areas of policy. Probably the major area in which central policy has been steadily ignored for thirty years is that of organizational autarchy, or self-sufficiency of supply. Central authorities in Moscow are quite aware of the cost advantages to be gained through the specialization of individual factories on particular products. Each separate industrial organization, however, is anxious to be as self-sufficient as possible, and thus achieve independence of its neighbors and of an often whimsical national system of allotting necessary supplies.

Since no ministry could be sure of getting the materials, parts, and equipment needed for its operations, the natural tendency was for each to try to expand the coverage of its production so as to supply its own needs. Each ministry was quite willing to pay the price of high-cost production in order to achieve independence. Thirty years of denunciation from Moscow, accompanied by reasoned explanations of the advantages of division of labor, had absolutely no effect.

In 1951, only 47 per cent of the brick production of the Soviet Union was accounted for by the Ministry of the Industry of Construction Materials. High-cost production, often with long railroad hauls, characterized the remainder. In 1955, 390 units of a particular type of excavator were produced. Two thirds were produced within the appropriate ministry, but the rest were produced elsewhere at a cost 50 to 100 per cent greater. Of the 171 plants in 1957 which specialized in machine-tool production, only 55 were under the appropriate ministry. The other plants were organized within ministries which used their machine tools.

Each ministry, in fact, seemed to act much like an independent nation engaging in foreign trade. Each inevitably dealt with other ministries, but cautiously, jealously safeguarding its independence. Self-sufficiency was treated as the keystone of this independence.

What made this situation even more difficult is that each individual plant copied the example of its ministry, and strove to become an autarchic principality within an autarchic nation. In 1956, the Urals Machine-building Plant, one of the nation's two giant heavy-equipment plants, grossly underutilized its powerful and expensive presses designed for production of forgings two hundred tons and over. Of all the forgings produced during January–September 1956, more than half weighed less than twenty-seven tons apiece. While this was scarcely what one would call small work, it was totally out of line with the capacity of the equipment.

In 1957, no more than half of the nation's standard tooling, nuts and bolts, and electrodes was produced in specialized plants. Yet it was officially recognized that the cost of producing such items in the consuming plants was several times as great as the cost of production in factories where economies of scale could be achieved.

As the thirty-year Soviet experience of factory autarchy illustrates, decentralization of decision-making has in fact gone a long way down the organizational ladder. Despite all of the formal centralization, the individual plant director in Russia seems to be much more successful in building his own little empire than is his counterpart in the American giant corporation.

This, however, is in no sense due to the greater belief in decentralization among Soviet top managers. There have been complaints of factory directors who disregarded "on principle" orders from the top-management organs of their industry. Plant managements are said to have virtually broken off "diplomatic relations" with these top organs and with other plants, and they have been reproached for considering themselves as feudal lords quite outside Soviet law.

The great strength of the Soviet factory, from an organizational point of view, is that it has been the only stable structure in all of Soviet industry. Ministries and their subdivisions have been split apart, lumped together in new combinations, and then once more splintered. This process continued steadily over a period of three decades, as the Russian leaders have alternately been revolted first by the problems inherent in having only a few large organizations, and then by the large "span of control" required for co-ordinating a multitude of smaller ones. In all of this shuffling, only the plant organization was left alone.

It is scarcely surprising that this single stable organizational unit should have amassed considerable decision-making power. It is also not surprising that any given plant management should be reluctant to become dependent upon a "sister" plant under the same parent body; for the chances were good that, within a few years, the two plants would be subordinate to different higher bodies.

The New Russian Organization Chart

The year 1957 saw a new type of industrial reorganization. At the end of March, Khrushchev published his "Theses" advocating the abolition of industrial ministries. This proposal appeared quite radical, since the tendency in the previous few years had been to strengthen the powers of these same ministries. Throughout April and early May, there was considerable discussion in the Soviet press of Khrushchev's proposal. On some minor points there was disagreement, although mainly the discussion was one of elaboration. We now know that disagreement within the top ranks of the Communist Party was considerably stronger than that expressed publicly, and that some powerful Party figures defended the old industrial structure. But in May, the Soviet parliament passed legislation which essentially incorporated Khrushchev's original proposals.

The industrial reorganization law ended the former system of grouping industry by product and technological process into national ministries. Instead, one hundred-odd regional councils were formed to administer all types of industry and construction within their respective regions. Administration had shifted from organization by type of product to organization by geographic region. What made this reorganization appear so drastic is that virtually all of the industry administrations had previously been centered in Moscow, while the new regional administrations were, in the nature of things, to disperse to the four winds.

One of the most important purposes of this reorganization was thoroughly to disintegrate the old empires above the plant level. With new organizations being formed on a radically different principle, the ancient autarchy within ministries and subbranches of ministries was bound to go. This autarchy had advanced so far that a root-and-branch eradication may have been the only type feasible.

It is true that new, regional autarchy may well spring up. Indeed, it did quickly appear in embryo form, and was as quickly denounced. While these denunciations show that the central authorities are well aware of the danger, the history of the past thirty years is that organizational forms have a compelling logic of their own which is much stronger than the force of denunciations from the center.

Nevertheless, it takes time for a new autarchic pattern to develop. "Take therefore no thought for the morrow; for the morrow shall take thought for the things of itself. Sufficient unto the day is the evil thereof." It will be time enough to reorganize again when the new form of autarchy becomes severe.

The second major purpose of the reorganization is to bring higher management into ready contact with plant management. Where previously consultations were difficult, and entailed trips to Moscow from factories scattered over one sixth of the globe, now they are readily convenient. Higher management, say Soviet writers, will now be familiar with local situations and will be able to make sensible planning and operating decisions.

One *may* interpret this desire for closer contact as simply representing an effort to improve the quality of higher-level decisions. But this strikes me as a naïve interpretation. Far more important, we have here an effort to regain central control. With top management really available for consultation, with red tape reduced, plant managements should no longer be under such great pressure to violate rules and to make their own decisions. As obedience to central orders becomes more practicable, it should also become more common.

While this co-ordination leads to loss of actual power by plant management, it represents a significant expansion in its recognized, legitimate power. For now genuine consultation and the serious treatment of suggestions made by plant management are possible. In contrast with the past, these managements can take the path of legality and legitimacy. From the reactions heard in the Soviet press, it would seem that Soviet managers welcome this shift.

In a talk with me, the chief engineer of a Leningrad food plant warmly supported the reorganization. His argument was that of improved communication between his plant and higher authorities. His plant falls under the jurisdiction of the food administration of the Leningrad region's industrial council. This particular administration covers sixty plants, and has fifty to sixty engineers at its headquarters. One of these engineers has the task of maintaining regular contact with this plant along with two or three others in the same specialty. Since the office of the contact engineer, as well as that of his superiors, is close to all the plants, conversations are easy to arrange.

A third purpose originally announced for the reorganization was that of reducing the size of the bureaucracy. It is, however, quite clear that this function—if it was ever important—will not be realized. Soviet administrators and scholars with whom I discussed this question either felt that there had in fact been no decline in the number of people above the plant level, or that at best the reduction was inconsequential. No real efforts seem to have been made to achieve such reduction. But perhaps this is not too surprising when we consider that the Soviet ratio of white-collar to manual workers at all levels in industry is only two thirds of the American proportion. The Soviet problem in this regard does not seem overly serious.

A problem which still remains unresolved in the reorganization is the question of how substantive it will all be. Someone still has to worry about total growth of different industries on a national scale, and someone has to enforce such decisions. So long as materials are allocated to particular industries and plants, some national organization in Moscow must do this job.

All of these tasks have been handed over to the greatly strengthened State Planning Committee, with a few special industries—such as chemicals, electric power stations, and military industries—receiving central guidance from outside the committee.

In this regard, Soviet industrial administration faces a ticklish balancing problem. If too much control is given to the State Planning Committee, then plant managers will really be serving under two masters. The plant's regional industrial council may guide it in one direction, while the appropriate industrial sector of the national or republic State Planning Committee pushes it in another. Apparently, this was a real problem during 1957. If this control, according to industry, should be pushed strongly, then the industrial reorganization may turn out to have only further weakened central control through having established strong and independent bodies in conflict with each other over supervision of factories. Factory managements would be forced into taking on additional power, at the same time that their hopes for legitimacy are frustrated.

But the opposite risk is also serious. The Russians have always stressed that there can be no serious planning without enforcement of the plans. If operational control is left solely in the hands of the regional industrial councils, one may wonder if each will not soon resemble a medieval principality with its barriers to outside trade. In private conversations in the Soviet Union, central control over investment decisions was pointed out to me as a key element which would prevent this from happening. However, it must be remembered that such control failed to keep the industrial ministries from expanding in undesirable directions. It is far from certain that investment control will work this time, unless it is accompanied by operational control from the center.

Thus the Russians are still fighting the age-old administrative battle to maintain central control while at the same time decentralizing operational decisions. There can never be any final "victory" in this sort of a struggle. For this effort resembles the walking of a tightrope, and "success" can only be defined as not falling off.

11. TWO WORLDS

Size of the Bureaucracy

In American industry, the growing number of administrators and white-collar servicing personnel is impressive—and frightening to many. In manufacturing-plus-mining, taken together so as to be comparable to the Russian data, the number of people performing white-collar functions as a proportion of manual workers has risen steadily during the past half century. From a low of 9 per cent in 1899, it had risen to 17 per cent by the end of the First World War, to 22 per cent by the end of the Second World War, and to 29 per cent by 1954. Thus over one quarter of the American manufacturing and mining labor force is today employed in the administration of our sprawling industrial complex.

Surprisingly enough, considering the multiplant character of our great corporations, only a small number of these white-collar employees are involved in co-ordinating the activities of different plants within the same corporation. In 1954, 90 per cent of all white-collar employees were employed within plants, and only 10 per cent worked in central offices of corporations. Between 1923 and 1954, in manufacturing, the number employed in central offices ranged between 6 and 13 per cent of the total. Thus, measured in terms of the proportionate number of employees involved, co-ordinating activity within corporations is quite unimportant as a user of manpower resources. The cost of this activity is minuscule: 2 per cent of the industrial labor force is involved.

British manufacturing has been studied in comparison with American, and shows a ratio of white-collar to blue-collar employees which is 3 to 5 percentage points below the American figures. However, the virtually unbroken time-trend upward in both countries is unmistakable.

Russian manufacturing and mining, however, display a different pattern. The left-hand section of the following graph compares the data for the United States and Russia, in both countries treating only those people employed on the plant level. While this treatment underestimates ratios in both countries, the understatement is by only a few percentage points. These statistics are much more reliable for both nations than are the estimates, shown on the right-hand side of the graph, which are needed to include personnel above the level of the plant.

The data is striking. Not only do Russian plants have a lower proportion of administrative and clerical personnel than do American plants, but—much more important—the trend since 1940 has been downward. While Parkinson's law of the self generation of administrative and office personnel can be readily read into the American statistics, and equally well into the prewar Soviet statistics, the "law" has been reversed in postwar Soviet industry. Moreover, this difference in trend between American and Russian industry is unaffected by differences between the two countries in the relative importance of different subbranches such as chemicals and apparel.

Russian data, like American, is a great deal murkier when we leave the level of the plant. Estimates for 1956, however, indicate that the total number of personnel in higher bodies who were involved in directing Russian plant operations, purchasing, and sales were perhaps one third of the number of white-collar employees in the plants themselves. This is roughly triple our percentage estimate for the United States.

Adding together the white-collar personnel working both within and above the plants, we find that they total to a lower proportion of manufacturing and mining manual workers in Russia in the mid-1950's than they do in the United States. As is shown in the following graph, the Russian figure is about 20 per cent; this compares with 29 per cent in the United States. These figures have been reached in the two countries through a substantial increase over the prewar statistic of 10

A— RATIO OF WHITE-COLLAR TO MANUAL WORKERS IN FACTORIES AND MINES
B— RATIO OF ALL WHITE-COLLAR INDUSTRIAL AND MINING PERSONNEL TO MANUAL WORKERS

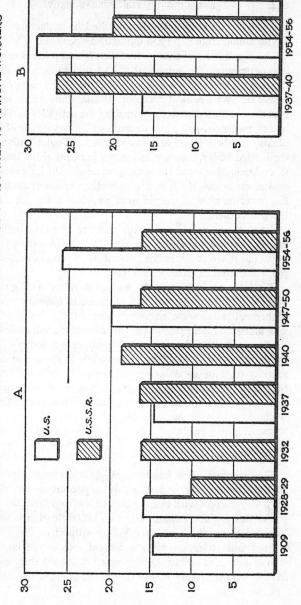

per cent in the United States, matched by a decrease in the Soviet Union from the 1940 figure of 27 per cent.

The significance of this mass of data is that it helps us to put into perspective the numerical size of bureaucracy in Russian industry. It gives us a better appreciation of the costs in manpower of Soviet central planning. While white-collar workers who are concerned with co-ordinating the activities of different plants, measured as a ratio of white-collar workers within the plants, are three times as numerous in the Soviet Union as in the United States, they are still only 4 per cent of the industrial labor force. Moreover, the extra personnel used for central coordination in the U.S.S.R. are more than counterbalanced by the fewer number of people used on white-collar jobs within the plants themselves.

Thus, if we simply count the number of warm bodies involved, the cost of central planning in Russian industry is not high. But if we consider the proportion of well-educated people, a different impression emerges.

We have no postwar data on this subject, but figures for 1940 show that 45 per cent of all those in industry who had higher education were employed above the plant level. This was indeed a high price to pay for central planning. But with the far greater numbers of college graduates in today's Russia, the proportion has doubtless fallen, while at the same time the scarcity of these men, largely engineers, is far less. The cost of central planning, measured by investment in human resources, has fallen, not only quantitatively but qualitatively as well.

Organizational Personality

Every organization has its own goals, its own personality. Many organizations find it highly important to indoctrinate all policy-makers with the organization viewpoint. One example of this is the strenuous effort of indoctrination which has gone on within the Tennessee Valley Authority.

Such indoctrination plays a critical role in the co-ordination of activities within the organization. As we shall see later in this chapter, truly objective standards for measuring the effect of decisions cannot be established. Individual judgment is of the essence in the evaluative process. But the judgments of many individuals can be co-ordinated through company policies and by means of a clearly defined company "personality."

For an illustration of this position, let us turn to a Princeton study of industrial relations in large American companies. In a number of firms, industrial relations heads stated that the most important co-ordinating mechanism which they had was a common philosophy of industrial relations. Explicit policies were never sufficient to obtain uniformity in treatment, but rather informal methods—operating over long periods—were essential to assure the acceptance of this philosophy. Original recruitment was directed to finding "our kind of people," and much emphasis was placed upon "growing up in the organization and having a feel of what the organization means and stands for." One company reported that the *average* plant personnel manager has gone through an eight- to ten-year indoctrination period at headquarters before being sent out into the field.

In all probability, the area of industrial relations is one in which indoctrination and company tradition play a peculiarly powerful role. But the same forces are also at work elsewhere.

It would seem reasonable to believe that this indoctrination problem is one key reason for the low mobility of American managers between companies. Moving from plant to plant, subdivision to subdivision, but always remaining within the company, the upward-bound executive gains breadth without losing his touch for the individual peculiarities of his corporation's personality. If he were to switch to another corporation, this subtle process of indoctrination would have to begin over.

In the Soviet Union, the Communist Party plays this indoctrinating role. Rare is the executive of stature who is not a Party member. For a non-Party executive has not been subjected to the full strength of the traditions of the Soviet administrative "personality," and so in a real sense is not fully trained for his job. Those few executives who are "non-Party Bolsheviks," as the term goes, are presumably men with other vital qualifications who are judged to have also imbibed enough of the Party personality to make them acceptable.

As an organization which is explicitly and formally concerned with indoctrination on a national scale, the Soviet Union's Communist Party plays an important administrative role which has no full counterpart in American business. Within any single American corporation, the Party's counterpart can be met in a combined formal and informal indoctrination program. But no such program can go beyond the limits of a single corporation.

The nearest American counterpart is the combination of the swing of national and regional conventions, the golf and country clubs, the six-week business-school courses for executives, the round of suburban living—so much the same in all parts of the nation. These do much to create a personality of "mid-century big corporation man" which differs drastically from personality types of other countries and of other times.

It seems to me, however, that such creation of a mid-century American executive type still has not fully met the indoctrination needs of American corporations. The executive may or may not, for example, be heavily oriented to the goal of growth of the firm, putting growth even above profits. He may believe in conservative operations—or he may be a plunger. He may be a firm believer in research and development, or he may accept it only as a momentary fad which must be paid its due of lip service.

In fact, the failure of this national American indoctrination to meet the needs of any specific company may go far to explain the existence and success of some decentralization programs within large corporations. General Motors, for example, long the epitome of decentralization down to the divisional level, has had a mixed pattern with regard to the splitting of authority below that level. Some G.M. divisions have been guided by a decentralization philosophy; others have followed the policy of strong centralization. Opinions have differed as to the contribution of these different organizational patterns to the money-making abilities of the divisions.

Peter F. Drucker, the management consultant, has raised an interesting question with regard to what is really produced by decentralized management within divisions. He cites one senior divisional executive in General Motors as attributing the efficiency of the corporation to the fact that it has a few large and centralized divisions which produce profits, and that it has smaller and decentralized divisions to produce the future management of the corporation. By giving real responsibility to juniors, decentralization should provide them with excellent decision-training. It may be that it is this educational process which is really the greatest contribution of decentralization in American corporations.

One might expect that training of management would be no real problem in the American economy, since our horde of small businesses should provide a fine schooling for future managers of large firms. There should be no need for large corporations to decentralize simply in order to provide make-believe small businesses in which to train the managers of tomorrow.

The fact is, however, that large corporations recruit very little of their top management either from small companies or from other large companies. In Warner and Abegglen's 1952 study of such large corporations, it was found that only about 3 per cent of the top executives questioned had ever been business owners. Forty-eight per cent had never worked as executives for any other company, and another 40 per cent had worked for only one or, at the most, two other firms. By and large, American companies seem to be faced with the problem of training their own top managers. In this task may lie the greatest advantage of decentralization down to low levels of management.

Russia's managers seem to be able to move, and be moved, much more freely than is the case in American business. This may be explained by the fact that the Soviet Communist Party serves as a means of providing the same organizational personality for all of the different management groups in the entire society. No matter where the Russian executive may go, he is already imbued with the fundamental "personality" of the management. In this sense, all Soviet business is like one large corporation. The usual limit to free American executive mobility—freedom within a given corporation but not freedom to move to another—is transcended in the Soviet Union through treating all Soviet business as a single organization with a single personality.

Communication Upward

One aspect of the communication problem is the bringing of lower- and middle-management personnel into the process of planning and decision-making. The value of such participation has been well recognized both in American and in Russian industry. It has been viewed as improving the quality of final decisions and, of at least equal importance, as giving these executives a great psychological stake in the fulfillment of the programs.

If there is any real difference in this regard between the two countries, it is that the Russians seem to have made a more prolonged and systematic attack on the problem of attaining this participation. Not only is there the customary informal consultation, but regular formal channels have been stressed since the very first of the Five-Year Plans in 1928. Plan proposals, for example, have always been expected to move back and forth from the national level to that of the shop; all management groups are expected to have a hand in formulating the final plans.

The difficulties of organizing such participation have been severe in both countries. Not only do frequent committee meetings and conferences wear out Russians and Americans alike, but time pressures for decisions are usually urgent and restrict the possibilities of widespread consultation. In late 1957, a prominent Soviet author recognized that the role of local managements in Soviet planning is in fact still comparatively limited; he mentioned a minor reshuffling of planning procedure which he hoped, groundlessly I think, would improve conditions.

In this aspect of communication, both American and Russian top managements have faced up to the same problem for much the same reasons, and neither has been markedly successful. The same sorts of difficulties bedevil top management in both countries.

Although we find that this similarity exists in the treatment of participation in the planning process, the two countries have radically different approaches with regard to keeping open the pipelines for the flow of information upwards. The Russians have placed far more stress than we have on keeping these channels open, and they have been willing to pay a high price for this attainment.

As pointed out earlier, one problem is to make sure that no individual can bottle up the communication channel. The Russians have tackled this difficulty by establishing alternative channels running through different hands. This approach, however, can be defeated by the creation of a "family atmosphere" among the groups astride the information channels, who may co-operate to prevent bad news from reaching higher authorities.

A typical example of the working of such a "family circle" might be secrecy concerning worker housing which the factory is expected to build. Where the plant is short of funds and building materials, the director may delay construction of housing in order to speed the erection of an additional production shop. The new shop may seem to him to be far the more urgent of the two projects under conditions where its completion is a precondition for fulfillment of the factory's production plan.

However, the director needs the assistance of the factory Party secretary if the delay in housing construction is to be kept from the ears of higher authorities. The Party secretary, who is also judged by his superiors partly according to the plant's production performance, may well go along. The trade union chairman of the factory local may also stick with the director—if only to hide his own feebleness in protecting locally the interests of the factory workers. If the editor of the town newspaper can be brought into the circle, to assure the suppression of indignant letters from the factory's workers, so much the better. If, in addition, the director's immediate superior, in the administrative organ above the factory, is himself willing to suppress any rumblings he may hear, then the circle is really a tight one.

This "family atmosphere" has been a perennial Soviet

problem, and it has been met resolutely, even though each time only temporarily. One device is to shift people around between jobs sufficiently frequently so as to prevent solid "rings" from being formed. A second, equally drastic approach, is constantly to reshuffle the organizations themselves. Both procedures have regularly been used in Soviet industry although, of course, they have not solely been directed toward the problem of communication.

In addition to the costs involved in keeping in flux both executive personnel and organizational charts, there is the morale cost of using an espionage system. This, too, is a price the Russians have been willing to pay. In fact, the Secret Police—in the form of "special sections"—has been openly used as an official organization with a recognized role in the factory.

A third cost which Russian administration has been willing to pay is that of sharply reducing the effectiveness of staff as advisors to middle management. Staff groups are specifically instructed always to report to higher bodies. They act as a check on management, and thus have difficulty in also functioning as a support. The clearest case of this is in the comptrollership department, and Russian administrators have been quite clear as to the nature of their difficulties here. Although Russian administrators would naturally like to eat their cake and still have at least some of it left, they have been willing to pay the price required to maintain the flow of information.

Thus the maintenance of channels of information upward is a management goal which seemingly is given much greater relative weight in Soviet than in American industry. In the hierarchy of management goals, those of stability, management contentment, and successful fulfillment of staff functions stand higher on the American business ladder.

Role of the Market

The Soviet administrative task is substantially more difficult than that faced in American industrial corporations. One reason for this, of course, is the sheer magnitude of the task. But there is more to the matter than size alone.

Soviet top managers operate an extremely high-pressure system. They are concerned with getting the maximum possible out of their plant and equipment, and their ideal is to run it steadily at a rising level of full capacity. The operation of the Russian steel industry at 80 per cent of capacity—a figure considerably higher than the American 1958 average— would be considered the worst of crimes.

Moreover, the Soviet industrial organization is completely integrated vertically with all output, running from that of fuels and raw materials right up to the final product, being administered under the aegis of the Council of Ministers. Only imports from abroad can serve as a source of supply to the Soviet industrial organization without first having been produced by this organization itself, and these imports comprise a very minor element in the system.

Thus a neat intertwining of inputs of one industry with the outputs of feeder industries is essential. The production of the clothing industry must be planned to mesh with its inputs of cloth coming from the textile plants. Since the national industrial organization also tries to get along on minimum inventories, tight scheduling is required. As expansion is programmed, a careful timing of investment in the different branches of industry is necessary. Planners must think several years in advance so as properly to gear the textile and clothing industry into one another's expansion programs.

An administrative system of this sort, which can run smoothly only with precise co-ordination, inevitably suffers from repeated bottlenecks. The cotton crop may be slightly smaller than usual in a given year; since only minimum inventories of cotton have been held over from the previous year, the textile industry now cannot get the expected supplies, and it in turn is short on deliveries to the apparel industry. When bottlenecks occur, some lines of trade are bound to suffer directly and their growth slows down, in turn causing further failures elsewhere. This sequence has been a perennial Soviet difficulty, and for very understandable reasons.

Large American corporations would seem to face a similar problem. They, too, must co-ordinate production in one division with production in another. They, too, would like to get the most out of their equipment. However, in actual fact, American firms seldom operate under the taut Soviet conditions.

One reason for this is that American corporations generally try to function with more slack than is found in Soviet industry. If orders unexpectedly expand, American firms wish to be in a position to fill them. Investment tends to stay ahead of the market—rather than barely keeping pace with it. A good example of this is the American steel industry, which increased its capacity in 1957 to 141 million tons, although its top annual production is still only 117 million tons. As a result, genuine bottlenecks are encountered much less frequently in American industrial administration than in Russian.

But a second and even more important form of slack for American corporations is the existence both of a market and of other corporations. An American firm which runs into a shortage of parts can meet the problem by giving out contracts for the work. Flexibility is achieved, although at a cost, by expanding the number of subcontractors and the amount of work given to each. The problem is thus shoved off to another organization. But the Russians cannot do this; for there is no "other organization" except on the world market.

Thus the Russian industrial organization must solve all of its own problems. An American corporation, no matter how large, can go out on the market and pay another firm to take over some of its worst difficulties.

The enormous importance of co-ordination, combined with the grave difficulties in achieving it, has pushed the Russian industrial structure toward great centralization. Production programs of all plants must be co-ordinated with one another, and a powerful co-ordinating device is the allocation of all important materials and fuels to each individual factory.

Not faced with such grave problems of co-ordination, American corporations have tended to operate with looser controls. To them, the "market" serves as the source from which bottleneck demands can be met.

As we saw in Chapter Ten, however, extreme formal centralization may simply result in the loss of central control. Decision-making may in practice be highly decentralized, with

activities in its plants. All insisted on more direct and immediate tests.

Thus American top managements are, in actual fact, forced back upon subjective judgment in evaluating the success of lower management. It is top management which sets company policy, and the divisions and plants must operate within this framework. But even inside the limits of explicit policy, middle managers cannot simply proceed to make those decisions which they think will lead to greatest profits, expansion of sales, and general efficiency. They must always keep in mind the individual slants and biases of the top managers who will be judging their performance. For there is no unequivocal test of "success." Where there is judgment, there must inevitably be bias!

Nevertheless, while subjectivity and bias do enter into judgments as to the quality of middle management in a large American corporation, let us not overestimate these unavoidable limitations on the calculable test of profitability. This test does serve as a basic standard by which American management can be judged. All sorts of adjustments must be made, and these may even reverse the results of the raw "test" as a standard of evaluation. Still and all, profitability does provide a starting point for evaluation of executives; it offers a reasonably firm jumping-off spot in this difficult process.

In the Soviet Union, the administrative machine also gropes in search of such a starting point for managerial evaluation. It has copied the example of capitalist corporations in trying to use profits for this purpose. But profitability of the individual plant has proved to be an exceedingly weak reed in the Soviet Union. The pricing of products, raw materials, fuel, and labor is too chaotic. Moreover, the key Soviet administrative problem is co-ordination of the different plants and industries. Profit serves as only the dimmest reflection of a plant's success in playing its allotted role in the over-all pattern. Detailed knowledge of the factory's production and of the specific materials, fuels, equipment, and labor which have been used is crucial for evaluation.

Thus Soviet administration has failed badly in establishing workable summary standards for evaluating middle management. Large American corporations have not done too well in this respect either; the problem is inherently extremely difficult. But American administrative practice can be rated a good deal higher than Soviet in this regard.

In summary, then, the existence of many separate industrial organizations in the United States, linked by an impersonal market rather than through administrative channels, has significant consequences for administration. It greatly lightens the burden of central direction, and particularly of co-ordination and scheduling, as compared to the Soviet Union. It lessens the pressure toward formal centralization, and thus makes it easier for each organization to maintain genuine central controls over its constituent parts. Finally, it makes it possible for the "test of the market" to serve as a useful starting point for evaluating middle-management performance. Soviet industrial administration is deprived of these advantages.

part five

WHO RUNS THE BUSINESS?

12. STOCKHOLDERS AND THE COMMUNIST PARTY

Who runs the business? During the last century, there was no question as to who was in the saddle. Labor unions were weak or nonexistent, in no position to tell the employer how to operate the shop. Government, by and large, stayed out of things. Business decisions were made by men who owned and, in that period, operated their own companies.

This is scarcely the case today. Unions, government, stockholders, banks: all have their own vital interests in business decisions, and all have the power to take a hand in the game. A decision by U. S. Steel to raise prices will create hazards throughout the entire economy, affecting both national income and the level of unemployment in far-distant industries. All groups are risk-takers, and all become decision-makers. Clearly the attitude of the Federal Trade Commission with regard to prosecution for price-fixing will affect the management pricing position. Nor can union reactions be ignored. Decision-making is a complex process indeed.

In the United States, these non-management groups are distinct and often antagonistic. There is no unifying body to provide central direction. Compromises, of course, are constantly being evolved; but these compromises are between independent powers, each with its own distinct goals and values.

Soviet decision-making runs a different course. In the last analysis, there is a small group at the head of the Communist Party which has the power to make decisions. A single unifying, ultimate quintessence of authority does exist.

Here we have a fundamental difference between the process of business decision-making in Russia and in the United States. But even this distinction can be overstated. In the

United States, opposing groups may meet in the market place
or at a conference table. Individual decisions on specific problems tend to evolve, although agreement is rare on general
policies to guide future decisions. In the Soviet Union, the
Praesidium of the Communist Party is really little more than
the ultimate conference table at which conflicting interest
groups reach compromises. The difference between the Russian Praesidium and an American conference is that the Praesidium can lay down long-range policies. This is what makes
it feasible to establish a national "plan" which will be a genuine guide to decisions—unless power structure shifts. But,
clearly, most issues work themselves out at levels far below
that of the Party Praesidium, and here compromise may be
achieved in a fashion similar to that found in the United
States.

It is not easy to answer for the U.S.S.R. our question of
who runs the business. "The Communist Party" is scarcely an
answer; it is like saying that a conference of disputants makes
decisions. Such an answer begs all the interesting problems.
Thus our question is as significant for Soviet industry as it is
for American.

At first view it seems incongruous to lump within the same
chapter American shareholders, the very personification of the
profit motive in capitalism, and the Russian Communist
Party. But in one basic sense, both groups play the same role
in their respective societies. Each represents legitimacy of
power. In practice, however, each is very much of a constitu-
tional monarch rather than an absolute ruler. While the parallel between the two groups is only partial, a comparison of
stockholders and the Communist Party illustrates some interesting features of both.

American Managerial Revolution

The story of the American managerial revolution has
often been told. Where once American business was largely
owner-managed, the development of our huge corporations has
led to a separation of management from ownership. As stock
ownership has grown increasingly diffuse, so goes the tale, no

stockholder or group of stockholders can today dominate the large corporation. It is management which sends out the proxies for stockholder votes, and it is management which to all intents and purposes re-elects itself into office.

Recent data to document this argument is missing. But Robert A. Gordon, an economist of the University of California at Berkeley, has compiled data of the year 1935 which cover three quarters of the two hundred largest corporations. For the industrial companies in this group, salaried executives of the corporation comprised 43 per cent of the total number of directors on the corporation's board. In thirty out of the eighty-four giant industrial corporations, salaried executives were an absolute majority on the board of directors; in fifteen additional firms, they were only one shy of a majority.

In the group of one hundred fifteen largest industrial corporations in 1939, there were only five in which a close direct link existed between management and ownership. These were the five companies in which the combined shares of stock owned by all officers and directors of the corporation totalled more than 30 per cent of the total stock outstanding. In over 80 per cent of the corporations, the officers and directors combined owned less than 5 per cent of the outstanding stock.

Such evidence as this points to separation of corporate control from ownership. It indicates that the vast majority of our great industrial firms have managements and boards of directors which do not directly own even a respectable minority of the corporation's stock.

But does this really mean divorce of control from ownership? Perhaps both corporation officers and boards are simply hands hired by stockholding groups not themselves on the boards or directly in management?

Here, naturally enough, opinions differ. An estimate for 1937–39 which was made by the Securities and Exchange Commission, after omitting companies which were subsidiaries of other firms, found that 36 per cent of the largest manufacturing corporations were outside the control of any stockholder group. Gordon, in reviewing the figures, felt that this one-third estimate should be raised substantially.

Whoever is correct, it seems clear that a large proportion

of American giant corporations are controlled by management in the absence of any substantial unified ownership. But it is also reasonably certain that this management control is far from a universal fact of American corporate life, although there are those like A. A. Berle, attorney and authoritative author on this subject, who seem to deny it.

The proxy fights of the 1950's have proven that managements are not secure, even in prosperous times. Well-organized raiders have been able to buy into corporations, and to combat the policies of existing management before the jury of the stockholders. The importance of the vote of even the small stockholder has been dramatized by these battles. Stock ownership and control seem once again to be linking together more closely.

But we should be careful not to overemphasize the role of the stockholder. The once-successful raider Leopold Silberstein observed: "It's very tough to buy control in the market if the management controls 10 to 20 per cent [of the shares]. I don't go into any situation where the management owns as much as 10."

In short, the managerial revolution, the separation of control from ownership, the relegation of the shareholder to coupon clipper and capital-gains speculator, is well advanced. But it is still a long way from having taken over American industry.

For those companies which are management-controlled, one may well ask—and indeed the question has been asked ever since Berle and Means' basic 1932 study of corporate control —by what moral right does management govern? Traditionally, the manager-owner was simply exercising the right of private property. He was the entrepreneur, risking his personal fortune on the success of his enterprise. He himself bore the losses of his business, and so it was judged proper that he should have the authority going with his responsibility.

In the company which has many stockholders, the owner of common stock also bears the risk. Workmen, tax collector, suppliers, banker, and bondholders: all must be paid before the stockholder can benefit. The stockholders, exercising control, seem legitimate counterparts of the nineteenth-century owner-manager.

But management? When it owns little stock, as we have seen to be typically the case, it bears little risk. The company's losses are not suffered by management, but by the stockholders. A careful study of the larger American firms whose stock is publicly owned revealed no clear relationship between profits earned by a corporation of any given size and the total compensation—including bonuses—paid to its executives. Contraction of markets is a loss borne by the workers who lose their jobs, while executives are relatively secure in their own positions. The spreading of losses to other industries is a risk borne by these industries and by the public at large.

In what sense, then, are the managers taking a chance? How can they be called entrepreneurs? What is the relationship between the moral right to manage of the old-time owner-entrepreneur and the power exercised by these non-owning managers? These are the questions which have challenged the legitimacy and, in certain quarters, the very claim to continued existence of the modern management-governed corporation. For, if the stockholders do not rule the corporation, if control by right of private property is not involved, why should not the government appoint the management? Why should the management be allowed to appoint itself?

Indeed, the issue pushes deeper. It has been presumed that owner-managers press for the largest possible profits, making decisions as to output and price in accord with this objective. Traditional economic theory has oriented itself upon this profit goal, and has explained the interlinking of the economy around this centerpiece motif through what amounts to an elaboration of Adam Smith's "invisible hand." As Smith put it, the owner-manager "generally neither intends to promote the public interest, nor knows how much he is promoting it. . . . By pursuing his own interest he frequently promotes that of the society more effectually than when he really intends to promote it. I have never known much good done by those who affected to trade for the public good. It is an affectation, indeed, not very common among merchants. . . ."

What happens with the divorce of management from ownership? The profit goal becomes only one among several. Managements are urged to consider and represent not only the stake of the shareholders, but also the interests of the employees, the consumers, the local communities in which plants are located, and the national public at large. Managements are asked to take the broad view, the statesmanlike approach. Or, to voice the same concept from the cynical side of our mouths, they are asked to act like politicians who are in office for life: who need not worry about what the public wants, but only about what the politician thinks is good for them.

Adam Smith found this statesmanlike approach "an affectation not very common among merchants." But the case is different today. Public service is a great watchword of management. And why should it not be? Prime allegiance to the interest of stockholders has no special appeal for management-dominated corporations, except for historic and sentimental ties which may well be fading away. What goal should such a management have? The public weal is as good as any other. Indeed, when management insists on searching still further for a goal, it often gets into such strangely tortuous situations as the pursuit of size for its own sake.

But this point returns us once more to the issue of socialization of management control. If managements are to pursue the common weal, as they interpret it, would it not be more reasonable for them to pursue that image of it which is held by the public itself? In short, should not corporate managements be responsible to elected officials? If private management voluntarily gives up the traditional goal which has bound the free enterprise system together, does the system still have its *raison d'être*, or should it be forced to evolve still further?

It is in the forestalling of these questions as to management-dominated corporations that the stockholder still plays his role. He is the link between such managements and the traditional legitimacy of business power. Even when the stockholders are powerless, they bring the cloak of legitimacy to the management. And of course, as we have seen earlier, the stockholders do play a controlling role in many—two thirds according to the SEC estimate—of all our large corporations. The managerial revolution has occurred in only a portion of our firms. But where it has taken place, the legitimacy function of the shareholder still remains.

Clash of the Commissar and Party Secretary

When we in America think of the Russian Communist Party, we are likely to have in mind Khrushchev, the Praesidium, and the Central Committee. For we know that the Communist Party makes the ultimate decisions in the Soviet state, and we realize that these decisions are virtually uninfluenced by the rank-and-file Party members. In the light of this, we are bound to think of the Communist Party as simply a fancy Russian name for the real government of the Soviet Union.

Certainly this conception has much to recommend it. Even Soviet legal textbooks tell us "that not a single major decision on general questions of state activity are taken by [government] organs without prior guiding instructions from the Party." The Praesidium of the Party can appropriately be considered as the top policy-making body of the Soviet Union, with authority for everything from levels of military spending to decisions as to what makes for good literature and who should be allowed to accept a Nobel prize. In this role, the Praesidium of the Party acts as the apex of an all-embracing administrative system. Both the Council of Ministers at one extreme, and the Union of Soviet Writers at another, can be viewed as executive organs of the Party Praesidium; their task is to iron out the "details" in their respective fields.

If this were all there were to the Communist Party, we would find nothing very unusual about it except the scope of its power. It would be simply one more national government —a little peculiar, it must be admitted—which has been given a different name for historical reasons.

In fact, we may follow further, into the area of legitimacy, this conception of the Party as the real government of the country. For what gives a Soviet plant manager legitimacy of power? In a strictly legal sense, his authority emanates from the Council of Ministers and ultimately from the Supreme Soviet, which is elected by universal suffrage. However, as we can see even in the quote given above from an approved Russian textbook in law, no one in the Soviet Union takes this legalism too seriously. Although the manager's appointment is made by an organ of the Council of Ministers, the source of the legitimacy of his power in the eyes of his factory workers is the backing of the Party hierarchy.

But what is it which lends legitimacy to the Party hierarchy itself? Three things, it seems to me. All three of them are consequences of the fact that the Soviet Communist Party is far more than simply Khrushchev and the Praesidium.

One of these sources of legitimacy is the doctrinal role of "Pope" which is played by the Party hierarchy. The hierarchy is the sole final authority for proper interpretation of Marxism-Leninism. It is the ordained voice of "science" in all aspects of Soviet life. Drummed continually into the ears of people at all levels of society, this doctrinal role becomes fundamental. It is not the State which gives legitimacy to the Party, but rather the Party which makes the Soviet State legitimate.

Linked to this doctrinal power is the aura cast by Russian heroes and martyrs. Some of these are purely nationalistic figures, men who gained their stature from furthering Holy Russia's national interests. Their politics are seen as irrelevant. Peter the Great is in this camp, as is the great general Suvorov, whose capture of Pugachev—the most formidable of the peasant rebels against the Tsar—is now completely forgiven. Such men are viewed as having earned their legitimacy by dint of services directly to the nation.

The modern heroes, however, are Party figures. Lenin is the chief of them. Purity of ideals, personality, and family life are represented by him. In Leningrad, Kirov—the city Party secretary whose assassination was the signal, although with the delayed reaction of a time bomb, for the terrible purges of the thirties—is talked of in the same fashion. Both were martyrs: one seriously wounded, and the other killed by enemies of the Party. Listen to a Russian speaking of these men, and you will realize the extent to which their names attach present-day emotions to the Communist Party. For Lenin and Kirov are remembered as Party, rather than as government, figures.

The third ground for legitimacy of the Party is that of "democracy"—Russian style. Government bodies do not really have this basis of support, for Soviet state elections are intended to do little more than rally the public around the chosen candidates in a festive occasion. But the Communist Party does meet the Soviet definition of democracy.

The essence of this definition is not the choosing of Party officials by the Party membership, although formal election does occur. There has still been no repudiation of the well-known statement about Party democracy in which Stalin asked: "What is democracy within the Party? Democracy for whom? If by democracy is meant freedom for a few intellectuals, cut off from the Revolution, to chatter on without end, have their own press organ, etc., then we have no need for such 'democracy.'" Stalin rejected the idea that the Party member must understand the Party program, for, he said, such a concept would lead to having a Party composed only of intellectuals. It is enough, said Stalin, for the Party member to "know" the program.

Clearly such a membership is not intended to evaluate decisions or changes in doctrine made by the Party hierarchy. It is true that the post-Stalin period has seen some extension of the concept of Party decision-making. Khrushchev successfully called upon the Central Committee to reverse the key decision made by the smaller Praesidium body which favored the Malenkov-Molotov-Kaganovich coalition. But the broadening of the power base has gone no lower than these two hundred and fifty men. There have been no signs of permitting discussion of controversial national problems among ordinary Party members, or of permitting them to vote for Party officials on the basis of the candidates' views regarding these issues.

The fact that the ordinary Russian is granted no power of choice between candidates for leadership is reflected in his marked indifference to the fate of individual officials. Even Beria's removal from power could not cause a ripple of excitement among the Moscow crowds, at least according to Western reports. The ousting several years later of Khrushchev's remaining powerful rivals was of even less interest. To use the expression of the Russian man-in-the-street, the choice of top leadership is a job for "them" rather than for "us."

The essence of Soviet "democracy" is the activity of large numbers of people in interpreting to their local scene the decisions made higher in the organization, of taking part in carrying out these decisions and in supervising their execution by others, and finally, of trying to mobilize support for these decisions by the general Soviet public. In short, *democracy consists of participation in everything except basic decision-making.* In terms of this definition, the Communist Party is indeed a democratic organization; and the Russians can make an honest case for the Soviet Union being more "democratic" than the United States.

This sort of democracy can have quite an impact upon the ordinary Soviet citizen. For it means that the Party can function as did the old-fashioned big-city political machine in the United States, but on both a vaster and more intimate scale. Millions of Party members play the role of the precinct captains, keeping in touch with the public throughout the year. Politics is not something far off in the Kremlin or even in city hall, but is represented by a neighbor who can fix a summons, clear up red tape, or see that garbage is collected properly. If nothing else, the Soviet citizen can at least pitch his beef into the ear of this sympathetic minor representative of the powers that be. This is politics with the personal touch.

In order to make the Communist Party democratic in this sense, a large membership is desirable. At the same time, if the members are to fill the desired role, this membership must be an elite. It should be composed of people who are both willing to take on the burdens of ceaseless, unpaid activity, and who are considered by those with whom they live and work as being of leadership caliber.

This membership must permeate all segments of society if it is effectively to initiate, mobilize, and supervise. Thus candidates for membership are not accepted purely on the basis of their personal qualifications, but due regard is given to the need for having members properly distributed throughout the national labor force. Party organizations have the right, when necessary, to send Party members into other lines of work and other geographic areas. As of early 1956, the Communist Party had seven million members out of a total Soviet population of two hundred million. In two factories concerning which I obtained information during my 1958 visit, Party members made up 14 to 19 per cent of the total work force.

Let us now turn to an examination of the Communist Party's role in Soviet industry within the frame of reference set by comparison with American stockholders. This comparison, of course, is intended for purposes of illustration and in order to highlight selected features of both organizational structures. The following chart shows the various levels of both Party and stockholder power.

The pinnacle of power in the Soviet Union is held by the Praesidium of the Central Committee of the Communist Party. In Stalin's day, one-man control was exercised through this organ. Unruly or undesirable members were readily kicked out of the club, and usually kicked further than that. Today, impression has it—although no one really knows—that there is more than one person of power within this body.

Similarly, an American corporation is headed by its board of directors. Depending upon the company and period, this board may be dominated by one man or by several.

Just as a high proportion of American directors are also officers of the corporation, so too there is a large but not complete overlap between membership in the Russian Praesidium and the holding of high administrative office in the state machinery. Of the disputants for power since Stalin's death, Beria, Molotov, and Kaganovich represented such overlap, while Malenkov and Khrushchev had their careers contained primarily within the Party apparatus.

The board of directors is elected by the stockholders. Since it is this fact which makes the board's reign legitimate, bows of obeisance are offered to the stockholders in even the most management-controlled of companies. Regular stockholder meetings are held, reports of some sort are sent to stockholders, proxies for ballots are assiduously collected.

Similarly, the top Party organs are ultimately elected by the Party membership. Eight million Party members in 1959 match the seven or eight million American shareholders. Reports are periodically made, and elections are held through an indirect balloting system. It is true that, since the mid-twenties, ordinary Party members have not had a choice of candidates for

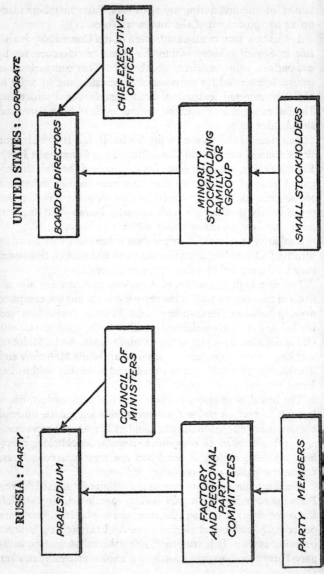

LEVELS OF POWER IN RUSSIA AND THE UNITED STATES

UNITED STATES: CORPORATE

CHIEF EXECUTIVE OFFICER

BOARD OF DIRECTORS

MINORITY STOCKHOLDING FAMILY OR GROUP

SMALL STOCKHOLDERS

RUSSIA: PARTY

COUNCIL OF MINISTERS

PRAESIDIUM

FACTORY AND REGIONAL PARTY COMMITTEES

PARTY MEMBERS

top office—and even then it was at peril of their lives that they voted wrong. But the American small stockholder is rarely, although not quite so rarely as the Russian Party member, offered a choice of candidates and of policies disputing for his proxy.

Having seen some similarities between the peaks of the two organizational pyramids, let us turn to the two foundations. Neither the small stockholder nor the ordinary Party member has any particular influence on choice of candidates for the top positions or of the policies they will follow. At the same time, it is they who give legitimacy to the entire superstructure in the eyes of the general public.

But both stockholder and Party member provide more than legitimacy. The stockholder supplies the risk capital upon which the corporation is founded. The giant company also hopes that he will support the firm as a customer, giving preference to it over its competitors. An important argument for stock ownership by workers of a company is that the dual role of the employee-stockholder will help improve labor relations from the company point of view.

The Party member provides the sinews of his organization. His is the unpaid labor which helps execute the plans of the higher organs, and which propagandizes, supervises, and integrates on the level of the shop and factory. He is the embodiment to the general population of the Party "personality." The government may be composed of a group known as "they," but the Party consists of neighbors and workmates who are certainly part of the "we" of the common man. Finally, and least important, the Party member's dues provide three quarters of the Party's total income.

Precisely because the Party member is the direct representative of power to the public at large, the demands of morality fall particularly heavily upon him. If he is convicted of a crime, the sentence will be more severe than for the ordinary Soviet citizen. If he is drunk regularly or beats his wife, his Party cell will discuss the matter in public meeting. The Party member is a marked man.

Take divorce. Divorce is difficult enough for the ordinary Soviet citizen. Not only are there the customary formalities, but the alimony award is rigid and high: one fourth of the man's earnings if there is one child, one third if there are two, and one half if there are more than two. But for the Party member, divorce is virtually a political offense. Particularly if the Party member is at all prominent, divorce is bound to bring him an official Party vote of censure. Often, I was told by one Soviet citizen, the best he can hope is that his Party unit will grant him tacit permission to live with his new love on condition that he remain formally attached to his wife.

One of the hit plays of the 1958 Russian theater season was the Czech play *Such a Love* by Pavel Kogovt. It is a moving love story, launching a powerful and dramatic attack upon the social and, specifically, upon the Party obstacles to true love. Peter, a young instructor in family law, is unhappily married. He and a university student, Lida, are in love. Peter intends to divorce his wife and marry Lida, but is dissuaded by the head of the personnel sector in the university. The personnel man who, it is explicitly stated, is a Party member, points out to Peter that divorce would be harmful both to society and to Peter's own career, since it would scarcely be in keeping with Peter's position as a specialist on the family. But if Peter's love for Lida is truly a "great love," the Party official says piously, Peter should in any case proceed with the divorce.

Peter is not a hero. He begs his wife to take him back, and Lida, overhearing the scene and overwhelmed by Peter's betrayal, falls off a moving train in a half-suicide, half-accident.

Who is to blame for Lida's suicide, asks the narrator? Who is to blame for the fact that, of all the play's characters, she is the only one who follows the morality proclaimed throughout the play in Peter's lectures? She is the only one who actively believes in love; who holds that the socialist family is indeed a new kind of family, based for the first time in history upon proper relationships between men and women, with love as its foundation.

All of the characters accept their share of the guilt for Lida's suicide. But who is to judge us? they ask. The narrator points to the audience as judge. It is clear that he expects the audience to find that the Party must take upon its own shoulders at least a large portion of the blame.

How can we interpret the smash success of this play, and its production simultaneously in many Soviet cities? Is this success a forerunner of relaxation in the Party's concern with morality, of an easing of the public judgment of the personal lives of Party members? Perhaps; for there are other tokens which might also be taken as signs of this. But it is safe to say that the Party member will for a long time continue to live much of his private life in the public eye, and will therefore be mindful of public standards of judgment.

What is the incentive to the Party member for taking on this heavy role? The shareholder in an American corporation measures his reward in hard cash. Dividends and—more important in these days of inflation and high taxes—capital gains are his payment.

The Party member receives most of his reward in prestige: he is one of the "rulers" of the nation. He is a member of the most select of clubs. A second part of his reward is in the feeling of service to the nation; in this respect, he is like an American active in his church or charity. A third payment is in improved chances for advancement in his regular work, although it is indeed difficult to weigh the importance of this. Least important of all, he may receive some monetary benefits. One retired pre-1917 Party member, now on pension, pays a lower rent for his apartment than he would otherwise pay precisely because he is an Old Bolshevik. But such money benefits are hardly likely to be greater, over a lifetime, than the sum of membership dues he has paid out.

It is in the middle tier of the Party and stockholder pyramids that the most interesting parallels lie. For it is here that we find the interaction between management and strong stockholding groups in the American corporation, and between management and strong Party groups in Soviet industry.

In the large American corporation, the individual holder of a large block of stock—or, more frequently, a family or other group-coalition of stockholders—is a power within the firm. It is rare that there should be any group of stockholders which holds an absolute majority of stock in a large company.

Whether the stockholder group holds 5 or 20 per cent of the stock, management had best pay close attention to its desires. This is true even when the board of directors is management-controlled—for boards can change.

This does not mean that management must obey the instructions of this minority stockholder group. Management, too, has power—and the stockholders will not lightly appeal to the board from a management decision. If the issue does go to the board, either side may win. Should the struggle continue on into a proxy fight over a new board of directors, management has powerful weapons available for such a battle. This struggle is one which both sides will normally prefer to avoid.

So, too, in Russia. The plant Party committees, the city committees, the regional committees: all are potent bodies, and their full-time secretaries are powerful men. One of their major functions is that of supervising industry: of seeing that all goes smoothly in the shop, the plant, the entire industrial regional administration. The build-up of industry is a fundamental ingredient in the program of expanding the strength of the Soviet system and thus of the Soviet Communist Party. The Party committees are there to protect the interests of the "stockholders," and they themselves are judged by their success in this regard.

In fact, the Party committees are extremely active in their "protection of the stockholding interest," far more than is the case of their counterparts in American business. With the duty and obligation of "supervision" over industrial management, they have in fact injected themselves deep into the management function. They have consulted with managers on day-to-day problems, set policy for them, and even ousted executives and appointed new ones. At times, they have acted like stockholders who were taking over the business.

Thus one powerful prewar director of a major plant, who seemed to be permanently on the outs with both the plant and city Party authorities, found himself a victim of harassment. His record was too good for the local Party people to attack him directly, but no sooner would he be off to Moscow on business than his major executives would find themselves in deep water. Once the plant Party committee, in the director's absence, tried to fire his chief of personnel. Another time, it sharply reprimanded the assistant director for leaving the plant during working hours without consulting the Party secretary —although he had gone on the director's orders.

Another director, newly appointed to a different important plant, was welcomed at the first factory Party meeting with the words, "We'll see how the new director works. . . . Doubtless, we'll whip him along." There was good reason for the new director to take this promise seriously, for it was only a short time since his predecessor had been illegally removed by this same Party group, and then had been turned over to the courts for criminal prosecution.

This procedure of direct Party interference has never worked too well, and the top Party organ—like any good board of directors—has tried to shield management from the Party eager-beavers. It has insisted that the managers must manage; it has proclaimed that, while assuredly they should pay attention to Party advice, it is on their own responsibility that they accept or reject it. The Praesidium has, in the past, strongly chastised city Party committees which have usurped the right to appoint and dismiss directors of factories. At the same time, it has wished to maintain detailed supervision by the intermediate Party committees over management, and it has held these Party committees to be responsible for any laxity in their stewardship.

The result has been an uneasy compromise. By and large, Party and industrial management men have tried to work in harness. Each group is too powerful to be needlessly antagonized by the other. When there is strife between them, there is the real danger that higher authorities may resolve it by ousting both the management and Party officials concerned, and by bringing in new representatives who can get along with one another.

Thus, the director mentioned above, who had been welcomed to the plant with the promise of whippings to come, soon ran into the expected difficulties. In a routine transfer of a foreman from one department to another, he met with resistance from the Party secretary. For, although the plant director has authority to transfer the plant personnel as he sees

fit, the factory leadership of the Party has authority over all
Party members. In this case, the Party secretary refused permission for the transfer. The minor issue became a major one.
Finally, the regional committee of the Party "helped" the factory Party secretary to see that he could—and had better—get
along with the director.

Still and all, disagreements arise which cannot be compro-
mised. Appeals can be taken higher both in the channels of
industrial management and of the Party. Few issues, of course,
will mount too far before they are settled. But what happens
when they go all the way to the top?

The "top" is the Praesidium of the Central Committee of
the Communist Party. In a formal sense, it is purely a Party
organ. It is elected and removed by the Party membership,
just as the board of directors of a corporation is chosen by the
stockholders. But, also like a board of directors, it has management functions. Its decisions are binding on all levels of industrial administration. Many of the members of the Praesidium play direct management roles as well. At the present
time, Khrushchev is not only first secretary of the Communist
Party—i.e., top representative of the shareholders—but he is
also chairman of the Council of Ministers and so chief management representative. He has only to change hats in order to
change roles.

Thus the Praesidium is a unique Party organ. In all intermediate Party bodies, the key figures are full-time Party officials who represent only the Party. As a result of their limited
role as Party representatives, they cannot issue final and un-
challengeable instructions to management groups. But the
Praesidium represents directly within itself management
groups. It has the final word, and its decision in any particular
case may go either to the Party or to the management appel-
lant. It is very much the board of directors of the Soviet Union.

In fact, we may take the parallel one step further. In the
last analysis, decisions of an American board may be appealed
to the stockholders. Similarly, we have seen one recent and
successful appeal from the Praesidium to a somewhat wider
group of powerful minority shareholders. I am referring to
Khrushchev's appeal to the Central Committee, which to a

large extent is composed of influential Party figures in the provinces. In a crucial power struggle, these large stockholders in the Central Committee received the vote which reversed the Praesidium and which elected a new majority within it.

Our parallel between the Russian Communist Party and American corporate stockholders is now complete. Both can be considered as absolute rulers over management only on the basis of treating the Praesidium and the board of directors as the top Party and stockholder organs respectively. But this is sheer formalism. For in both these bodies, powerful forces are at work which represent other than solely Party or stockholder interests. Both the Praesidium and board of directors are appropriately viewed as arenas in which stockholder and management forces reach agreement, and in which they occasionally lock horns.

13. LABOR

Informal Groups at Work

The time-and-motion study boys have a fabulously successful record of prediction. American industrial engineering theory holds that workers on incentive pay should be able to produce some 20 to 30 per cent above "standard" output. This standard is the volume that workers paid by the hour would be expected to turn out. Remarkably enough, the vast bulk of workers in all industries which employ piecework systems do seem to produce almost exactly according to prediction.

Unfortunately, the high quality of these predictions cannot be credited entirely to management and the industrial engineers. Some of the predictive success must be attributed to the workers themselves who, when producing on incentives, are careful to see that management's expectations are not disappointed. Output restriction must often be awarded the chief palms in the battle to reach, but not exceed, the predictions of the industrial engineers.

Part of the reason for such output restriction is a distrust of management on the part of labor. If workers in a shop should begin regularly to produce 200 per cent of standard, it seems a reasonable guess that the standard would be changed. Where a labor contract or management policy forbids an altering of standards unless there has been prior change in working conditions, it is assumed that management will be sufficiently ingenious to find a need either for redesign of the part produced according to the loose standard, or of the process used to produce it.

Probably more fundamental than labor distrust as a cause for output restriction is the fact that both labor and manage-

ment in the United States wish to achieve certain managerial
results which management alone simply cannot accomplish.
Both groups, by and large, would like to avoid juggling of
the standard for volume of output on a job. Labor demands
this as a precondition for interpreting an incentive system as
anything but a thinly disguised speed-up; management accepts the demand as justified, and considers stable standards
as fundamental to a successful incentive wage system. At the
same time, however, both management and labor are insistent
that earnings in a plant must really be organized into some
sort of a sensible pattern. When semi-skilled recruits earn more
than highly skilled twenty-year men, because of "loose" and
"tight" standards respectively, no one would call this a workable system of rates. The amount of labor trouble found in the
occasional plant or department which glides into such a situation is a surprise to no one.

Given a piece-rate system, there seem to be only two ways
to achieve these twin goals of stable standards and maintenance of an appropriate earnings pattern. One method is for
management to loosen up standards so that they accord with
the loosest one extant. Adam Abruzzi reports cases "where
even an hourglass would have shown a job could be done in
X minutes, yet the production standard was knowingly set at
2X minutes." This procedure, of course, can render a plant
totally non-competitive. Abruzzi reports a few cases in which a
company could be restored to competitiveness only by up and
moving to a distant geographic area, leaving behind it the
building, the workers, and the loose-standards tradition.

The second, and fortunately the vastly more prevalent,
method of achieving these joint management-worker goals is
to depend upon labor itself to keep in line the earnings of
different skill groups. Output restriction, informally enforced,
is the standard procedure. If none but a handful of ratebusters
produce more than 125–130 per cent of "standard," regardless of whether the standards are loose or tight, then everyone
is kept happy. Management can maintain stable standards,
have a workable wage pattern, and still get the one-fourth
increase in productivity promised from its incentive system.
Labor can gain the extra take-home pay, while preserving so-

cial stability by ensuring that relative earnings meet the workers' sense of equity, and at the same time avoiding rate changes
and resulting speed-up. Even the "scientific minded" among
time-and-motion-study men are happy, for the standards they
set have been proven to be "scientifically sound" and accurate
within a 5 per cent margin.

There are no really good statistics as to the prevalence of
piece-rate systems in American industry. Perhaps the best estimate is still the one which came out of a wartime survey by
the American Management Association. Here it was found that
62 per cent of direct producers and 17 per cent of indirect
producers worked under some sort of incentive system. The
division between the use of individual and group incentives
was fairly even. Eighty-five per cent of the companies surveyed were using the same wage system that they had had
four years earlier, thus indicating that the war did not see the
introduction of drastic changes.

From this study, it would appear that the proportion of
American manual workers who are paid according to some
sort of piece rate is not overwhelming; the proportion is kept
down by precisely the sorts of administrative problems we have
been discussing. Yet the figure is sufficiently high to warrant
the consideration we are giving to the problems implicit in
these piece-rate systems.

As labor takes over the managerial task of maintaining a
workable wage pattern under existing piece rates, it frequently
finds it imperative—or at least useful—to become involved in
other management functions. In the Lapointe Machine Tool
Company of Hudson, Massachusetts, for example, the workers
—not through their union but rather acting as informal groups
—played a powerful role in the scheduling of production. They
were strongly interested in the question of timing as to when
jobs on "loose" standards would actually be begun, and when
work on "tight" standards would have to be pushed through,
since they felt it important to maintain a daily rate of total
production which would appear constant. As one executive of
the company put the matter: "You couldn't schedule work.
The operators, particularly in grinding, would pick the good
jobs from the rack and hide them. Eventually they would ring

them in, but in the meantime we would lose track of them."
Such worker management of scheduling is a potent device for
maintaining constant earnings while varying effort as the
workers wish. If jobs with loose standards are saved for Blue
Mondays, then earnings on these days need not suffer as a
result of hangovers. The tough jobs can be saved for the middle of the week.

Matters such as organizational and equipment changes
within the factory also become subjects of labor concern. For
these lead to changes in the standards, and such changes may
be bad for the workers concerned. Unsatisfactory changes can
be resisted: the new standards may prove "impossible" to
meet, and the methods changes may lead to poor-quality product. As a result of all this, one may properly ask: Who is performing the management function on the shop floor?

Precisely this question was asked in one American automobile plant with 15,000 employees. Academic investigators interviewed foremen and shop stewards and inquired as to
whether the foreman or the steward had most to say about
what was going on in their department. For 63 departments,
the answers ran:

17 departments: both agreed that the foreman had the
power;

13 departments: both agreed that the foreman did not have
the power;

23 departments: the foreman thought he had the power,
while the steward believed he himself had it;

10 departments: neither foreman nor steward was certain as
to who had the power.

In this last case, a unionized plant was being studied. Here
the shop steward was the formal representative of the department's workers. But worker restriction on output, control over
aspects of scheduling, etc., are well documented for unorganized plants as well. Where a group of workers does not have
a shop steward, it usually turns up one or more informal leaders to play his role. Worker management on the shop floor
may be just as widespread in non-union plants as in union

ones, and it appears to take pretty much the same forms within the shop.

Worker restriction of output, of course, is not purely an American phenomenon. Russian industry has faced the same problem, and for virtually the same reasons. It is true that the Soviet worker is rarely afraid of working himself out of a job. Rising production quotas for factories have assured what we in the United States would call overfull employment—overfull in the sense that it creates great pressures for wage-push inflation—and thus they have taken care of the layoff worry for most Soviet workers. Even so, those in plants which have fixed output quotas—perfume factories, for example—may still wish to restrict output so as to avoid forcing some workers to shift to jobs in other plants less convenient for them. More important, all the other powerful motives which exist in the United States for output restrictions are also present in the Soviet Union. Just like American workers, Russians are concerned with avoiding speed-ups which lead to more work for the same money; they also wish to protect inefficient workers from being shown up before management; they also want to assure an earnings pattern which meets their idea of justice. All these motives make for strong pressures against upping productivity.

During the 1930's, Soviet management faced an extreme form of the work-restriction problem. As modern technology was introduced into Soviet industry, enormous labor productivity gains became feasible. But in the first years of the 1930's, these gains could not be realized. Raw labor was pouring in from the countryside, and it had to be factory-broken before productivity could rise. Probably even more important, management at all levels was itself poorly trained. A period of years was needed for absorption of the new technology; only then could productivity really mount.

Given this situation, the setting of standards for the piece rates governing the Soviet wage system was a difficult task. In the first years, it was necessary that these standards be very low in order for them to be at all realistic and acceptable to the workers. But later, if Russia were to become a powerful industrial nation, it was essential to raise them rapidly to internationally respectable levels. It is true that this lifting of standards is an issue which often accompanies the introduction of new equipment into American plants, and it is commonly met by raising the output volume required of workers according to a "learning curve." But in the American case, the learning process takes weeks or, at the most, months. In the Soviet case, it was a matter of years. Russian management would have had a hard time selling the argument that the "learning curve" philosophy could properly be extended over such a long time period.

Soviet management, of course, had certain powerful weapons for dealing with the problem of raising the standard. It did not have to fear strikes; these were illegal in practice, although not in theory. Secret police informants, as well as Communist Party members distributed throughout the factory work force, were major aides in weakening group restrictions on output. However, overheavy reliance upon these supports might well have boomeranged through the medium of a collapse in worker morale. Appeals to nationalism and to ideology, in the form of "building socialism," made a heady drink for many; but such appeals were also insufficient supports to carry the burden.

The year 1935 saw the flowering of a fabulous effort to raise labor productivity: namely, the Stakhanovite movement. Launched and kept aloft in a publicity campaign far beyond the capacity of Madison Avenue—combining dominance of the newspaper pages, control of the sound waves through loudspeakers and radio and, most important of all, use of face-to-face contact through millions of "agitators"—it was enormously successful. Stakhanovism was partially directed at bringing forth more work-effort, but the potential gains from this source were recognized as relatively small. Primarily, it was aimed at motivating workers to use improved techniques on the job, and to innovate new ones. Its emphasis was thoroughly modern, being on rationalization rather than on sweating.

The rewards offered to individual workers were high. Stakhanovites became national heroes, honored with medals and with their pictures in the papers. Glory was the payoff; but also cash. Some 70 per cent of all workers were paid by piece rates, and large numbers were switched to progressive-piece-rate systems (under which the payment per unit produced rose sharply in a number of stages once the standard was met). Many individual semi-skilled Stakhanovites earned more than did the directors of their factories. Simultaneously with the rise in earnings, the rationing of consumer goods was ended in order that the new money wealth might mean genuine purchasing power.

By December 1935, four months after the movement began, the payoff to the state was clearly evident. Within heavy industry, half of all the workers produced more than 150 per cent of standard, and a bare tenth fell below 120 per cent. It seems a fair guess that these results were to a large extent achieved by breaking through work restrictions which had previously prevailed. While some Stakhanovites doubtless were given a rough time by their workmates, the resistance was remarkably feeble. A combination of a stick and a large carrot had finally brought into motion a labor force which was only a few years off the farm.

The time had come to raise the "boguey." The Soviet government wished to reduce labor costs; in addition, it felt impelled to do something about the widely differing degrees of looseness which had now become apparent in the standards. During early 1936, quotas were set for factory-wide cuts in the piece rates; managements were to use judgment in raising individual job standards to meet the over-all factory quotas. By July, only some 15 per cent of the workers in heavy industry were producing over 150 per cent of the new standard, and some 25 to 30 per cent fell below standard.

At this point the issue arose squarely: What would have to be done so that management could continue to raise labor productivity, motivating workers once again to push their output far beyond the "standard"? The official government policy on standards was clear-cut: whenever any changes were made in the job, the standard for the job should also be altered. But changes were being made all the time; could a piece-rate system survive constant juggling of the rates?

Plant managements seem to have answered in the negative. Since they were far more interested in production than in wage costs, and since obviously the way to motivate workers to higher production was to leave the rates alone, the managers opted for loose standards. Over a period of three years, they ignored official instructions and kept constant the output standards for different jobs. Only in 1939 did national authorities tighten up through a new national campaign, complete with plant quotas.

In the prewar period, this practice of not reducing rates except in times of national campaigns paid off fairly well. Despite the drastic dislocations due to the political purging of management ranks and to the shift to military production, labor productivity did not fall and even continued to rise. Between 1936 and 1940, workers in heavy industry—the giant segment of industry whose production was of real concern to the government—produced an average of 130 to 160 per cent of "standard." By mid-1938, one third to one half of all these workers were again producing more than 150 per cent of standard. This was quite a recovery from the low point of July 1936, when only one seventh of heavy industry's workers were in this production category.

However, when Soviet plant management opted for stabilizing piece rates to the best of its ability, it could not simultaneously rescue the principle of preserving a pattern of earnings related to skill. There were some attempts to argue that existing earnings really did comprise a system of sorts, in that a worker turning out high output on a job with a low classification was really more skilled than a worker with only average production who was filling a higher-graded place. But, generally speaking, there was agreement as to the confusion and disparities in the existing earning structures.

A good indication of such disparity in earning structures is the intensity with which workers search for the "loose" rate. Often such search can be carried on within a given factory, but frequently it takes the form of quitting one job and getting another in a different plant. The years 1938 through mid-1940 saw the annual rate of separations running at about 80 per cent of total employment in all industry. Despite the increasing obstacles to changing jobs, virtually all of these separations were actually quits. Incentives to remain in the same job were offered; housing and minor pay increases, together with old-age, sickness, and accident benefits were linked to seniority in the plant. But the quit rate remained at a level which has not been approached in American industry except during the last war.

In recent times, however, Soviet management seems to have developed a startlingly successful solution to the problem of combining a real incentive system with a balanced earnings structure. Average piecework output as a proportion of "standard" has continued to mount; in 1950, the figure for all industry was 139 per cent of standard, and by December 1956 it had reached the fabulous average level of 155 per cent. In 1955, piece workers' earnings were almost double their "base" rates. On the face of it, in view of the rapid rise of labor productivity in Soviet industry combined with the fact that worker output has continued to rise as a proportion of standard, we can conclude that Russian management has continued to motivate workers to do other than restrict output to a predetermined overfulfillment of standard.

At the same time, the unbalanced earnings structure of the prewar years—at least in so far as this is reflected in a high labor-turnover ratio—seems to have been corrected. Soviet writers have ceased to complain about high turnover. In 1954, the ratio of "separations" to employment in Soviet industry was down to almost 20 per cent—compared to an annual average of 80 per cent during 1938–40 in the Soviet Union, and an annual average during 1951–57 in the United States of 46 per cent. This low 1954 Soviet industrial-turnover rate, it should be noted, occurred some four years after Soviet authorities had ceased to enforce laws prohibiting the free change of jobs by workers.

In one Moscow plant I visited, 15 per cent of the labor force had gone off the payroll during 1957. Of this group, 3 per cent had been fired, 4 per cent had been retired on pension, 2 per cent had quit to go back to school, and the remaining 6 per cent had taken other jobs, been drafted, transferred by the Party organization, or had left for some other miscellaneous reason. Here, certainly, is a picture of a factory with a stable work force.

How was this never-never-land combination of true incentives for output and a balanced earnings structure achieved? How could management permit and encourage individual workers to continue increasing the gap between actual output and standard, and yet avoid violating their sense of "equity" in relative earnings and thus set them off once more on a wave of job changes in search of the "loose" rate. The evidence points to the hypothesis that there has been a management policy of not raising standards even when output rose because of technological and organizational changes, and so of permitting rates to become quite loose over a period of time. As individual rates in a factory became loose, and threatened to overturn the balance of the earnings structure of the plant, other rates would also be loosened in order to once more rebalance the structure. Thus there has been a continual loosening of Russian factory standards as compared to potential output at the moment.

Although standards were "revised" annually until 1956, the revisions cannot have been particularly stringent. A Soviet author, discussing the annual revisions of standards, reported that it was not infrequent for plants to "revise" the standards for items which had already ceased to produce. Examples are available where a given job, performed under identical conditions, was timed in one plant as requiring one hour, and in another as needing four hours. During 1954, entire industries failed to meet their labor-productivity plans, and yet average worker output in these industries was paid as being at 160–170 per cent of standard. Clearly, there was no necessary relation between the standards laid down at the plant level and the labor-productivity targets set by higher administrative levels.

The Russian manager has kept his eye firmly on output and ignored labor costs. He has not attempted to tighten standards sharply as they were exceeded, nor has he wished to incite his other workers into quitting by treating them unfairly. The result was that in 1955 Bulganin could complain that, although industrial base rates had hardly risen from prewar levels, actual take-home pay had doubled. Bulganin quite properly placed the responsibility for this remarkable development upon universal looseness of standards.

Even in Russia, however, such a policy of loose standards has its cost. In the United States it can lead to bankruptcy for the individual company. In Russia, with all managements following this policy, the cost is of a different nature.

Up to 1949, loose standards led to higher costs of production and continued inflation. Workers got their hands on extra money faster than the government was willing and able to produce consumer goods; so prices rose. But since 1949, the standards have been further loosened without accompanying price increases; indeed, there have actually been substantial price reductions. This halt of inflation was made possible by the fact that, between 1950 and 1956, the goods available to the Russian workers increased some 40 to 50 per cent. A vast outpouring of production for consumers was concentrated within this period, when for the first time standards of living were raised above the prewar level. The great expansion of money wages in the pockets of consumers was matched by the increase in goods which they could buy. True, the Soviet policy of price reductions has been a victim since 1954 of rising money income, for prices could not continue to go down in face of the additional purchasing power. But this sacrifice of a deflationary policy has not seemed an overly high price to pay for the results. Failure to reduce prices does not create the popular fears and antagonism aroused by ever-mounting prices.

Unfortunately for Soviet management, there are limits to this policy of maintaining both high worker incentives and an appropriate earnings pattern through the progressive relaxation of actual standards relative to potential ones. In a period when Soviet policy and capabilities led to a flooding—judging by past Russian practice—of the consumer goods market, this policy was feasible. But as Russian policy turns to a much slower relative expansion of consumer goods than in the early 1950's, money earnings cannot continue to increase as rapidly without new inflation. Perhaps as a result of this fact, there has once again been concern with tightening up the standards. Russian plant management cannot continue to live in an "ideal" environment.

Thus, Russian management may well have to turn about

and face the American dilemma of choice between management goals. The new approach adopted in the Russian system
may well be that found in American industry—output restriction by workers. The alternative would seem to be a return to
the high labor mobility of the 1930's.

Trade Unions: Immature and Overripe

In 1945, a National Labor-Management Conference was organized under President Truman's auspices. Its purpose was
to draft a basic statement marking out those fields of business
decision-making which fall within the scope of unions' legitimate interests. But no agreement was possible. The union representatives wrote: "We cannot have one sharply delimited
area designated as management prerogatives and another
equally sharply defined area of union prerogatives without
either side constantly attempting to invade the forbidden ter-
ritory, thus creating much unnecessary strife." The management men concluded that "the only possible end of such a
philosophy would be joint management of enterprise."

Two years later, General Motors President Charles E. Wilson declared: "If we consider the ultimate result of this tendency to stretch collective bargaining to comprehend any subject that a union leader may desire to bargain on, we come
out with the union leaders really running the economy of the
country. . . . The Union leaders . . . will have the deciding
vote in all managerial decisions, or at least, will exercise a veto
power that will stop progress."

One need not go all the way with Mr. Wilson in order to
agree that American trade unions play a strong role in influencing certain types of traditional management decisions.
Their influence goes vastly further than that of labor in unorganized companies, where informal groups of workers exercise their power only in the making of shop-floor decisions.

The union's role is really twofold. On the one hand, it bargains as to wages and fringe benefits, such as medical insurance, pensions, and guaranteed-annual-wage plans. In a significant sense, none of this negotiating is really interference
with managerial decision-making. A bargain is struck, and

management is then left to operate as best it can within the framework of the union contract. This contract is similar to the agreement made with a customer, which may also stipulate not only price but, in addition, "fringe" elements such as delivery times, method of packing, and procedures of inspection for quality. The bargain remains fixed until the next contract period. The real difference between wage-negotiation and negotiation as to sales conditions is that the company management is legally obliged to enter into negotiations with the union, while there is no legal pressure to negotiate with a prospective customer. Whether this legal distinction is of great importance so far as management's rights are concerned is another matter.

But American unions do more than this sort of negotiating. Typically, although not invariably, they have been concerned with seniority as the key determinant of promotion and layoff, and through the interpretation of seniority they have played a major role in determining the make-up of the plant's work force. They have bargained as to work loads and as to the speed of assembly operations, formalizing in this area the earlier informal and often unspoken dickering. They have taken a hand in preventing entirely or, more commonly and particularly so in recent years, in easing the transition to new machine technology.

At the extreme, American unions have been interested in companies' pricing policies and even in their advertising. Since the wage bargain depends partly on the company's ability to pay, unions are vitally concerned with this ability. The barbers' union, for example, is quite concerned with raising the price of haircuts. In 1938, the president of the Steelworkers union protested against cuts in the price of steel—since he was afraid that they would lead to pressure on steelworkers' wages. On the other hand, the United Automobile Workers union has engaged in strong public protests against increases in the price of automobiles. In this, it has doubtless been influenced by a desire to disassociate wage and price increases in the minds of the public. In the General Motors 1945–46 negotiation and strike, the union demanded a wage increase without any accompanying price increase, and when price increases were in fact instituted it tried to fight them in the federal courts.

Unions may also be vitally concerned with the issue of plant location. In 1956, the Hat and Cap union discovered that an Illinois manufacturer was building a plant in Kentucky. On the basis that in the future this might mean closing of the existing Illinois plants and abandonment of the company's present unionized employees, the union struck. It won an agreement providing that the company could not transfer work to Kentucky without making payments to the union at the rate of $.50 to $1.50 per dozen caps transferred.

Concern with wages and working conditions can push unions into an interest in all phases of management activity. Moreover, since managerial policy must be flexible in pricing, marketing, and production areas, and since management decisions cannot be made only at the set periods when union agreements are negotiated, union policy must also be flexible. The desirability of continuous union concern with all matters which underlie bargaining as to wages and working conditions has been strongly asserted by many union leaders, and they have increasingly entered into day-to-day management decisions.

One may view these developments as natural consequences of traditional union functions. On the other hand, one might consider them as nothing more than reflections of the "immaturity" of American unionism. This latter approach gains strength from the fact that, in general, the older Western European trade union movements have not followed this path at all.

In England, for example, union locals normally have jurisdiction over all workers within a given trade in a particular locality, and these locals thus cut across plant lines. As a result of this structural pattern, British unions are not well organized for bargaining on an individual company basis, and they make no attempt to do so. Instead, bargaining occurs between unions, or even federations of unions, on the one side, and employers' associations on the other.

A system of shop stewards functions on the plant level. But these stewards are elected by all employees, and not just by union members. Since, typically, there are many unions functioning within a single plant, shop stewards' committees could not be linked to any union even if they wished to be.

British national labor bargaining covers a narrow range. Primarily, it is concerned only with wages, although hours, holidays, vacations, and weekly-pay guarantees may also be specified. The unions tend to oppose any bargaining on an individual company or plant basis, and wish to negotiate only with associations of employers rather than with individual firms. They resist getting into matters such as layoff procedures, labor transfers, and production standards; for only people on the spot could work out these questions, which are not easily susceptible to industry-wide bargaining. Even seniority provisions are rarely included in formal agreements.

This union resistance to broadening the scope of collective bargaining is due to the fact that such negotiations would have to be carried on with reference to local situations, and so would be under the shop stewards and outside the control of the national unions.

In this framework of national bargaining, there is no strong membership control over union leadership. In fact, officers are often selected on the basis of examination and are even given tenure until retirement. Such leaders can afford to be "responsible" and to put national interests—concern with inflation and international balance of payments—above the narrow desires of their union members for higher wages. The weapon of union-authorized strikes has been atrophying in England for lack of use. With such a tradition of "responsibility," it is no surprise that observers should find that "the gap between the top level of unions and the membership in the plant has tended to widen in most unions during the past two decades," and that wildcat strikes have been increasing.

From a management point of view, this absence of interference in management functions by the "mature" British unions would seem ideal. But each rose has its thorns. While the goal of economic control is not pursued through collective bargaining, it is pursued through political action. British unions are typically closely attached to the Labor Party; they strive for their social objectives through political rather than through economic action. Their concern is not so much with maximum gains for their members; thus, wage claims on all companies are geared to the ability to pay of the firm with average, or even lowest, efficiency. Instead, the unions aim at winning gains for the "working class" as a whole at the expense of the "capitalists."

If British trade unionism is mature, Russian is even more "mature." The civil-service role of union officialdom has reached its ultimate. Shvernik, long-time president of the trade unions, also held for seven years the honorary position of head of the Russian state—a position comparable to that of the Queen of England. Top union officials may be ousted, but this is normally done by others than their members. When the Soviet Union's industrial administration was reorganized from an industry to a regional basis, existing industrial unions were also predictably reshuffled. The unions perform for the state such functions as those of administering parts of the social security program, helping to organize competitions for higher output between shops and plants, and checking on management's enforcement of safety regulations.

A recent proclamation of the Central Committee of the Communist Party has declared that "the central tasks of the trade unions are to mobilize the masses in the struggle for the . . . further strengthening of the economic might and defensive power of the Soviet state . . . for technical progress, for continuous growth in labor productivity. . . ." Only at the tail end of the proclamation was there mention of the goal of "further growth in the standard of living and culture of the workers." There are no antimanagement overtones in this document, or in the many similar ones which have preceded it during the past three decades.

By American standards, this is indeed a strange type of unionism. But for a British unionist, it would not seem quite so strange. For if the proper purpose of a trade union is to promote the interests of the "working class" as a whole, rather than of the union's own members in particular, how can this be done once the "capitalists" are no more? Only by promoting general national interests. It is precisely this that the Russian trade unions do; these "national interests" are defined by the

Communist Party, and the trade unions' task is to help achieve them. Here is a broad, "mature," civil-service concept of trade unions, pursued to its limit.

This is a point important to understand. Soviet communists are not cynical in the role which they give to the trade unions. Grant them their basic propositions that the Soviet Union is a "workers' state" and that the Communist Party is the legitimate prophet of the nation; grant them also the appropriateness of the European socialist trade union tradition of, at least theoretically, pursuing the common interests of all workers and not solely those of the union membership: then Soviet trade unions are the genuine article. Membership control over higher levels of officialdom can scarcely be taken as the *sine qua non* of legitimate unionism; if this were our standard, we might even have to write off some unions this side of the Iron Curtain. Soviet factory managers are quite sincere in testifying to the genuineness of the unions in their plants, although hearty approval of unions by management may sound a bit strange in American ears.

Unfortunately for the Soviet trade unions, it is not clear that their own membership approves of their functions quite as strongly as do the Communist Party and the various management groups. It is quite true that it would be difficult to organize a reliable public opinion poll on the subject. Nevertheless, it is worth pointing out that, back in 1935, Stalin himself indicated that the entire Russian union movement was passing through a serious crisis. The rank-and-file membership was dissatisfied with the unions, he said, and it saw no prospect of change. The average worker was even beginning to wonder, he declared, whether trade unions really have a place in the Soviet Union.

Stalin deplored this weakening of trade union prestige. And well he might. Unions do have their role in the Soviet factory, and at least potentially it is an important one to the Soviet government.

One of their functions is that of political propaganda. Unions are esteemed as "the school for Communism" and as a "transmission belt" between the Party and the workers.

Their second function is administrative. Unions help to settle worker grievances, thus serving as a check on shop and factory management. Union and management representatives meet together on grievances; decisions must be unanimous and based on legislation, the contract and rules of employment, and the existing administrative regulations. The union in fact has a role superior to management, since the plant committee of the union is empowered to make the final decision if there is conflict at the first stage of grievance settlement. The management can appeal to the courts, but only on the grounds that the union's decision conflicts with some particular law.

Here is an area where plant unions may restrict management functions. Grievances run the traditional gamut of dismissals or transfers, payment for overtime and time laid off, claims to bonuses, rates of pay during periods of probation, etc. However, such restrictions on management seem minor indeed measured against the American pattern.

Other administrative functions of unions include supervision of safety standards, checking of wage systems, and examination of dining halls and public housing. In all these cases, the union is used as an inspection body to ensure the execution of official Party policy.

There is also a tradition of union activity in ensuring proper working conditions and social amenities. Details covering these are included in annual contracts drawn up on a plant level between the management and the union local. Emily Clark Brown, an economics professor at Vassar, has analyzed three such contracts in force during 1954 and 1955. In two cases, the clauses seemed to be quite standard, but the contract of the third plant included numerous clauses which bore the earmarks of local negotiation.

The participation of the union in the allocation of funds for improving working conditions and for social amenities seems a useful one, both from the viewpoint of Soviet leaders and of the union members themselves. It would appear that the union local has little influence on the total amounts spent for these purposes, but it can affect their distribution. Here is a means, then, for getting the greatest morale benefits from a given expenditure. Of course, there is the danger of a backfiring of morale due to the fact that plantwide discussion of next year's contract may raise the aspiration level of the workers in the factory. But this is a risk which Soviet leaders seem willing to accept.

The last, and really most important, function of the trade unions is to act in such a way as to enlist the "participation" of the workers in the actual running of the plant. From management's point of view, such "participation" may spell real interference. But the union is not alone in having this function, and clearly the role of the Communist Party is even more important in this regard. Here is a function which deserves separate treatment.

Suggestions and the Boss's Ego

Long before our current crop of human relations experts began pushing the thought, it was obvious that factory workers do have some good notions on how to improve productivity in the shop. It is clear that the man at the bench often gets ideas as to how to turn out a job faster. The innumerable stories of the home-made jig, kept hidden in the worker's locker for use solely at times when he wishes temporarily to speed up production, are testimony enough for this. If only the operator could be persuaded to contribute his ideas to management!

But there is another dimension to the participation puzzle. Motivation is obviously a key element in increasing productivity, and a group given the power to share in decisions seems—by this very fact—to feel more of a stake in the production results. Moral: Give production workers a share in making production decisions, not necessarily because the decisions will be better—they may even be poorer—but because they will be carried out more effectively.

All of this seems straightforward enough. It is true that everyone recognizes that losses of time in conferences and meetings result from such participation, but this extra cost scarcely outweighs the results. The problem is not in these losses. Rather, it lies in the fact that workers are not the only ones who like a bit of authority, and who get a kick out of making decisions.

Take some of the stories Americans bring back of family-owned factories in southern Europe. Here, the boss still sees himself as the feudal *patron;* his shop is an extension of himself; *he* makes the decisions—all of them. Let the worker simply follow instructions; discretion is not part of his job. Naturally, production suffers; quality is uneven; changes are resisted; the worker is "irresponsible." But the shop "belongs" to the boss— it is under his thumb and is a direct projection of his personality—to an extent quite different from that found in any American business. The plant may produce less; but profit is not everything for the employer, any more than wages are everything for the worker.

This picture may seem extreme and quite irrational. But is the American foreman always happy to receive suggestions from his workers, even when these suggestions cause the department to make a better showing? Do the methods engineers always welcome these ideas? When American management accepts schemes such as the Scanlon Plan to give employees a share in the profits and a feeling of ownership, does it always rejoice in the interest of these new "owners" in the sales, pricing, and financial policies of the firm? Are the managers always delighted when their costly boners are pointed out to them?

None of this argument should suggest that management need only accept workers as co-makers of decisions in order to increase productivity. In one experiment in a Norwegian shoe-assembly plant, an academic experimenter persuaded a hostile management to permit several groups of workers to participate in the production decisions needed for a changeover in shoe styles. The workers did in fact take an active and interested part in these decisions, but productivity remained unchanged. The stopper was a plantwide informal agreement among workers as to maximum daily production; ringing in the workers on decisions as to methods and organization of production was not enough to persuade them to change their decision as to output restriction.

The largest-scale American effort to enlist worker participation was during the last war. Under the persuasion of the War Production Board, some five thousand union-management programs were established. Although co-operation in raising productivity was the announced goal, actual co-operation could be better observed in the staging of bond drives and in the collection of blood. It is estimated that not over 10 per cent of the plans made any direct contribution to production. Once the moral pressure of wartime ended, the "co-operation" programs collapsed.

Worker participation in Russia encounters, of course, the same human obstacles met in the United States. But the Russians seem to have been more successful with it than we have.

While worker participation is a difficult thing to measure, the number of suggestions made by workers for improving production methods is one statistical piece of evidence. Here, the Russian figures are quite impressive. During 1956, for example, one or more suggestions were submitted by one and one third million employees—in other words, by five out of every hundred working in industry, construction, and transport—and 1.4 million suggestions were put into practice.

In a Moscow plant, I was shown a booklet of about fifty pages which the management had prepared as a guide to innovators. In it, there was a listing of individual machines used in the plant, defects in each which were causing problems, and results hoped for from suggestions as to how to correct these defects. Clearly, the booklet represented quite an investment of managerial time. The director of the plant told me that rationalization suggestions made during 1957 had yielded economies of production in that year which were 0.6 per cent of the factory's total annual production and 3 per cent of the factory's annual wage and salary bill. Other Russian data suggest that this plant was reasonably typical in its savings from its suggestion system. These figures do not seem so high as to be unbelievable, and yet they indicate quite a fair contribution to efficiency.

Aside from these individual suggestions, the principal form of worker participation is the production meeting. Basically, there are three types of these. One is the meeting of all employees in a given shop or even in an entire factory. A second sort is a meeting of the "active workers": the known innovators and the particularly experienced workers, meeting with the management and engineers to contribute their ideas. The third variety is the Communist Party meeting of a shop or plant; in a factory where 15 to 20 per cent of all employees belong to the Party, a Communist Party meeting cuts a broad swath through the work force.

All of these meetings, and particularly the Communist Party gatherings, must often strike the management officials as peculiarly designed to embarrass them. For nothing is sacred. Finance, procurement, production schedules: everything and everyone is fair game. And woe to those managers who refuse to answer questions on the grounds of "management prerogatives"!

To say that management is always delighted with full participation by the workers in the plant would be somewhat of an overstatement. The officially recognized rarity of general worker meetings, as well as their frequent lack of content, must be partly a result of good management planning. But management is operating under severe ideological and practical handicaps in its efforts to keep down worker criticisms. One factory director interviewed by an American in 1955 implied that production meetings were a real ordeal for him. But at a question as to whether workers dared criticize openly, he said, "Any director who suppressed criticism would be severely punished. He would not only be removed, he would be tried."

Soviet ideology has it that Russia is a "workers' state," and thus that workers have a genuine owners' interest in seeing that things go well in the factory. This being the case, the obvious blocking of such interest—even when the interest is expressed in embarrassing questions and in implications that the manager is a numbskull—can be interpreted as a serious political offense. Such an interpretation would be particularly probable in cases where this interest was expressed at Communist Party meetings—which is precisely the place where it is most likely to appear.

As is usually the case in such matters, more powerful forces than ideology alone are at work in supporting this sort of participation. Soviet leaders antedate our own human relations experts by several decades in their strong belief in participation as a means of improving morale and, thus, productivity. Moreover, they are firm supporters of adopting successful technical and organizational ideas—whether these come from a Russian benchworker or from the capitalist West. Finally, as we have seen in an earlier chapter, they are great believers in establishing a multitude of information channels leading upward. What better channel can there be than a meeting where the man who is actually doing the production job can say his piece?

All this participation, of course, normally stops short of criticism directed at the top levels of national leadership. Within the higher administrative organs, for example, the Communist Party units—made up of janitors and ministers, indiscriminately—are not given the same power of "supervision" over officialdom which is held by similar units at the shop and factory level. Soviet counterparts of our human relations men are careful to try to protect themselves from this nefarious system. But they find it quite appropriate for the lower echelons.

There seems no good way for us to evaluate the success of Soviet efforts in enlisting participation in the factory. Certainly, these efforts run up against major managerial resistance—and, in any society, plant and shop management have means of handling the malcontents. Workers must frequently ask themselves: Why go to a lot of trouble thinking up ideas, only to end with my neck out? If my foreman has it in for me, for example, won't I wind up getting only tough jobs with "tight" piece rates? Soviet leaders have constantly shown themselves disappointed that more worker participation was not forthcoming. This disappointment has been particularly strong with regard to the general meetings for which the trade unions are responsible. Despite the counterpressures, however, there is little doubt that worker participation goes considerably beyond that found in American firms; its official sponsorship alone would assure this.

14. THE CIRCLE OF CONTROL

To paraphrase Clemenceau, "Business is too important to be left to businessmen." This is a basic point upon which both American and Russian society agree.

There was a time when the American public believed that the businessman took all the risks of business, and thus had a right to make all the decisions. Today, he is more often likened to the army colonel who waves his men ahead into battle, saying, "Go ahead! I'll take the responsibility!" There are many doubters of the dictum that "What is good for General Motors is good for the country."

So everyone gets into the act of management. Professional managers, unorganized workers, shareholders, and trade unions: all crowd into the pitcher's box together. The Department of Justice and the Federal Trade Commission each has its own slightly different interpretation of the rules of the management game, and each tries to umpire the decisions. Congressional committees are ready with new interpretations. Even the Internal Revenue Department gets into the umpiring, with decisions as to which expenses are or are not deductible; such decisions, of course, can be a major influence on the future play of the game.

Partly, all this is simply a struggle over the changing ground rules under which managers operate. But when congressional committees investigate specific price increases made by individual companies, more is involved than ground rules. When unions work out detailed agreements for the orderly introduction of automation and retraining of workers, they are soon forced into the business of partaking in day-to-day managerial decisions. When banks make loans to weak companies, they may do more than force an agreement as to financial ratios which must be maintained by the company. They may put a man on the board. Different groups have different interests, and all want to be in on the day-by-day interpretation of the letter and spirit of the rules.

Management is more than a technical procedure of scheduling tasks and balancing alternatives. Some goals are considered more important than others, some intangible costs higher than others, some risks worse than others. All power groups involved want "in" on this weighing of intangibles, and the entire society is involved.

In Russia, Soviet theory goes to the extreme in downgrading industrial management. All management—even the highest level in the Council of Ministers—is seen as the errand boy of the Communist Party, working out the detailed implications of the Party's decisions. There is no question in anyone's mind of "leaving business to businessmen."

As I have argued in Chapter Twelve, however, the lower and middle levels of the Communist Party are only participants in management decisions, not the final arbiters. Heads of factories and economic regions are in a strong position to argue back. At the highest level of the Party, the Praesidium of the Central Committee, decisions can be made which are at least as final as those made by top bodies in other countries. But the Praesidium is best viewed as an arena in which all interested power groups fight matters out and vote them to a decision.

Thus American and Russian industry are alike in that their fortunes are governed by changing combinations of interest groups, all busy sharpening their own axes at the grinding wheel of business policy. But the industries of the two nations are dissimilar with regard to the arena in which decisions are finally ground out. In the United States, decisions are made piecemeal, without the existence of any set, organized procedure for bringing the conflicting groups together. The market place, the picket line, the courtroom, and the conference room: all are arenas in which the groups establish contact, two at a time. No decision is final, for the next interested party is still to be heard from.

In the Soviet Union, there exists the ultimate arena of the Communist Party Praesidium. Here a decision can be made.

Such a decision is as "final" as a policy decision can be in any organization. Namely, time is required before it can be weathered away through administrative interpretation.

In this sense, there is a core of central direction of decision-making within Soviet industry. True, it is a limited core—little more than an irresistible pressure on all power groups to come together at some point, make a decision, and stick to it until their relative strengths shift. But even this is a core which is normally absent in the United States, and which has been temporarily improvised only at moments of crisis such as the last war.

The Praesidium of the Communist Party has various control bodies and devices at its disposal. These have the task of preventing—or at least delaying—the erosion of its decisions.

One means of carrying out the Praesidium's policies is through the power of the Communist Party to transfer its members at will from one job to another. Since the Central Committee of the Party has its own personnel section in charge of appointments of the more important Party figures, the right of transfer can be potent in enforcing central Party decisions.

In actual fact, however, this power seems to have been used somewhat less than we might expect. Prewar data from secret Party files, captured during the war by the Germans and then in turn by us, indicate that regional Party bodies have normally given their routine approval to transfers in business posts—rather than themselves initiating these transfers. Published Soviet data show that the Central Committee has usually not played an active role in choosing Party officials to function in individual factories, even when these officials were formally responsible to the Central Committee itself. Instead, it has depended upon regional Party committees to make the choices in everything but name.

Thus the right of Party transfer of members—while doubtless occasionally important—appears to be utilized as a regular control device to a much lesser extent than one might have thought.

The State Bank is an organ which has been depended upon for policing industry. Since it is in charge of the sinews of economic policy—money—it has been chosen as a watchdog of national policy. All monetary transactions must go through its hands. Unfortunately for its control functions, it has often shown itself to be well indoctrinated with the tenets of international sound-banking policy. It has frequently shown more concern for the safety of its own cash and loan position than for anything else. In justification, it should be said that at times when it has tried to exercise control, it has often found the Party unwilling to back it. Thus the Bank has seldom been particularly successful in enforcing the official policy that wages should grow less rapidly than labor productivity.

A final organ of enforcement which we might mention is the Secret Police. This detective agency seems to have lost much of its power in the post-Stalin days. Earlier, however, it was a control body of no mean dimensions. In the mid-1930's, for example, it took its job so seriously as to make short work of much of Russian top industrial management, military leadership, and even of the Communist Party hierarchy.

By and large, however, while the Secret Police has sometimes seemed on the verge of running away with the ball of power, the Party hierarchy has always succeeded in reasserting its own authority. In fact, the Party has been so successful in this that, with hindsight, we may regard a man's appointment as Minister of the Secret Police as having been virtually a delayed death sentence.

In brief, the control bodies at the beck and call of the Praesidium have not been as reliable as was doubtless hoped. Each developed its own special interests; each either followed the example of the State Bank and looked for easy ways to carry out its job, thus restricting its functions, or it tended toward the opposite extreme of empire building. The problem of policing the policemen had been perennial.

Thus we are brought back to the limitations of the Soviet Party Praesidium as the core of central power. Not only is the Praesidium limited to the function of an arena of decision-making, but it is also constantly faced with the need for checking on those bodies which it has chosen to supervise the execution of decisions. In this form, the original decisions inevitably come up for review again and again. The reviewing body is that same old mixture of power groups which was earlier faced with the need for making the original decisions.

part six

INSIDE THE FACTORY

15. FACTORIES EAST AND WEST

Picture yourself in Kharkov. You came to town on the midnight plane, and stopped at the Intourist office first thing in the morning. The pleasant, middle-aged lady in charge asks what you want to see, and without too much hope you suggest a factory. Any preferences? she inquires, and you throw forth the name of a factory you have read about. Then you go off with your guide to see the sights of the town.

Two hours later you are back at Intourist. Kharkov is full of factories and universities—but not much else. The grand tour of the city does not take long. Now that you have returned, you are amazed to learn that you're dated up for the afternoon to visit the factory of your choice. You express combined thanks and surprise, since in most Russian towns Intourist is not very good at making such arrangements. Your hostess answers that, in Kharkov, Intourist must be prepared to display factories and collective farms; what else is there for the foreign visitor to see?

Now, if you are serious about the factory visit, you are faced with a puzzle. This plant you are about to see will have to represent Russian industry to you. How can you decide whether it is doing a good job or a bad one? What standard of comparison should you use? Presumably, your standard will be American industry. But what in the world does a *typical* American factory look like?

Is a typical American plant one so highly automated as to make you doubt that the automation will ever pay for itself; a plant whose production line is a Roman holiday for the design engineers and a nightmare for the company treasurer? Or is it the plant compressed into tight quarters, and with such narrow aisles that hand trucks comprise the ultimate of mechanized materials handling?

Is it the factory laid out on a production basis, with materials flowing neatly in one door and finished products flowing out the other? Or is it the "tote box" plant, where work moves from top floor to the bottom and up again in a Chinese maze?

Is it a factory which weeds out equipment as soon as the machinery begins to lose its competitive edge? Or is it the plant which still has its equipment left over from the 1920's, and which uses belts and pulleys to run all the machines in a shop off a single giant motor?

Within the same American shop, one can find a packaging line virtually untouched by human hands side by side with another, handling the identical job, where all operations are performed manually. Which is typical?

In short, American industry is so variegated that the word "typical" has almost no meaning. Virtually any plant, seen anywhere outside of Asia, perhaps, has its counterpart somewhere in the United States.

This being the case, what will you be able to learn about *Russian* industry simply by going through a single Russian plant? You may learn a good deal about this one specific factory, but that is hardly what you want. How can you use this visit to help you compare a Russian plant with an American one? When you think about it in this fashion, you are likely to throw up your hands and wonder why in the world you should want to see the factory at all.

I had to face precisely this problem. It was easy enough—in Kharkov—to duck the question and to go ahead with the visit. But now, faced by a demanding typewriter, the question is plaguey indeed. The harsh answer seems to be that one can learn rather little about Russian industry just by walking through one factory or even through a handful of them. Fortunately, however, there is other information against which I could check my impressions.

For the fact is that Russian factories are different from American ones. Each individual plant may have its American counterpart, but in the mass they are of a different breed. How do we know this? From the Russian statistics and from their accounts of average performance.

Size

To begin with, let us take the question of size. Russian factories are of all dimensions, but mostly they run big. In Moscow, for instance, clothing plants run three hundred to three thousand employees apiece. Considering the nature of this industry, and the fact that such plants are often hole-in-the-wall in the United States, these are large-scale factories.

For industry as a whole, the data is even more striking. The following chart shows the proportion of workers found today in different-size factories in Russia and the United States. Although there are only about six hundred and fifty giant Russian factories with more than four thousand employees apiece, 38 per cent of all Russian workers are employed in them. In contrast, barely 20 per cent of American industrial workers are employed in plants with over twenty-five hundred employees. However, if we were to think of American companies rather than factories, close to half of all workers are in companies of over five thousand employees.

How can we explain the fact that Russian factories seem, on the average, to be so much larger than our own? A big part of the answer lies in the way we measure size: by number of employees. Soviet industry still requires two or more workers to do the job of one American worker, and thus the Soviet plant, in general, produces no more than the smaller American factory. Nevertheless, employment in a factory is the most important single measure of the burden and responsibility borne by the factory's management.

A striking feature of the typical Soviet plant is the large number of workers who are busy doing some manual job other than directly working on the product. In Soviet manufacturing as a whole, perhaps half the manual labor force is made up of these "auxiliary workers." In the iron and steel industry in 1954, these auxiliary workers outnumbered direct production workers almost one and one half to one. The same thing was true during 1953 in the mass-production industries of automobiles, tractors, and agricultural equipment. Auxiliary work-

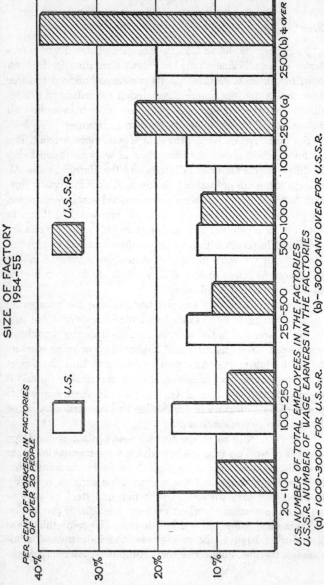

SIZE OF FACTORY
1954-55

PER CENT OF WORKERS IN FACTORIES
OF OVER 20 PEOPLE

40%

30%

20%

10%

20-100   100-250   250-500   500-1000   1000-2500(a)   2500(b) & over

U.S.
U.S.S.R.

U.S. NUMBER OF TOTAL EMPLOYEES IN THE FACTORIES
U.S.S.R. NUMBER OF WAGE EARNERS IN THE FACTORIES

(a)- 1000-3000 FOR U.S.S.R.   (b)- 3000 AND OVER FOR U.S.S.R.

ers are principally involved in transport within the factory, in inspection operations, and in maintenance.

Materials Handling

In the Russian iron and steel industry, 20 per cent of all workers are involved full time in transporting inside the works the necessary materials, fuel, and the product itself. This is as large a group as the sum total of all those employed at the blast furnaces and the open-hearth furnaces taken together. Or choose another example. Within the giant machinery industries, which hire almost one third of all Soviet workers, the proportion of transport workers to all employees is something like double the American figure.

The most important reason for the high proportion of materials-handling workers in Russian industry is that the international revolutionary wave in this technology has still not reached the Soviet Union. The 1920's and 1930's saw an American revolution which eliminated most hand trucking and manual handling. The great mass of unskilled labor which had previously been absorbed in these operations was now forced out. The gasoline and electric fork trucks, and the skids on which items are loaded so as to save handling, have been the symbols of this revolution. In the 1940's and 1950's, the revolution crossed the Atlantic and began to transform British industry. But it will be the 1960's, and conceivably even the 1970's, before Russia is similarly affected.

In the Soviet Union, an industry producing small materials-handling equipment simply does not exist. Powered fork trucks are conspicuous by their absence. In the Kharkov plant I visited, the management had skillfully equipped a machining line with small electric and pneumatic hoists with which to move the parts being worked upon. But in order to install the pneumatic hoists, the plant first had to produce them itself. They were virtually unobtainable on the market.

There is also a second reason for the large numbers of Soviet workers engaged in materials handling. Not only is this process relatively unmechanized, as explained above, but, in addition, there is tremendous pressure for materials-handling operations to be completed rapidly in order to avoid the need for storing large inventories of materials between processes, and at the same time not to hold up these production processes.

The American steel delegation which surveyed the Russian steel industry during the summer of 1958 remarked on this pressure. They pointed out that twice the number of cranes were available in one of the Magnitogorsk open-hearth shops as would be found in a similar American shop. The Russian objective was to assure that there would be no possible delays, and thus that maximum steel production could be achieved.

The same emphasis on speed can be observed in the loading and unloading of freight cars at factory railroad sidings. All plants are obligated to clear freight cars off their sidings as rapidly as possible and to get them back onto the main railroad lines. In this way, the number of freight cars needed in the Soviet Union is drastically reduced; but a price is paid in the form of stand-by crews of freight handlers.

The economic forces at work are fairly simple. Labor is relatively plentiful in the Soviet Union compared to the United States. Russia is still a country which can afford to use women with brooms to keep the streets spotless. But machinery and gadgets are expensive. Freight cars are expensive. New investment is still concentrated upon increasing production, and not on saving labor. It is still cheaper to use seven men with hand trucks instead of one man with a power truck. When this situation changes, as it long ago changed in the United States and has recently changed in England, we may be confident that fork trucks will find their way into Russian plants. Until that time, the Russian leaders are sufficiently good businessmen to keep their wild-eyed engineers under wraps.

Quality Control

The same principle applies in quality control. Any modern industrial system must be concerned with the quality of its product, and the Russians care as much about this problem as does anyone else. However, just as in the case of materials handling, they prefer to do the job with cheap hand tools instead of using expensive control apparatus. The result of this, of course, is that a large part of the Russian labor force is engaged in checking on quality. In 1955, according to Soviet authors, 20 per cent of all the employees in the vast machinery industries were engaged solely in inspection; one million people had inspectors' jobs in these industries alone.

Inspection work, however, has its own special problems rather different from those of materials handling. Whether you decide to move goods by power truck or on your back, the same task can be accomplished. But this is not true when it comes to controlling quality.

One early postwar Soviet study worth reporting was an investigation into the accuracy of measurement in an instrument plant which the Russian author of the study seemed to feel was typical of the industry. The engineer writing the article had re-examined items which plant inspectors using the types of gauges most common in Soviet inspection practice had passed as "unconditionally satisfactory." The engineer found that, of those items accepted as being of high quality, between 15 and 61 per cent—depending upon the particular type of item—in fact violated the plant's quality standards.

In the same plant, three highly experienced inspectors were chosen to conduct an experiment. All three, using the factory's normal inspection devices, examined the same instrument parts. In 7 to 23 per cent of the cases—the exact percentage differing with the part being examined—they disagreed among themselves on whether to pass the work as acceptable.

In view of these results, it should be no surprise to learn that, in 1951, 11 per cent of the nation's production of agricultural equipment, after having been passed by plant inspectors, was rejected by the purchasing agents of the Ministry of Agriculture. This high rejection rate occurred despite the ministry's urgent desire to get the equipment out to the farms in time for the season's work.

There is no question but that Soviet industry has recognized the quality problems inherent in the use of simple inspection devices, and that it has begun shifting over to more automatic and sensitive equipment. In some plants which have been visited by American engineers, the Russians have moved as far in this direction as we have. It seems reasonably safe to hazard the guess that their military industry, for example, is well equipped with the latest quality-control devices.

Two serious problems, however, confront Soviet managers in their efforts to modernize inspection equipment. The first of these is simply time; the process of revolutionizing a major area of factory work such as inspection is bound to require many years. This is the case not only because of the pressures of inertia, the need for redesigning production processes to mesh with new inspection procedures and quality standards, and the requirement of retraining labor. In addition, quality-control departments must first win large investment allocations for inspection equipment from their competitors, who are voracious and powerful traditional recipients of investment funds. Inspection can hardly expect to win overnight its rightful place as a functional area in which to sink major sums of money.

The second problem confronting inspection is the peculiar structural organization of Soviet industry. As we saw in Chapter Ten, Soviet factories have grown up in the tradition of self-sufficiency. Not only do plants produce much of the special machinery and tooling which they themselves require, but as late as 1957 they produced half of their own needs for *standard* tooling, nuts and bolts, and electrodes. When a plant is compelled to produce its own tooling, then the purchase and maintenance of specialized inspection apparatus for such tooling becomes enormously—perhaps prohibitively—expensive. This Soviet organizational structure of factory self-sufficiency has stubbornly resisted change for thirty years, and both it and the problems which arise from it are unlikely now to disappear rapidly.

Maintenance

The third large group of auxiliary workers in Soviet factories are those engaged in maintenance and overhaul. A reliable Soviet author writes that during 1955, in the main branches of industry, between 15 and 25 per cent of factory workers were engaged in maintenance. In contrast, a 1958 authoritative American source book, the *Production Handbook,* quotes a comparable figure of 2 per cent as the proportion of manufacturing personnel engaged in maintenance in four presumably typical American fabricworking plants, and 5 per cent in twenty-seven metalworking plants.

In three Soviet plants whose managements gave me figures during 1958, the proportion of maintenance workers was only 8 to 9 per cent of the factory labor force, compared to the 15 to 25 per cent figures quoted for all Russian industry. But even these lower proportions were double the American figures cited above, and they were more than double the percentage of maintenance employees working in three American machine-tool plants which I myself visited.

Soviet maintenance workers are so numerous partly for organizational reasons. It is normally not feasible for a Russian plant to send out its equipment to be repaired even when it is in need of a major overhaul. No organizations are available to do this kind of work. Thus, every plant has its own repair shop. Even worse from a works manager's viewpoint, it is often impossible to purchase parts required for equipment repair, and the plant is faced with the necessity of producing in its own repair shop many of the items needed.

In contrast, the plant superintendent of one American company told me that he dislikes getting involved in any major repair on the equipment in his plant. Although his is a machine-tool factory, and therefore peculiarly capable of repairing the machine tools it uses, this superintendent feels that the cheapest policy is to call in a representative of the original equipment manufacturer for any significant repair. As a result, he keeps only a skeleton maintenance crew.

Clearly, this factory's maintenance policy is not followed by all American manufacturers. But, at a minimum, all would buy the parts they need rather than follow the Russian make-it-yourself practice. The Soviet manager has no option as to his maintenance policy.

The second reason for the large number of Russian maintenance workers is the pressure on the Soviet manager to keep his equipment in operation as long as possible. It is not easy for the manager to get new machinery to replace old; demands on production from new factories, being equipped for the first time, are too great. Thus, we can read in the Soviet magazines of equipment being overhauled when it is clear in advance that it would be cheaper to throw the old machine away and buy a new one. The manager, however, although he cannot get permission to buy another machine, does have the manpower available to overhaul his present equipment; he acts accordingly.

An impressive example of this pressure to keep machinery in operation is the operating life of automobiles which is expected by the authorities. One driver of a medium-sized Intourist car told me that his car was expected to go 300,000 miles before being scrapped. True, this driving was to be exclusively on city streets, and Russian cars probably follow the West European tradition of being built for longer wear than are American cars. Nevertheless, one can imagine the maintenance required in order to achieve this mileage. When I was a passenger in this car, it had already clocked 95,000 miles and still provided quite a comfortable ride.

The Product and Plant Changeovers

Russian factory operations are strongly influenced by the traditionally casual approach of Soviet industry to the consumer. We have seen earlier in this chapter what happens to the typical factory in its role as the consumer of products from other industries, and how it has been forced onto a thirty-year do-it-yourself jag. But when the factory management turns to work on its own final product, it reaps all the advantages of the consumer-be-damned attitude. The Soviet manager is still in the enviable position of old Henry Ford during the period when he could get away with his famous 1909 slogan: "Any customer can have a car painted any color that he wants—so long as it is black."

Thus the Russian factory, in general, produces a fairly standard item. Whether turning out dresses or lathes, it need not pay much attention to the customer's desire for variety and special features. The Gorky automobile plant, for example, started production of the "Victory" car in 1945. This model was not replaced until 1957, when the "Volga" began to come off its assembly line. One change of model every twelve years places no great strain on the ingenuity of the production department. This way of doing business would be an American production engineer's fondest dream—and a marketing man's nightmare.

By and large, the Soviet production manager faces a different sort of problem than does the American. He will have longer production runs of the same item, and will have a more limited range of products about which to worry. The product designers will not constantly be coming in with wonderful "minor" design changes which just happen to end up doubling production costs, and so the production manager will not be locked in continuous battle with these designers. The production manager knows what his shipments should be next month and the month after, and he need not speculate as to whether the sales manager's forecasts really make any sense. The consumer may be as fickle as he wishes in his tastes, but it will not matter much so long as there is still a seller's market in Russian industry.

Free of these problems, the Russian manager can concentrate on two other types of production issues. One of these is the question of how to wrestle with scarcity of necessary materials, since supply is always uncertain. The manager must be a master of the art of substituting on short notice one material for another, one shape or thickness for another. This is no task for the novice.

The second type of production issue is more orthodox, but has perhaps greater importance in Russian than in American conditions. This task is that of designing both better methods and new equipment for producing an old product. An American company will generally be better advised to put its brains into designing product improvements instead of more efficient production processes. The American firm forges ahead by developing new products; the Russian plant managers win bonuses and medals through upping production and cutting costs on a standard product.

This picture of Russian factories and of the task of their managements is a highly generalized one. There are, of course, many Soviet plants which face quite different problems.

Leningrad, a great pre-Revolutionary industrial center and

the most western-spirited of Russian cities, is noted for its experimental factories geared to working out the production "bugs" in new products. Once a product gets thoroughly "shaken down," it is transferred to some other plant in another city where it can be put into mass production. Presumably, Leningrad industry is given this breaking-in role for the Soviet industrial complex because of its traditional advantages of high-grade management and labor force, as well as of closeness to first-rate research institutes. Leningrad's strengths are much like those of southern New England.

A somewhat more typical Soviet operation is that of the "Hammer and Sickle" factory in Kharkov. An account of its production history and change of products over half a century should be informative.

The "Hammer and Sickle" plant dates from the nineteenth century. Before the Revolution, it was one of Russia's largest producers of agricultural equipment. At the end of the 1920's, still one of the two big plants of the industry, it converted from horse-drawn equipment to heavier, tractor-powered threshing machines. By 1932, it was supplying the entire needs of the Soviet Union for these machines.

Until 1938, the plant continued in this field. Then, with the gradual conversion of the Soviet machinery industries to military output, the factory was shifted to the production of motorcycles. Threshing-machine production was gradually removed to other plants, and by 1941 at the latest, the "Hammer and Sickle" plant produced nothing but motorcycles.

With the outbreak of war, the plant's equipment was dismantled and evacuated east. The two plant engineers with whom I talked in 1958, both of whom had been working in the factory during 1941, insisted—under my questioning—that only obsolete machinery had been abandoned to the Germans. After 1943, when Kharkov was retaken by the Red Army, most technical personnel and many of the evacuated workers of the plant were returned to Kharkov. The equipment, however, was left in the east and new machinery was provided.

Virtually all of the buildings of the plant had to be built anew, for the Germans had done a thorough job of demolition. On a tour of the factory, I pointed to one ramshackle structure and asked if this also was a postwar creation. No, I was told, the Germans had left that standing. My engineer-guide facetiously expressed the wish that the Germans had been more thorough with regard to destroying that particular building.

When the plant was rebuilt, it was returned to its earlier production of tractor-powered threshing machines. In 1949, it produced fifteen thousand of these machines.

In 1950, however, the plant was given a new production program. It was converted exclusively to the production of gasoline motors for combines. This conversion, I was told, was connected with a decision to change the type of metal from which these motors were to be made. The Kharkov plant personnel, apparently, were considered more capable of solving the related production problems than were the personnel in the plants where these motors had previously been produced. At least, this is the story told by my Kharkov engineer-guide. I did not have an opportunity to query his counterparts in the other factories.

These internal-combustion motors were produced from 1950 through early 1958. In March 1958, the plant's product was changed to diesel motors also intended for combines. This product-change was announced simultaneously with a decision virtually to abandon the production in the Soviet Union of the older-model gasoline engine. The factory began actually to prepare for conversion at the end of 1957, having been forewarned of the product-change.

In the summer of 1958, when I visited the plant, it was still in the process of conversion. The new final-assembly lines for the diesel motor were scheduled to be set up within about one month. In the meantime, work was proceeding by using a temporary line which was soon to be torn down. This same process of production on a makeshift basis, while installing permanent equipment and lines, was going on all over the plant. In this year of conversion, production was expected to reach one quarter of the capacity output planned for 1960.

This mass-production factory is a heavy user of special-purpose machinery. As such, the conversion of product necessitated a substantial re-equipment of the plant. Six hundred and eighty tools were being purchased or produced by the plant itself during 1958—four times the number added in the more normal year of 1957. Yet with all the destruction, rebuilding and conversions of the "Hammer and Sickle" factory, it is interesting to note that its labor force in 1958, virtually unchanged by this latest reconversion, was within 5 per cent of the figure it had reached in 1929.

Shift Work

Both the United States and the Soviet Union seem to share the characteristic of widespread use of a second shift. In the years 1951–56, for example, U.S. government studies of the percentage of manufacturing workers engaged in a second, third, or fourth shift showed a range running from 12 per cent in New York City to 32 per cent in Detroit. In the Soviet Union, some 40 per cent of all manufacturing workers, as an estimate on my part from a variety of data, seem to be on one or another of these multiple shifts.

Other countries have also tried to use their plants and equipment for more than one shift. The British government, for example, has for some time exhorted industry to adopt shift operation. Clearly, considerable savings of investment are possible when a plant is worked for sixteen hours a day instead of eight. Yet in Britain in 1954, shift work within any given industry was still less than one third as common as it was in the United States. The big problem in Britain seems to have been the dislike of workers for an evening shift, and the unwillingness of employers to experiment with it during a period when their workers had a multitude of opportunities for jobs in other plants.

A natural question to ask, at least in periods when industry works two shifts and is still expanding new capacity, is why American and Russian managements do not generally adopt a three-shift program. Three shifts were common in the United States during the last war; in the early 1930's and during the war, the Russians also pushed hard for this type of work schedule. Since the war, however, round-the-clock work has been rare in both countries, except in industries such as steel and chemicals where the technology requires it.

In speaking about this to American and Russian management people, I received a miscellaneous group of reasons which sounded much the same in both countries. Difficulties of management and control, difficulties of foremanship, maintenance problems, lowered productivity in the third shift, desire for excess capacity in order to meet demand (by saving the possibility of a third shift for emergencies): all these reasons were given. Maintenance was particularly emphasized in the Soviet Union as a problem encountered in three-shift operations, since repair of a piece of equipment is more likely to be a lengthy procedure there than in the United States. This longer repair-time requirement is due to the greater need in Russia to fix broken or worn-out parts, instead of simply substituting a new part purchased from the factory which originally produced the machine. In the United States, the reasons given to me did not lay stress on maintenance considerations so much as upon the desirability of having equipment reserves to meet expansions in the market.

In both countries, however, the main stumbling block seems to be the same one met in Britain: the employees don't like to work at night. American and Russian workers seem more willing than Englishmen to accept evening work, but apparently they are equally adamant with regard to the graveyard shift. Except in unusual cases and in emergencies, this worker unwillingness seems decisive as an obstacle. In this matter, the Russian worker seems quite capable of swinging his weight.

Women

Women comprise 45 per cent of total Soviet industrial employment. In no sense are they concentrated in offices or in special industries such as textiles. Rather, women are seen everywhere in Soviet factories, even on the floors of iron foundries.

In discussing with Russian managements the question of "women's work," one can meet executives who state their policy as being that of giving women only physically-light tasks. One delicate assembly operation which I observed had a 100 per cent female staff. This feminine monopoly, I was told, was due to the fact that women are more skillful than men in rapid manual manipulation of small objects; the same reason is given in American plants for using women on similar assembly tasks. By and large, however, a policy of keeping women off heavy jobs is unlikely to be carried out in Russia until the never-never era of Communism, with its two free mink coats per customer. At present, the construction job of hod carrier seems—at least to my casual observation—to be treated as a purely feminine job, in the same fashion as is the assembly of watches.

The reasons for the omnipresence of women in all types of work are not far to seek. There is not only the East European tradition of peasant women doing heavy field labor; not only the Soviet drive for sex equality, matched by provisions for the care of young children; but, most important of all, there is the tremendous shortage of males resulting from the war losses. With a population badly out of balance in the age group thirty-five years old and up, Soviet women must perforce do much of the hard physical labor of industry.

However, although there is not much sex-specialization by broad occupational category, there does tend to be such specialization with regard to fields of higher education. At the end of 1956, women comprised three quarters of all Soviet doctors, and two thirds of those Soviet teachers who had college degrees. On the other hand, only 28 per cent of the country's engineers were women. This specialization of the sex doubtless accounts for the fact that women seem to be relatively rare among factory managements.

The percentage of women who are well educated is striking. Although at the end of 1956, women made up only 45 per cent of the total labor force, they comprised 53 per cent of all those with higher education; as to those with specialized secondary education, 66 per cent were women. In the economy as a whole, men tend to be proportionately less educated than women; but among those working in industry, men are far in the lead.

The Worker Goes to School

Russian managers are great believers in education, far more even than are American managers. One important consideration in the promotion of a Russian factory worker is his willingness to engage in formal study related to his work. While an American skilled worker or foreman has generally picked up his know-how on the job, the Russian has often gone to a special technical high school.

In a Moscow plant I visited, 28 per cent of the labor force were attending night school. Five per cent were still getting a general education and were registered in courses pitched at all levels from fourth grade through high school. Another 5 per cent were registered in courses at one of the city's many technical colleges. But the vast bulk—18 per cent—were attending technical high schools. These were the future toolmakers, setup men, and foremen of the plant.

It would seem reasonable to assume that the morale of a factory gains from having this large proportion of people who combine work and training. Perhaps this combination is partly responsible for the success of the Russian plant's suggestion system. On the other hand, one could well imagine morale problems occurring later if there are no openings for advancement of these workers once they complete their technical training. This is a danger which would be most likely to face a static economic system, but even in rapidly growing Soviet industry it might well be an embarrassment for individual plants. When I raised this problem with one factory director, he agreed that his workers might later be forced to move on to other plants if they wished to find jobs in keeping with their new training.

Research, Development, and Design

Research, as anyone who has engaged in or managed it knows, is a most disorderly process. The fruitful idea peeks out of the unexpected context. The payoff from any single research project is unpredictable.

This unpredictability, of course, diminishes as the character of the research becomes more practical and less basic. But even out-and-out applied industrial research is difficult to fit into a mold. Doubtless there are, for example, research departments which are busts so far as turning out commercially significant results, but which are invaluable to their firms in keeping the managements *au courant* with research done elsewhere. Someone has to read the technical literature and translate it into terms meaningful to general management, production, and sales; this translation process may spell the difference between expansion and decay of the firm. A company with such a research department may be well advised to keep up its "research" even though the product—judged as research alone— is markedly substandard.

Maintaining an applied research unit within the confines of a plant has marked disadvantages. This is particularly true if the plant is not located in a great metropolis, for it is difficult to lure first-rate researchers out to the sticks. When the stimulation of like minds is absent, motivation and creativity may suffer. The tremendous advantage to the researcher of talking things over with the "guy down the hall," possible in a university or research institute, is lost. In the case of Soviet industry, all the problems of industrial recruitment are magnified by the fact that researchers are paid just as well in an academic setting as in industry—and often better. Industry in Russia must compete for engineers and scientists without one of the prime drawing cards which it possesses in the United States.

Aside from recruitment and creativity problems, the maintaining of research within the plant is likely to create administrative problems, especially for a conservative management. This is true in either Russia or America. Research types of personalities are difficult to integrate into a factory organization. They tend to take unkindly to punching a time clock, and even to the more subtle manifestations of a routinized workshop operation.

Nevertheless, the rejection of factory research and the concentration of applied research within special institutes is far from a perfect solution. Close contact between the research department and other divisions of the firm is bound to be severed, and the catalytic effect of the researcher's presence is lost. In addition, applied research which is out of touch with production and marketing functions may be quite wasteful. This is true not so much because the research is inapplicable, although doubtless this is a real danger, but because the bread-and-butter departments of the firm build up sales-resistance to the research process and results. Once they are personally out of contact with the research men, they inevitably tend to look upon their proposals as coming from outsiders rather than from members of the management team. Since selling the idea of research is a key function of the research department, it makes as little sense to put obstacles in the way of this department's selling effort as it would to block off the salesmen of the company's product.

Soviet industry has no tidy solution to this problem. Fundamental research, whether basic or applied, tends to be concentrated within the research institute-graduate school combination which has proliferated over the Soviet scientific *corpus*. But how about design of machinery, improvement of production processes, development of new metallurgical or chemical properties?

This type of work may be done anywhere. It may be included by the Soviet government as a portion of the planned program of some research institute. It may be done in the labs of a single factory, or of a group of factories, by factory-employed personnel. A plant may take up the problem as its own and yet, not having the necessary personnel or facilities, contract out the job on a cost-plus basis to an established research institute. Alternatively, the factory may hire individual consultants, themselves part of a university or research institute, to tackle the problem. Most likely of all, some combination of these procedures will be used.

In short, this type of narrow, applied research is handled in the Soviet Union rather similarly to the way it is tackled in the United States. Perhaps the Soviet research institutes are drawn upon a bit more than are American universities, commercial research outfits, and government laboratories. But the distinction is purely a matter of degree.

The real difference between the Soviet industrial research effort and our own is that the American is product-oriented, while the Soviet is far more concerned with improving the processes of production. But this is a matter of ends—not of research means.

Curiously enough, however, Soviet and American industry are much further apart in the way that they organize traditional industrial functions than in the manner in which they handle their respective research efforts. Now that we have treated the basic structure of the Soviet factory and of its product, we are ready to turn to the differences between the Soviet and American factory with regard to how fundamental activities are organized.

16. RUNNING THE FACTORY

Shop Management

When thinking of problems of shop management, I often recall a visit to an American machinery company which had reorganized its production operations several years earlier. The company had changed its organizational structure so that some single production department would do most or all of the machining work on any given part, rather than each department specializing in a particular class of machining operations. As a result, work no longer had to be shifted from department to department for successive operations. A good deal of planning had gone into making possible this reorganization, movement of equipment had been necessary, and retraining of foremen in the variety of different machining processes was required.

The plant executives with whom I spoke were very proud of their new system. But when we got down to analyzing what had been accomplished in the reorganization, it turned out that the really important change was in the time required between the placing of an order with the firm and the shipment of the order out of the plant. Production was greatly speeded up simply because of a halving of the waiting time needed between machining operations on each part. Before the production reorganization, when machining operations were performed in different departments and under different foremen, the factory scheduling office computed the total time needed for a given order as actual work-time plus three days between each operation. Under the new system, where the same foreman was in charge of most of the work performed on a given item, this waiting time between processes had been cut from three to one and a half days.

This plant has ever since symbolized to me the importance of management structure in affecting production organization. By placing responsibility for a given item largely on one foreman, instead of continuing an organization system which required co-ordination among different foremen, there was perhaps a one-third reduction in the total time needed to get out the work.

If we look at Soviet industry, we find quite a different management setup within the plant than is typical in American firms. It would be surprising indeed if this difference did not have implications for Soviet production.

Back in 1934, a Soviet administrator wrote a newspaper article describing his reaction after visiting some thirty American machine-tool factories. He appeared particularly struck by the difference between Soviet and American plants in the relationship existing between shop management and the central factory-management bureaus. He was amazed at the degree of centralization of the management function in all of the American plants he had seen. He was surprised that office and bookkeeping work should be centralized for the plant as a whole; that each shop should receive its blueprints and dispatching schedules from the main office; and that even the technological flow of work should be determined centrally rather than separately in each shop. All this was quite different from Soviet procedure, where management was far more decentralized to the shop level.

This article, written in 1934, could be republished today. Even at the end of 1956, more than half of all the administrative and technical staff of plants in the machinery and textile industries worked within the shops, which are subdivisions of the factory; only a minority were engaged in central bureaus of the factories. As a result, the typical Russian plant is to a considerable extent composed of a group of semi-autonomous shops, over which the plant management has only a rather loose control.

To some extent, the semi-autonomous nature of Russian shops arises from the fact that many of them are quite large. In 1956, a Soviet author made a study of the number of workers in shops of representative plants. In the electrical industry, 75 per cent of the shops had over fifty workers apiece. In heavy machinebuilding, 43 per cent of the shops had over one hundred workers apiece.

Primarily, however, the shops' autonomy would appear to be due to the desire of Soviet managers to simplify their problems of control. Although Soviet administrators have complicated their lives by building large factories and combining all the industry of the nation into a single administrative system, they have tried to ease the resulting situation by decentralizing much responsibility to the shop level. This decentralizing effort has been a continuing one; even during the postwar period, the number of technicians and administrators in the shops seems to have grown much more rapidly than has the number within the plant bureaus. In many firms, a shop superintendent will have not only foremen as his subordinates, but he will also surround himself with his own shop-planning and dispatching bureau, his own shop bureau for determining the technical processes by which to perform the given jobs, his own bookkeeper, his own time-study and wage bureau, and even his own procurement sector.

Budgeting and Production Targets

Given such autonomy of the shop, a serious problem arises in trying to assure identity of interest between the administrations of the shop and the plant. This issue has been tackled in the Soviet Union by placing the individual shop—just like the entire factory—on a budget. It is hoped that being on a budget will cause the shop superintendent to show concern for all aspects of his shop's work. The system of departmental budgets in the United States, of course, has a quite similar function.

This system of budgeting, although it has had its ups and downs in the Soviet Union, its expansions and contractions of scope, by and large goes rather further in Soviet factories than it does within American plants. This fact is not particularly surprising, in view of the greater independence of the shop in the Soviet Union than in the United States. If the entire Soviet factory is to keep money costs from mounting beyond receipts, and if it is to live within its allocation of materials and its programmed budget of labor force, then the individual shops which comprise the plant must do likewise.

The difficulty in using the budget system for the Soviet shop, however, is precisely the same difficulty which exists in the case of the factory. Although the shop superintendent is *told* to keep his eye fixed sternly on his budget, he and his shop are *judged* primarily on the basis of their output. This conflict between fiction and fact is well exemplified by recent complaints concerning bonus systems now in force for shop-management personnel.

Soviet economists have argued that it is grossly unfair and, worse, harmful to the economy, to give bonuses to managements solely in accord with whether production is above that planned. It is true that Soviet managements must meet planned targets for costs, labor productivity, etc., if their output bonuses are to be received in full; but, by and large, there are no added bonuses for doing better than planned in regard to the cost factors. The shop superintendent who just meets his output target, but produces sharply below planned cost, will get far less of a bonus than will the superintendent who succeeds in beating his production goal at the expense of barely hitting his cost target.

The result of this premium and judgment system is that each shop management is primarily concerned with its own production plan for the month, quarter, and year. Close scheduling ties with other shops, improvement of work in one shop so as to make the job of the next shop easier: these are the sorts of considerations which fall to one side. In a sense, each factory is composed of many distinct little factories under the same roof.

Storming

Production-scheduling is a favorite subject for self-castigation in Russian industrial management circles. Scheduling of materials into the factory, of the work through the various shops, and of the finished product out onto the railroad freight cars is notoriously poor. As a result, Soviet industry is highly subject to a practice which the Russians fittingly call "storming."

"Storming" is the practice of gearing the factory's work to its production plan in a remarkably shortsighted fashion. The basic time unit of the production plan is the month. At the beginning of the month, work moves slowly. The deadline is far off; shortfalls in production can be made up later. If precisely the right materials are not in stock, work can still be postponed until they arrive. But as the month moves along, things begin to pick up. Efforts are speeded; substitute materials are used; work truly gets under way. At the end of the month, all is in a flurry. Management bonuses are hanging on the month's production; management heads may roll if the target is not met. Regular production-scheduling gives way under the need to "push through" those items which will build up the month's production total. The regular weekly holiday for the factory may be switched from a Sunday near the end of the month to a weekday in the beginning of the next period. "Storming" is under way.

The production target is met; the fortress of the production plan has been successfully stormed. Now the new month begins. But production slackens off as workers recover from their efforts. The disrupted production schedules must be reorganized. A recoupment period is needed. And so the first part of the new month passes into oblivion.

Much Soviet factory data has been presented as to the extent of this "storming." Most of it has appeared as documentation for speeches and articles castigating the practice. Perhaps more convincing than such data, which is clearly selected so as to make an argumentative point, is some material on the subject which I found in a Russian Master's essay. Copies of all Masters' essays and Doctors' dissertations written in the Soviet Union must be filed with the Moscow Public Library, and it is rather fascinating to an American college teacher like myself to work one's way through the Library's special dissertation catalogue. I chose a handful of titles which seemed promising, put through the usual library call slips, and proceeded to examine the results of my fishing expedition.

One essay which I came across in this rather random fashion

was written in 1952 by a student in Kiev. He had studied three major machinery plants in Kiev, presumably choosing these particular factories simply because they were conveniently located and because their managements were willing to open doors to him. For three hundred pages, he proceeded to describe and criticize their operations. The factories were named in the report, and the job of description was quite a good one. Among the subjects treated briefly was "storming."

Data were presented as to the proportion of each month's production which was completed, on the average, during the last ten days of that month. Each of the twelve months of the year was treated separately, and the average for two twelve-month periods was presented.

FACTORY	PERCENTAGE OF WORK COMPLETED DURING THE LAST TEN DAYS OF EACH MONTH	
	1950	1951
Factory producing automatic machine tools in large numbers	67	78
Job-shop plant	78	73
Motorcycle plant	54	41

Here we have a very marked concentration of production within the last third of each month. Yet this is probably quite typical of Soviet fabricating industry. From this essay as well as other sources, we can say that roughly twice as much work gets done in the last period of the month as would occur if production were evenly spread throughout the entire month.

Such "storming," however, is not a peculiarly Soviet problem. It is also characteristic of some of American manufacturing: for example, the machine-tool industry. In one American machine-tool plant I visited, one third of the month's production was shipped out during the last week; in other words, shipments in this last week typically were half again as great as they would have been if the month's shipments had been evenly distributed.

Why this bunching up? Explanations which I received from American machine-tool managements essentially boiled down to two: First, delivery promises to customers are in terms of shipment within a specified month; second, plants or divisions of companies often draw up monthly profit-and-loss statements with only actual shipments counting as income. In short, the American factory has a monthly target or "boguey" of shipments—precisely as the Soviet plant has a monthly "plan" of production. Both speed up at the end to meet the target.

While one does not encounter in American industry anything like the concern and fuss about "storming" which exists in the Soviet Union, these scheduling problems are nevertheless treated as a real headache in the American machine-tool plants I have visited. It is recognized that they are costly. Why, then, isn't production evened out? "A matter of human nature," one superintendent explained to me. "The men and the foremen work best under pressure. It's wasteful to have a 'boguey' with resulting uneven production, but if there was no 'boguey' there might be no production and nothing available to waste."

However, even aside from the apparent relative unimportance of "storming" in American industry as a whole, there is a very important difference between the character of "storming" in Russian and in American factories. In American industry, this practice finds its expression in uneven shipments of finished goods out of the plant. But most of the American shops whose operations take place fairly early in the production cycle function at quite an even pace. The factory planners and dispatchers schedule the work out of these shops in a rhythmic fashion. It is primarily in assembly operations, where parts produced in many different shops are put together, and where last-minute design changes have their impact, that "storming" is serious.

In Russian industry, on the other hand, the greater autonomy of each individual shop makes its influence felt. Each shop has a production "boguey" for the month, and the bonuses of shop management personnel are linked to their meeting these "bogueys." Thus the problem of "storming" in the Soviet Union is not just that of piling up of shipments out of the factory, but also of the piling up of shipments from one shop to the next in the production cycle. As a result, "storming" has a much greater effect on production through the entire Soviet factory than it has in American industry. Here is one more price the Russians pay for the autonomy given to shop management.

Maintenance Organization

In view of the general Russian localization of responsibility to the shop level, one would not expect Soviet practice to be at the opposite end of the centralization spectrum so far as the performance of maintenance and inspection are concerned. In fact, however, the Russians do tend to centralize responsibility in these functions a good deal more than is done in American factories.

A Russian plant's entire maintenance system is organized according to a schedule of prophylactic maintenance. It is the responsibility of the chief mechanic of the factory to work out a schedule of inspection, minor repair, major repair, and rebuilding for each piece of equipment in the factory. For example, a single complete cycle of maintenance for metalcutting machine tools now averages about five and one-half years, and, at least in theory, the schedule is drawn up when the machine tool is first installed in the plant.

The actual maintenance work may be performed by a separate maintenance department; it may be done within the individual shops; or, by far the most common, production-shop personnel may do most of the maintaining of equipment in the individual shops while major rebuilding and production of spare parts are carried on in the central repair shop. In any case, whatever the procedure used in the particular Russian factory, it is the chief mechanic of the plant who establishes the maintenance schedule for each piece of equipment and who has complete authority and responsibility for maintenance decisions—from tightening nuts and bolts to rebuilding equipment.

How can we explain this centralization of decision-making in the hands of the chief mechanic, so unlike the usual Russian approach to factory functions? My best guess is that this centralization is inspired by a wholly justified concern for the state of the equipment. The shop superintendent—even though officially he works on a money budget—is in fact concerned primarily with short-run production results. His earnings and his advancement are closely geared to these results. Is it likely that he will pull equipment out of operation so as to carry on preventive maintenance, or rather that he will tend to work his machines to death and hope to be able to catch up with maintenance during some slack period which may conceivably occur in the future? Quite clearly, Soviet top administrators fear that his choice will be the latter. The situation in the early 1930's, when rapid industrialization was first under way, certainly gave them grounds for this fear.

In order to protect the equipment, it is considered best to put responsibility for it in the hands of one man: the factory chief mechanic. Since his sole responsibility is maintenance, presumably he will not have divided allegiances. In the past, the various organizations supervising the factories have attempted to further strengthen the chief mechanic's hand by establishing industry-wide maintenance schedules for particular types of equipment; but these schedules never seem to have been intended as more than rough guides to the factory chief mechanics, and as supports upon which they could lean in their inevitable arguments with production men.

Still and all, it is impossible to shelter maintenance considerations entirely from those of production. Soviet administrators are not interested in protecting the equipment for its own sake, but rather in order to get out production. There must be a means by which production needs can have an influence upon maintenance schedules. In any dynamic economic system, there must be some way in which genuine production emergencies can take precedence over maintenance routines.

The necessary unity between production and maintenance responsibility is achieved through the standard organizational pattern of the Soviet factory. Not only do the shop superintendents report to the works manager, but so does the chief mechanic. It is thus the works manager who is expected to balance off the demands of production and maintenance at any particular moment.

Given Soviet conditions, this is not a bad managerial solution. In actual fact, in view of the pressures upon the factory as a whole, it is clear that immediate production goals will take precedence over everything else. Maintenance must be sheltered, but it cannot be divorced entirely from production considerations. Thus it is given a relatively, although not completely, sheltered position in the Russian factory organization chart; the forces of *Realpolitik* are counted upon to prevent the maintenance people from ignoring the immediate needs of production.

An interesting comparison to this Soviet management solution is a maintenance scheme adopted in an American metal-fabricating plant which uses mainly complex, special-purpose equipment.

The founders of this American firm had been strongly oriented toward engineering, and had an overwhelming interest in improving the production process and equipment for its own sake—regardless of the financial justification. In the early period of the company's history, all maintenance was concentrated in the hands of a special department which was the particular province of top management.

As the firm grew and as its market stabilized, new influences took over the company's management. Personnel changed, and top management became basically oriented toward finance rather than to engineering. In order to root out the perfectionist influence in maintenance, decisions as to maintenance were transferred to the production departments, although a special maintenance department was retained to do all of the actual work. This organizational change quickly justified itself in terms of a sharp drop—which has continued over more than a decade—in maintenance costs per million dollars of production. With production men making the decisions, maintenance came to be viewed as a service rather than as an end in itself.

This new organizational pattern for the making of maintenance decisions in this firm has certain technical absurdities inherent within it. The production foreman using a particular piece of equipment decides on whether and when maintenance work is to be done on his machine. Maintenance costs are charged to his departmental budget. However, as a general rule in this company, the production foremen do not have detailed technical knowledge as to the construction of the machines they are operating. Although the foreman can call on the maintenance department for advice, his decision must be made without a full understanding of the technical considerations involved. Technical knowledge is isolated within the maintenance department, while decision-making power is kept strictly out of its hands.

This organization chart for the making of maintenance decisions would certainly seem ridiculous if one were not aware of the very special historical conditions which have acted as a driving force on the management of this particular American firm. The fact that maintenance costs have declined over the period of a decade supports the correctness of management's decision to give more weight to organizational considerations than to those of technical know-how. It is a good example of the fact that different managerial organization structures may work quite satisfactorily in different environments.

This American management case is worth reflecting upon when judging Soviet maintenance policy. Russian centralization of maintenance decision-making may well be an apt managerial solution to the particular organizational and motivational problems facing Russian industry.

Quality-Control Organization

Quality control is a second functional area which has been highly centralized in the Soviet factory. The factory's inspection department not only has the right to reject output, but it also can stop production on individual machines and even in entire shops. Moreover, in order to make sure that the inspection department takes its job seriously, willful shipment of substandard products has long been established as a criminal offense.

The inspection function is even more separated from production than is the maintenance function. Not only is inspection carried on under a separate factory department, but this inspection department is entirely outside the scope of authority of the works manager. The chief inspector is directly responsible to the plant director, and his orders can be overruled only by a written order from the director. In order further to assure that such written orders will not be given lightly, administrative authorities above the plant level must be immediately notified in all cases in which the chief inspector is overruled.

Such organizational isolation of inspection from production might, in other environments, be disastrous. Inspectors might play safe in approving production, insisting that it be of unnecessarily high quality quite regardless of the costs of achieving this quality. But in the Soviet factory, with the strong general orientation to output, organizational isolation seems a desirable counterforce.

Centralization of the inspection function, however, creates an additional hazard. The more that responsibility for quality is taken over by the inspection department, the less responsibility and interest is left to the operator and the production foreman. Thus, centralization of the inspection function can create a major motivational problem.

On occasion in Soviet factories, this problem has been recognized and some responsibility for inspection has been turned back to the shop superintendents. In one plant I visited during 1958, a major effort had recently been made along these lines.

Previously, the inspection department of the plant had consisted of twenty-three inspectors. Now, it had been cut down to seven, and most inspection had been turned over to the shop superintendents; sixteen inspectors had been put to work directly under the production superintendents, quite out of touch with the inspection department.

The director of the plant seemed quite happy about the change. He believed that, for the first time, the production superintendents felt a real responsibility for quality. Clearly, he was attempting to grapple with the same motivational problems in inspection which are faced in American industry.

Flexibility and Size

What is it that keeps the small American manufacturing firm alive? It cannot turn out volume production. It cannot buy raw materials at low, volume prices, or engage in an all-out marketing campaign. It cannot afford specialized management services or specialized equipment. All the advantages of size are against it. Yet, the small company continues to survive and prosper.

The explanation would seem to lie in the ability of the small American firm to turn around on a dime. Management decisions involve few people and can be made quickly. When demand booms for a new product, it is often the small firm which can get in first to meet it. The hoola hoops in the 1958 craze were produced by small outfits. It is these firms which can look for special bargains in materials, since the amount of their needs are small. Their management organizations are simple, and overhead is low. No red tape slows them down. Relations with employees are often casual and informal. Few people doubt that the small firm has a permanent place in American industry.

Russian small plants, however, have none of this American flexibility. They receive their materials allocations and their production plans through the same bureaucratic channels as do large establishments. Their degree of red tape is almost the same as that of the large plant.

I questioned a number of Soviet experts on the subject of the small plant. Not one of them saw such factories as having any particular advantages. One of the leading Soviet authorities on industrial administration perceived the role of the small industrial firm as lying only in such functions as minor repair work and flour-milling for collective farms. In other words, according to him, its proper place was solely in geographic locations where volume requirements were small.

During the past year, however, some efforts have been made to cut down the managerial overhead within the small plant. This has occurred through a movement to eliminate shop superintendents and their staffs in small factories, and to replace them by foremen without staffs; in short, to centralize all staff functions. Certainly this is a healthy tendency, but the fact that this movement began to develop only in 1957 shows how rigid and hidebound management organization has been in the Soviet Union.

This is an important management distinction between American and Russian industry. Managerial flexibility, both within the firm and in its relation to the outside environment, is what provides the small plant with its secure niche in the American economy. The absence of this flexibility in the Soviet Union tends to make the U.S.S.R. a land of giant factories, for nothing countervails the production economies arising from their high volume of output.

The Foreman

Despite all the marked differences between the Russian and American factory, there is at least one major problem they share in common. Managements in both countries have regularly wrestled with the issue of what to do with the foreman; they have come up with virtually identical theoretic solutions; and they have shared the same disappointment with the practical results achieved.

The foreman is a key figure in any industrial operation. It is he who is the point of contact between management and the workers. He is the man directly responsible for supervising the work, for seeing to the job training of those workers who need it, for handling production emergencies, and for maintaining peace, order, and at least a minimum degree of worker contentment on the shop floor. Bad foremen can ruin the best of plants.

Yet modern industrial technology and social conditions have steadily evolved in such a way as to make the foreman an unhappy man. This evolution has whittled away his power and changed the nature of his task. Not that he has become obsolete; no, indeed! Rather, the foreman's tragedy is that his job has been changing more rapidly than has his own conception of what the job should be.

There was a time when the factory foreman was virtually an independent businessman. He did his own hiring and firing, his own production scheduling, and made his own decisions as to how a job was to be done. He was bound by only the loosest schedules for delivery of his product to the next department of the factory. In some cases, he even set the rates of pay for his men; and when this was not done officially, it was often accomplished informally through kickbacks to him from those who wanted promotion or, in hard times, wanted simply to keep their jobs.

But as technology became more complex, and as the need for better factory planning and co-ordination was recognized, managerial staff departments were organized within the plant. Planning and dispatching, methods and time study, engineering, quality-control departments: all these grew up around the foreman. In one functional area after another, the foreman became the man who executed the decisions of these staff departments rather than himself making the decisions. In American industry, the staff departments are plantwide; in Russian industry, they are often on a shop level and under the shop superintendent; but so far as the foreman is concerned, the difference is nil.

Not only have production requirements changed, but social needs have also altered. As trade unionism engulfed the work force in much of American industry, union contracts were signed which spelled out the grounds permissible for firing workers, disciplining them, promoting them, transferring them, and giving them overtime work. These matters ceased to be treated as purely management prerogatives. Uniform policies had to be followed throughout the plant, for violations of the union contract would be appealed to grievance machinery and beyond to final arbitration. Such union pressure on management to achieve uniformity in the execution of personnel policy helped to strengthen the already-developing personnel departments. American foremen lost the right to hire and fire, promote and discipline, determine overtime and layoffs.

In the Soviet factory as well, power over personnel has evaporated from within the foreman's fist. The Soviet trade union, like its American counterpart, has a grievance procedure. In Russia, in fact, this procedure is designed primarily to eliminate precisely the sort of individual inequities which arise from distributing down to the foreman level management's right to reward and punish.

The result of this biforked development of factory technology and unionism in both countries has been to turn the foreman into a badly disheartened man. His ideology and aspirations are still very much those of the independent executive running his own business. This orientation to independence is reinforced by the slogans reaching him from the highest levels of management on both sides of the Iron Curtain: that the foreman's department should be a "cost center" to be operated by him as though it were his own company, and that the factory's staff departments are there to "help" him rather than to make the decisions for him. These fine words express what the foreman too thinks should be the case, but they have long had only a tenuous link to actual factory conditions.

In fact, it may be argued that, increasingly over the years, the foreman has achieved success only as he has taken up a position independent both of management and of the workers he supervises. If he tries to execute all of management's instructions, enforce all rules, and sternly combat work restriction, he can only succeed in cutting his own throat. Shorn of the powers he once had over his work force, he can now only be the loser in a struggle with his men. On the other hand, he cannot fully identify with the workers under him; for if he does not maintain some pressure upon them, management will soon fire him out of his job.

In short, the foreman must try to be the shop-floor mediator between management and the workers. This is as true in Russia as it is in the United States. But, as mediator, he is the "man in the middle," and this has never been an enviable spot.

During the last war, foreman dissatisfaction took a dramatic turn in the United States with the formation of the Foreman's Association of America. By December 1944, this independent trade union had reached a membership of 33,000. A special panel was appointed by the National War Labor Board to look into the motivation for this unionization and for the new union's dozen wartime strikes in key industries. The panel found that the principal motivating factor was neither dissatisfaction with salary nor with working conditions, but was rather concern over the foreman's job insecurity and his relationship with management. It required the Taft-Hartley Law, with a provision freeing management from its previous obligation to bargain collectively with foremen, in order to halt this unionization.

Perhaps more important than such unionization by foremen

—shock as it was to American management and to most foremen themselves—is the negative feeling of many American manual workers toward the possibility of promotion to a foreman's position. A prewar study of New Haven workers found "a rather general lack of enthusiasm for such promotion." In a postwar *Fortune* poll of factory workers, 58 per cent of those interviewed said that they would not "care particularly" to be foremen.

The same negative attitude appears to have developed in the Soviet Union. Industrial literature, and even official government decrees of the prewar period were filled with references to the difficulty of persuading the best manual workers to accept foremen's positions. Although I have not seen such explicit statements in postwar Soviet writings, a major 1955 government decree complains of the continued prevalence of all the old difficulties in the foreman's position.

The heart of the problem may lie in the fact that, in both countries, management efforts have been directed primarily at bolstering the foreman's traditional role. In American companies, it is often argued that functional departments of the plant should do no more than "advise" the foreman, who is compared to the president of the company in the sense that both men call upon the functional departments for help. In the Soviet Union, the government has issued powerful and well-publicized decrees intended to rebuild the foreman's traditional power. But the American comparison of the foreman with the president is barefaced chicanery, and can do little more than maintain false aspirations leading to increased bitterness. The Soviet decree of 1955 is essentially a repetition of the government's 1940 decree, and it seems no more likely than the first decree to achieve anything but further reduction of foreman morale.

In the United States, the foreman's post has been typically thought of as the "top of the ladder" for the manual workman. Only the rare exception moves from foreman to higher ranks of management. Traditionally, the job has been filled by men with long experience but without college training or technical education. Although in some companies one hears talk of the need for more educated foremen—even graduate engineers—such a change seems at most only beginning.

The Soviet Union has much the same problem—including the talk of a "need for a change." Despite the Russian use of recent engineering graduates as foremen, a usage which is intended primarily as a training device, most Russian foremen are much like American: long on experience and short on formal education.

Nevertheless, we should not overstate this limitation of the typical foreman's education. In both countries, the foreman often has more formal training than most of the workers he supervises. Ely Chinoy, in his study during the late 1940's of a large American automobile plant, came away feeling that high school graduation is now an important—although not a formal —prerequisite for promotion to foreman in this factory. For Russia, we have recent data for one heavy machine-building plant in the Urals with a labor force of 25,000. Here 40 per cent of the foremen had completed high school. This plant, however, is almost certainly atypical, for it is an extremely high-priority factory in a technically complex industry.

EDUCATION	URALS FACTORY	
	All Workers (1953)	All Foremen (*June 1, 1955*)
	(Percentage)	
Less than seven years	70 ⎫ 92	23 ⎫ 50
Seven years	22 ⎭	27 ⎭
Completed technical education (either secondary or college level)	Less than 8	36

In all probability, it will be difficult to develop a different and better-educated foreman in either country until some improved *modus vivendi* is developed between the level of position to which the foreman is encouraged to aspire and the realities of his factory world. But, aside from position in relation to management, another matter which clearly requires attention is the size of the foreman's salary.

A 1953 survey of American companies on the subject of foremen's pay indicated that only a small proportion of the firms offered any guarantee to their foremen that they would earn a minimum dollar amount more than the employees under them. A similar 1958 survey, this time of firms with over one thousand employees, showed that in 70 per cent of the cases the foreman earned only 15 to 24 per cent more than the highest-paid man under him, and that in 19 per cent of the cases his differential was even less than 15 per cent. Particularly when workers were paid on an incentive system, concern was expressed by members of management that the foreman might actually earn less than individual workers whom he was supervising.

The same threat to the foreman's traditional income differential exists in Soviet industry. There, in fact, the situation seems to be even worse. In the 1955 government decree previously cited, the Council of Ministers insisted that the minimum salary of a foreman should be greater than the base pay of the most skilled workers under him; but the differential it provided was not overly generous, ranging only *up to 15 per cent*. This decree, it should be noted, was intended to improve the foreman's conditions.

In one Russian plant I visited, average workers earned 700–800 rubles per month, skilled workers earned 1000–1100 rubles, and foremen received base salaries of only 800–1000 rubles. In this plant, it must be said in amelioration, workers were not eligible for bonuses, while foremen averaged monthly bonuses of 300–400 rubles. Yet one would hardly consider the foreman's job one which a skilled worker would dream about nights as he plotted how to increase his income.

In short, it seems rather apparent that American and Russian industry have nothing to learn from one another in the area of foremanship. Managements in both countries have faced the same sorts of problems, have had the same stand-pat ideas as to what to do about them, and have been unable to prevent further deterioration of the situation.

While we have seen wide variations between many practices of American and Russian factories and factory managements, clearly these do not penetrate into all areas. Foremanship is a key example of an area untouched by national and social-system differences.

Economic and Organizational Pressures in the Soviet Plant

The Soviet factory is not simply one more anonymous product of the international factory system of the nineteenth and twentieth centuries. On the contrary, in many respects it bears the distinctive marks of present-day Russian society.

The immensity of the typical Russian factory, compared to the American, is an outgrowth of a variety of pressures. The fact that labor is cheap while machinery is dear leads to the presence of a large labor force in Soviet plants. This force does the work which could be accomplished with fewer people if more machinery were available. Such is the case particularly in materials handling, quality control, and in the maintenance function. The scarcity of machinery also leads to further enlargement of the maintenance crew in order to keep equipment operating as long as is physically possible.

There is also the organizational pressure compelling each factory in Soviet society to be as independent as possible of the need for outside supplies. The desirability of such independence from the viewpoint of factory management, obvious in the light of the traditional Soviet seller's market, has tended further to increase the size of plants. Factory managements try to produce for their own production needs, and they even go so far in this regard as to make the spare parts needed by their maintenance crews.

Operational inflexibility deprives small factories of the major advantage which, in the United States, accrues to them in comparison with large plants. This advantage of flexibility being lost, it is no wonder that the forces which make for large factories in the Soviet Union have things pretty much their own way.

The very size of Soviet factories leads in turn to pressure for decentralization within the factory. This pressure is a large part of the explanation for the extensive devolution of management down to the shop level.

Once much of the factory management function is decentralized in this fashion, new problems are bound to arise. Because Soviet shop managements are highly oriented toward physical output from their own shops, no matter what the cost, "storming" throughout all shops has become the rule. Co-ordination between shops is weak. Critical factory functions such as maintenance and quality control, which would be slighted by shop superintendents in the interests of immediate production, have thus had to be taken out of their hands and have been highly centralized. As a result, despite and even because general decentralization in the Soviet factory goes far beyond that normally found in an American plant, the functions of maintenance and quality control have moved to the opposite extreme and are considerably more centralized.

Yet when all this has been said, it must still be remembered that the industrialization process has its own imperatives. Soviet and American managements both tackle the same industrial problems, and the nature of these problems sets limits to the differences which can exist between approaches which prove feasible for handling them. In certain managerial areas— specifically, those of industrial research and the treatment of the foreman—the Soviet managerial approach has not differed significantly from the American. The Soviet and American factory systems are two different species, but they are both of the same *genus* created by the modern industrial revolution.

part seven

RUSSIAN INDUSTRY AND THE WORLD

17. ECONOMIC COMPETITION

There are two quite different perspectives from which one might look at the operations of Russian and American business management. One of these is the comparative approach which I have used up to now, analyzing not only the methods by which each type of management does its job and recruits its successors, but also the environment in which managers function on and off the job. Following this approach, we have looked for both similarities and differences between Russian and American business problems and environment, and between the different problem-solving methods employed.

A second possible approach is that of examining the interrelationships, direct and indirect, which connect American and Russian industry. Managements in these two countries have helped create, and are now operating, titanic industrial structures which serve as the economic underpinning for the two societies. What can we say about the roles of American and Russian business in the international political struggle between the two nations? This is the question to be faced in these last two chapters.

The Rate of Growth

One form of international competition in which the United States and Russia are engaged is economic growth. Whether we have entered wholeheartedly into this competition, and whether its outcome will turn out to be of real significance to anyone, are questions we may put aside for the moment. The fact is that a number of our most influential American politicians have suggested that economic growth should now be given a high place among our national objectives, and that such growth has long been accorded one of the very highest priorities in the Soviet scheme of things. Growth means increase in economic power; and economic power is viewed as a potent force in the minds of the people of the uncommitted parts of the world, in the cold war, and in the calculations of the military of both sides as to the outcome of any potential hot war.

Comparison of the American and Soviet rates of growth has, for several years, been giving concern to American policymakers as well as to the American public. There is little question that the Soviet economy is growing at a rate at least double that of the United States. More than this is difficult to say. There are all sorts of statistical pitfalls in comparisons of rates of growth for any group of countries, and these pitfalls are particularly serious when dealing with the Soviet Union. But, after all, this limitation is not too important. Precise numbers are not the issue. The important fact is that there has been and still is today a major gap between the growth rates of Russia and the United States.

Is this gap likely to continue into the future? Khrushchev obviously believes that it will, and that as a result he will "bury" us. Many Americans also fear that the gap in growth rates will continue, and that it will lead to the Soviet Union becoming the dominant power of the world. In the eyes both of the Russians and of these American observers, we are fighting a losing battle against time. It is held that the dynamism of Soviet industry will ring the death knell of capitalism.

Other Americans, thinking about this problem, find succor in the fact that official Soviet figures as to the present rate of growth in industry show a decline compared with the past. But this is small comfort. We know that, until 1950, Soviet growth statistics had incorporated within them major elements of bias which were removed in that year from all future figures. The decline in official Soviet percentages may reflect virtually nothing except the cessation of statistical manipulation. Moreover, Soviet agricultural production recently has been growing much more rapidly than was the case under Stalin. It is possible that agricultural improvement has more than compensated for any decline which in fact has occurred in the rate of industrial

growth. In short, we are completely in the area of conjecture.
Differences in official Soviet figures of past and present rates
of growth are well within the possible margins of error.

Putting statistics aside, what are the forces which in the future will affect the present gap between national growth rates?
Can we not make a qualitative analysis?

First, it should be noted that not only the Russian but also
the American economic system is highly dynamic. Fears of
American economic stagnation died with the 1930's. Both systems have proved themselves over a sufficient period of time, so
that we can state with reasonable confidence that both will
continue to grow.

Each of the two countries is self-sufficient, quite independent
of imports from abroad and of foreign markets for its goods. Of
the two, Russia is somewhat more self-contained; but, compared to West European countries, the difference in this regard
between the U.S. and the U.S.S.R. is not worth a picayune.

Up to the present, both nations have leaned heavily upon
individual incentives. American economic incentives have taken
the form of opportunities for high profits and capital gains,
while the Russian incentive system has operated through sharp
differences in wage and salary levels and through high bonus
and incentive pay potentials.

Within both countries, however, there has apparently been
some movement in recent years away from the incentive system. The postwar years have seen a greater degree of equality
of personal income after taxes in both nations, and more of the
same is promised in the Soviet Union during the current plan
running through 1965. To the extent that differences in individual incomes contribute to economic growth by creating
strong incentives for increased effort—and, despite all the talk
on both sides of the issue, no one really knows much about
such an effect—this movement toward greater equality should
slow down the rate of growth in both the United States and the
Soviet Union.

Another influence on growth rates is the depletion of natural
resources, with the resultant need of falling back upon poorer
or more distant supplies of raw materials. In the light of pres-
ently known resources, it would appear that the Soviet Union

is likely to suffer more than we. On the other hand, it must be recognized that Russian mineral reserves are not nearly so well explored as are our own, and thus that there is greater likelihood for discovery of important new deposits in that country. To the extent that new types of resources may come to substitute economically for old—for example, atomic energy for coal and oil—both countries will benefit. In short, there is no reason to believe that either nation will have a substantial edge over the other in regard to resource depletion.

The Soviet government's particular distribution among rival users of the nation's total production has, in the past, been a major cause of Russia's rapid growth. Personal consumption has been held down by the government in order that military expenditures and, even more important, investment in new production facilities, could be increased. By utilizing the lion's share of the growth of income for the expansion of new plant and equipment, the wherewithal for further growth has been constantly and rapidly augmented. While in the United States, private investment financed out of voluntary individual and corporate savings has made expansion possible, no such voluntary saving has been necessary in the Soviet Union. The Russian government has paid for expansion by taxing the Russian public; the rate of expansion of the stock of productive facilities depends upon the Soviet government's tax decisions.

It is extremely difficult to make forecasts as to whether this heavy Soviet emphasis on investment in further growth facilities will continue in the future. One can readily point to two conflicting influences.

On the one hand, as a country grows more wealthy it may become easier, psychologically and politically, to increase the proportion of national income growth which is directed into investment. This is the case because there is less pressure to use a high proportion of the income growth for the improvement of immediate living standards. For example, let us consider a country with a per capita income of $1000 and an annual rate of growth of 5 per cent. If it is decided to increase the standard of living by $25 per person per year, then half of the growth will still be left for capital investment and for various government expenditures such as armaments. But when the country has reached a per capita income of $2000, and if it still has the same 5 per cent growth rate, it is easier for it to put a higher proportion of this growth into new investment. Twenty-five dollars per person per year can still be added to the standard of living, and yet three quarters—instead of the previous half—of total growth in income can be channeled into investment, armaments, et al.

In short, a country can still maintain the same absolute growth each year in its standard of living while diverting an ever-higher proportion of the total income growth into new investment. The implication of this fact is that Soviet investment in growth may easily increase as a percentage of Soviet national income.

However, there are two elements of the contemporary Russian situation which are pushing the Soviet Union in the opposite direction. One of these is the desire to increase consumption very rapidly. Since 1950, for the first time in Soviet history, standards of living seem to have been rising steadily and markedly above the level reached under the Tsar before the First World War. The Soviet public has been demanding, and getting, better food, clothing, and furniture. A large bite out of total Soviet investment has been going into improvement of the abysmally bad housing conditions. Hours of work have been cut from 48 to 44 per week, and they are planned to be further reduced to 40 hours by 1962, and to 35 hours per week by 1968. In short, the Soviet public has been getting—and seem scheduled to keep getting—higher living standards both in the form of more goods and more leisure.

Second, the Soviet government is increasingly faced with the necessity of entering upon investment projects which in the past have continually been postponed. For example, Russian authorities delayed expansion of railroads and highways as long as they could, since such facilities do not directly increase the nation's output. But the limits of this policy have been reached, and now resources are being poured into transportation.

To take another example, the Russian population on the farms is still extraordinarily large when compared with the American. As Soviet agriculture becomes modernized, and as the Russian peasants resume their inevitable movement into the cities—as has been the pattern of American farmers since the beginning of the last war—the Soviet Union will have to put increasing funds into providing these urban newcomers with housing, electricity, sewage disposal, and all of the other public services. Russia still faces enormous costs of urbanization which we have already mainly paid. The American farm population is now largely resettled in the cities. This relocation job is still to be done in the Soviet Union; one can hardly doubt that it will be enormously expensive.

Thus, we can see that there are powerful forces pulling down the Russian potential for maintaining its old rate of expansion in growth facilities. It is quite likely that these forces are even greater than the others which are increasing the Soviet potential to do this job. But where the balance will in fact turn out to lie is impossible to say.

A major factor retarding American growth is the periodic upsurge of unemployment. Russia has eliminated this particular economic roadblock.

But Russia buys its advantage at a high price. She achieves and maintains full employment by means of a highly centralized planning system, beset with all the management rigidities which we have seen displayed in earlier chapters. She suffers major production inefficiencies, as well as much hoarding of labor on the part of managements who fear that if they lay off workers they will never be able to hire them back. It is by no means clear that the absence of unemployment in the Soviet Union is, on balance, a force making for faster economic growth over the decades. It is quite conceivable that the cost to growth, in rigidities and in other hidden losses within the economic system, is greater than the benefits won.

Finally, Russia has the advantage of pursuing standardization far more single-mindedly than we do. Soviet industry has not provided diversity of products, whether of dresses to final consumers or of machine tools to other factories. Its standardization policy not only keeps down development costs, but makes possible all the gains to be derived from mass production. Russian industry has concentrated its best efforts on the lowering of production costs. Just as American industry has gone far beyond Western Europe in this regard, so Russian industry has pushed the emphasis beyond the point to which we have carried it.

To the extent that Russian consumers become more demanding, diversity of consumer goods must increasingly appear. Already, one can hear the first mutterings about style from Russian women. The same decline in standardization may also be expected with respect to machinery and other factory equipment, since there is growing demand for special-purpose equipment to run automatic processes.

Thus, increased Russian diversity of products must be expected, and part of the Soviet advantage from standardization will tend to be lost. Nevertheless, substantial gains will be retained until such time as the Soviet Union begins to change styles regularly, as we annually change automobile models, in order deliberately to create "style obsolescence." Such a development in the Soviet Union is at best far enough off in the future so that it can be disregarded.

Internal dynamism of the economic systems, freedom from the vagaries of international trade, strength of incentives to individuals, depletion of natural resources, investment in growth facilities, unemployment, hidden rigidities of the economy, degree of standardization in production: all these affect the relative rates of economic growth in Russia and in the United States. These, of course, are not the only factors which will determine whether the gap in economic growth rates between the two countries continues at the current level. But, it seems to me, our analysis of these variables has pointed up such a complex relationship, with such an uncertain outcome for growth rates, that only a soothsayer would dare to make a prediction from it.

But, when all is said and done, is it clear that we should really be much interested in the relative rates of economic growth of the United States and of the Soviet Union? For one thing, as we shall see below, these rates are not particularly important in influencing the amount of aid which the two nations can give to underdeveloped countries. Simple political decisions as to what Americans and Russians wish to do, as well as the human-relations skill with which they do it, are overwhelmingly more important. So too with competition in the field of trade. Relative American and Soviet economic growth may be much less important in deciding the cold-war struggle over the neutralist world than one might at first think.

How about the appeal to the imagination of the world's poverty-stricken nations? Certainly, growth makes its appeal; we know this to our sorrow. But, probably at least as vital an appeal as growth is that of the standard of living which a country provides for its own people. Russia has, to a considerable extent, made its giant strides in economic growth precisely because the Soviet government was long able to hold down living standards. Is it certain that growth which is won at such a price is really appealing to men's minds?

Most important of all is military potential. One may well ask, with the world as it is today, whether the accumulation of further economic power has much to do with military strength. Perhaps both we and the Russians are already sufficiently powerful industrially so that each can support a military force capable of destroying the other. More economic strength may have no relevance here. Or again, to the extent that economic might is relevant to military, the really vital issue may not be the amount of total economic power, but rather the proportion of its economy which each country is willing to devote to military output. The hydrogen bomb may well have made obsolete for military purposes any comparison of rates of economic growth.

The Underdeveloped Countries

While the United States and Russia are competing—sensibly or otherwise—in the area of economic growth, they are also contesting for the good will of the underdeveloped, noncommitted nations of the world. Both are heavily in the business of aid. Both countries are concerned with linking themselves through the ties of trade to the neutralist world. What is the present state of this competition, a competition which in its essence rests on the industrial might of the two competitors?

Our own aid program is a widely diversified one, while the Soviet program is concentrated on a considerably fewer number of countries. Our aid is given primarily in the form of grants; the Soviet, in the form of low-interest loans. Both countries, apparently, hope to reap political returns from their money aid.

Through 1957, the Soviet Union and the other members of its Bloc had delivered goods under aid agreements to only fifteen countries other than Russian allies and Yugoslavia. These countries were Afghanistan, Argentina, Burma, Cambodia, Ceylon, Egypt, India, Indonesia, Lebanon, Nepal, Paraguay, Sudan, Syria, Turkey, and Yemen. Let us concentrate upon the Soviet-American competition in aid to these fifteen nations.

During 1956, the amount of non-military aid which was delivered to these countries by the entire Soviet Bloc was only 25 per cent of the volume delivered by the United States; in 1957, the Bloc's aid rose to 57 per cent. If we consider the aid delivered by the Soviet Union alone, its proportion to American aid rose from 16 to 42 per cent. Actually, this is an overstatement of the Soviet percentages since, in the total for American aid, we are excluding all disposal of American agricultural surpluses. In addition, it should be remembered, Soviet aid is granted almost entirely in the form of loans which must be repaid.

Nevertheless, Soviet aid to these areas has now risen to a substantial proportion of our own. If we look upon aid as a form of competition in winning friends, as a means whose efficacy for this task can be measured by the number of dollars spent, then the Soviet Union is becoming a formidable competitor. Moreover, since aid still comprises only a minuscule proportion of either country's national income, Soviet aid programs could in the future be multiplied many-fold if the Russian government should desire this.

One may wonder, however, whether it is true that allies can be bought through aid. Our own efforts in this direction have not been notably successful; Iraq is an outstanding example of failure. In 1956, Russia put some 52 per cent of its total aid expenditures outside of the Soviet Bloc into shipments to Yugoslavia; some 25 per cent of Russia's aid went to Yugoslavia in 1957; yet one would hardly say that today Yugoslavia is a loyal Russian ally. Similarly, the large amounts of both military and economic aid which have been provided by the Soviet Union to the United Arab Republic have created a situation in which this country is said, at least by some observers, to be at the moment the greatest single obstacle in the way of Soviet ambitions in the Middle East.

Perhaps economic aid should not be looked at in terms of competition. From an American viewpoint, economic aid might better be seen both as a form of worldwide income equalization—Henry Wallace's "milk for the Hottentots"—and as a means of lending greater stability to poverty-stricken areas. If we view economic aid in this fashion, then we should welcome Russian aid programs rather than consider them as an attack upon us. One type of sensible American foreign-aid budget would be a global one, with our own foreign-aid expenditures being *cut,* rather than competitively increased, when Russian expenditures grow. From this same point of view, joint programs through the United Nations would seem a desirable implementation of American foreign policy.

Of course, if we were to adopt this viewpoint it would be necessary for us to make sure that the Russian aid program could not in the future be used for political blackmail against recipient nations. We would have to be ready to fill the Soviet Union's place in aid to any country which was threatened with being cut off because it did not do Russia's bidding. But, aside from the need for our setting aside reserves as backing for such an insurance program, we might welcome Soviet economic aid as a contribution to our own international policy of warring upon poverty and upon political instability.

Aid is only one type of economic tie with underdeveloped countries. In the case of the Soviet Union, however, it is a major tie. During 1956, the fifteen underdeveloped countries receiving aid from Russia financed 36 per cent of their total imports from the Soviet Union solely out of this aid. In 1957, the percentage had risen sharply to 50 per cent. Moreover, 82 per cent of total Soviet exports during 1956 to the non-satellite countries of Latin America, Africa (excluding the Union of South Africa), and Asia (excluding Japan) went to the above fifteen countries; in 1957, the percentage was 85 per cent. Thus, the percentage of all Soviet exports to the underdeveloped, non-Soviet world which were financed through direct aid rose from 30 per cent in 1956 to 42 per cent in 1957.

This still leaves, of course, a substantial role for Soviet trade financed either through direct Soviet imports from these countries or through other normal trade channels. But for the United States, the relative importance of normal trade and private investment is far greater than it is for the Soviet Union. In the case of those fifteen nations which accepted Soviet aid, only 13 to 19 per cent of American exports were financed by aid during fiscal 1956–58. For all underdeveloped countries in the world—using the same definition of "underdeveloped" which we employed earlier when treating Soviet exports—our aid was scarcely 6 to 7 per cent of our total exports directed to these countries during fiscal 1956 through fiscal 1958. (In the figures for both aid and exports, I am excluding our disposal abroad of farm surpluses as well as our "defense support" designed to "provide the supplemental economic resources required if the participating countries are to carry out adequate defense efforts and sustain minimum economic growth.")

As for the underdeveloped nations themselves, regular commercial trade is far more important than economic grants or loans. A relative decline in the price of their exports—such as we have seen in recent years—can more than counterbalance aid funds received from all sources. The issue of whether economic interest will link these nations to Russia or to the United States is far more likely to be decided by ties of trade than by ties of aid. This point would hold even without the fact that many countries have shown a strong preference for "paying their own way" instead of receiving alms.

At the present time, the United States is far ahead of the Soviet Union in its trade with underdeveloped nations outside the Soviet Bloc. While a bare 4 per cent of total Soviet exports went to these countries in 1956, and 6 per cent in 1957, 31–32 per cent of all American exports in 1956 and 1957 went to these politically critical areas. Moreover, these high American percentages are from a total of worldwide American exports which was vastly larger than the Soviet total.

How can we explain this Soviet failure to expand trade connections with the neutral, underdeveloped world? Primarily, the explanation would seem to lie in the nature and biases of Soviet planning and of the Soviet administrative organization.

The Soviet Union has always been a highly self-sufficient nation, trading as little as practicable with the outside. Earlier, and partly even today, this has been due to a fear of becoming economically dependent upon any other nation or group of nations; such economic dependence, the Russian government thought, might be turned into political dependence. Increasingly, however, as the relative might of the Soviet Union has grown during the postwar era, such fears have diminished.

Probably more important today are those forces which, within the country, cause the individual Soviet plant to try to produce its own supplies instead of purchasing them from other factories. Just as the Soviet factory takes the route of producing its own needed supplies in order to achieve some security in a seller's market; just as the Soviet industrial ministries likewise have sought self-sufficiency; so too the national State Planning Committee follows the same path. Even trade with such allies as mainland China and the countries of Eastern Europe seems to be restrained. These allied countries have their own plans to fulfill, and the Russian State Planning Committee has greater authority over Russian factories than it has over Chinese or even East European plants. The Russian Planning Committee is better able to assure deliveries scheduled from Russian than from Czech factories, as well as being in a superior position to change the type or amount of orders which they will fill. There are major advantages to be gained through concentrating on internal trade.

It is such organizational forces which have kept the total level of Soviet foreign trade compressed to such a point that Russian trade is only half as large in proportion to Russian national income as American foreign trade is compared to American income. But even this limited foreign trade is heavily concentrated in the parts of the world allied to Russia: barely one fourth of Soviet trade is left for the rest of the world. Small wonder that the Soviet Union carries on little commercial trade with the third-force underdeveloped nations.

There is a third difficulty from the point of view of the Soviet Union which is inherent in international trade. This particular difficulty arises out of the nature of the Soviet pricing system. In the case of a great many products, Soviet planners find it virtually impossible to calculate whether the country will gain or lose economically from a given foreign trade transaction. How can a planner decide if it would be cheaper for the Soviet Union to produce item A for export while importing item B in exchange, or to reject trade and produce directly at home the desired item B?

In a private business economy such as our own, the solution is simplicity itself. An item is imported if it can be bought abroad more cheaply than it could be purchased from a producer within the country. The workings of the market take care of all necessary adjustments in the relative prices of imports and exports.

But in the case of the Soviet Union, all foreign trade is monopolized by a single government agency. This agency must decide whether a given lot of imports is worth more to the country than the exports which will have to be shipped in payment. But how determine this? By comparing the price of these goods on the domestic Soviet market? No, for Soviet pricing is highly erratic. In fact, pricing is so chaotic that an argument has been raging for some time in the Soviet economic press as to whether machinery prices should not be doubled while leaving stable the prices of consumer goods. If there is this much leeway and dubious calculation involved in present-day Soviet prices, then these prices can scarcely be taken as a proper guide for Soviet foreign trade operations.

This pricing problem was emphasized to me most forcefully in a 1958 discussion with a leading official in Polish economic administration. The Poles carry on their trade in much the same fashion as do the Russians, and the official sorrowfully admitted that Polish pricing was so confused that the Polish Planning Commission could seldom really be sure whether or not a given foreign-trade transaction was advantageous for Poland.

Why does such chaos exist in the Soviet price system? Essentially, because pricing is not too important in the Soviet scheme of things. As long as factory managers produce the items they are told to turn out and do so in the quantities ordered, and as long as they require allocation orders to get raw materials, fuels, and equipment—instead of just buying what they wish—then it is not terribly important whether the prices of goods relative to one another really make sense. It would be convenient for Soviet planners if the pricing system was orderly and reflective of reality, but it is not sufficiently vital to be worth putting a great deal of effort into the task of making it so. Only the prices of one type of consumer good compared to another must be reasonable—since consumers alone have money which they can use as they wish. But there is no great necessity for rhyme or reason in the pricing of those goods which are sold to businesses.

In view of the great difficulty in determining whether any particular foreign-trade transaction is advantageous for the Soviet Union, a simple escape from the problem is extremely tempting. The less foreign trade, the fewer such problems, and the less numerous the difficulties for the foreign-trade agency which are inherent in its defense of any decision it may make. Soviet policy-makers may not on principle object to the "dumping" of Soviet goods on foreign markets at prices below cost, but at least they would like to know when such dumping is going on. At present, they can seldom be sure if a given sale was at a favorable price or was really a case of unprofitable dumping.

Here is a tremendous bureaucratic reinforcement for other Soviet tendencies to self-sufficiency. In a small country such as Poland, where foreign trade on a large scale is a necessity obvious to everyone, this difficulty in deciding about particular transactions is no great obstacle to foreign trade. The difficulties must be faced. But in the Soviet Union, where under the best of circumstances foreign trade would be relatively minor, the difficulties can be avoided simply by rejecting all trade except in those cases where the economic or political advantages are abundantly clear.

All of this discussion leads to the conclusion that at present the United States has a tremendous edge on the Soviet Union in the competition to weave a network of normal commercial trade with the underdeveloped nations. Yet there is one element, which has not been considered, which in the future may possibly cause a change. This element consists of the internal economic structures of the United States and Russia.

The great American problem in trade is not that of supplying goods which are desired by underdeveloped nations, but rather of absorbing their products in exchange. They are exporters of foodstuffs and natural fibers, and these products are blocked from our shores so as not to worsen our own domestic farm problems. Some underdeveloped countries are exporters of oil, and petroleum is embargoed so as to protect American domestic producers. Our problem in trade is that of purchasing the imports which would provide dollars to the underdeveloped countries.

The Russians—*if* they could overcome their desire for national self-sufficiency, eliminate their organizational obstacles to trade, and develop a rational internal price system—would have an advantage here compared to the United States. Basically, Russia is a poor country agriculturally, with a bad combination of soil and rainfall in most parts of the gigantic land mass which comprises the U.S.S.R. The Russian farm problem is one of insufficient production. In terms of Russia's geography, it would make perfect long-run economic sense for her to become a great importer of foodstuffs and textile fibers in exchange for machinery and other manufactured goods. In short, Russia has considerable natural advantages over us as a trading partner for the underdeveloped portion of the world.

But this is an issue for the future, and perhaps the distant future at that. For the present, Russia's bias toward self-sufficiency and the inherent organizational problems of its planning system are the overwhelmingly dominant factors. We are far and away ahead in the game of trade—and likely to remain so. Moreover, this game seems to me to have a much higher payoff than the game of aid which is going on side by side, and in which the Russian hand is much more nearly equal to our own.

18. BUSINESS HANDS ACROSS THE IRON CURTAIN

In the days before the First World War, all knowledgeable men were aware of the fact that lengthy fighting between major nations on the continent of Europe was a political impossibility. Incredulity as to major war was fostered by the fact that there were two great forces in Europe which, although perpetually at each other's throats, shared in common the absence of strong national ties. One was the powerful Second Socialist International, whose members owed their allegiance to the internal working class rather than to any particular nation-state. The second force was large-scale business management, whose interests covered the world and whose allegiance was strictly to its international investments. Neither of these powerful groups would permit the politicians to involve them in self-destructive warfare.

The dream of international brotherhood of the working class seems, by now, to be dead. But the concept of "business without a country" lingers on. Consider, for example, the early-1959 visit to the United States of Anastas Mikoyan. Mikoyan apparently believed that there were special advantages to be gained from his addressing himself to American businessmen. As one businessman to another, he could appeal to their deepest interests. Apparently, this approach was expected to be far more persuasive than would be that of a Russian trade unionist appealing to American union leaders, or of a Russian diplomat dealing with American diplomats.

Trade Makes Friends—and Enemies

International trade is sometimes cited as one of the prime bonds existing between businessmen the world over. Such trade has been described as a great civilizing force making for international friendship. Partly, it is argued, this is because it leads to common economic interests. Far more important, however, is the fact that trade results in regular, businesslike contacts between citizens of all countries. In doing this, it breaks down national parochialism and provides each nation's business community with an appreciation for other nations' customs and for their means of carrying on the daily economic life of society.

This argument may have merit for many West European countries, those for whom international trade is the very lifeblood of the economy. Postwar German businessmen have learned to adapt to other countries' ways of doing business; for, if they had rigidly insisted upon others adapting to them, their trade would not have expanded as it has. Japan is another country whose exporters have shown considerable flexibility in their relations abroad. Of course it must be admitted that even before the last war Germany and Japan were leading adapters to conditions of foreign markets; this fact casts doubt upon the argument that such trade necessarily creates international good will.

In any case, neither the United States nor Russia has shown any of that flexibility in business relations which is said to promote internationalism. Both countries are colossi with enormous internal markets. Soviet exports total no more than some 2 per cent of Soviet gross national product, and our own exports are only some 4 per cent of the American gross national product. As a result, business in both countries is primarily directed inward. In both nations, managers are perfectly willing to engage in foreign trade—but it is up to the foreigner to make the necessary adjustments in his habits.

American business, of course, is notorious for its inflexibility in foreign markets. The foreigner can buy a product designed for the American market—or he can take his custom elsewhere. He must learn to conduct his business in English rather than in his native tongue. In short, it must be he who provides the adjustment. While this picture of American business is considerably less accurate today than it was before the war, it is still not very much of a caricature.

Russian foreign trade relations are, if anything, even more

inflexible. It is quite true that, on occasion, Soviet negotiators can move rapidly and show extremely sympathetic understanding for local conditions. Usually, however, this occurs only when some specific political object is perceived to be at stake in the negotiations. More normally, where trade is entered upon with the object of advancing the economic interests of both sides, and where there is no exceptional problem such as that of breaking into special markets, it is the foreigner who must do business in the Russian manner.

Doing business Russian-style involves becoming deeply involved with the top-level planning bureaucracy of the country. Red tape is the rule. Negotiators for business contracts have reported a trading procedure in which they would tortuously reach detailed oral agreements, and find that after all the bargaining was completed they would then first be asked to put their *proposal* into writing. Oral agreement is only the first step in the paper shuffling. Authority to make trade decisions in the Soviet Union is usually highly centralized, and months may be required before even an appointment with the right person can be arranged. Agreements are best made on the spot in Moscow, and a successful negotiation may well require the negotiators to settle in there literally for months.

It is hard to see how this method of conducting international trade relations does much to break down national hostilities or feelings of "strangeness." The home pattern of trade is maintained—and often, as in the Russian case, even further rigidified. There is little "broadening" experience for the people concerned.

I do not see Russian-American trade as much of an influence for reducing animosity between the nations. On the other hand, neither does it seem to be exacerbating the situation.

Periodically, both in the past and more recently, there have been scares in American business circles that Russia was dumping goods onto American or foreign markets, and even that this was being done deliberately in order to destroy American industry. Butter and oil in the early 1930's; aluminum, tin, basic chemicals in the last couple of years: these are the items which have been the *causes célèbres*.

Despite all the noise of the moment about these sales, the

transactions soon enough come to be seen in a more normal and innocuous light. In 1957–58, for example, the Soviet Union needed foreign exchange to finance imports, as it preferred not to dip further into its gold reserves. In order to enter in a time of recession into markets which were new for it, Russia followed a not unusual competitive practice of shading the going international price. Quite possibly, and if so with good sense, it followed this policy particularly with items in which it had temporary excess capacity relative to its capacity for processing these semi-finished goods. In all this, there is no need to look for Machiavellian policies aimed at the ruin of our own American giant corporations. In actual fact, of course, Russian industry is far down on the list of foreign competitors whose actions are studied with concern by American firms.

All in all, then, it would seem that neither American trade with Russia, nor competition with her in the markets of other countries, is likely to have much effect toward either a permanent improvement or worsening of our mutual relations. Such trade and competition are essentially irrelevant to the basic political issues which divide the world.

The "Managerial Class"

Just as Anastas Mikoyan seemed to hope for greater success from a Russian appeal to American businessmen than could be achieved by a similar call on American trade unionists or politicians, so too there are those in the West who regard Soviet business managers as the carriers of the world's prayers for peace.

The view is not infrequently voiced that a managerial class has arisen in the Soviet Union, and that the dust of world politics should gradually settle as this class takes over the reins of power in the Soviet Union. For, it is argued, these managers are reasonable business folk, concerned with running their own factories and industries, and having strong vested interests in the *status quo*. They see the world much as do businessmen anywhere else, and this similarity of viewpoint is bound to increase. Soviet managers are not Party fanatics, like those who have ruled the Soviet Union up to now and who link their fate with that of world revolution. It is hoped that, as the new management class captures increasing power, ideological differences between the Soviet Union and the United States are bound to diminish and to lose their cutting edge.

The idea that there exists a special managerial class in the Soviet Union needs examination. For, if no such class exists, the above position falls to pieces. But what is meant by "class"?

The view of class which is expounded by Marxists is quite straightforward. One must only look at the relationship between individuals and property, and use this relationship as the distinguishing mark. Those who own property and hire people to work for them, who earn a profit on their investments, belong to one class; those, such as independent shoemakers, who own their own shops but employ no labor, belong to a second class. The third class—the proletariat—is composed of those who work for wages.

Here is a very simple and purely economic concept of class, quite easily applied to categorizing the population of a capitalist country. No public opinion polls are needed; a man's class is an objective fact, not a matter of what he thinks it is. But, quite evidently, those Westerners who talk of the existence of a "managerial class" in the Soviet Union do not attach this meaning to the term "class." The Soviet factory director and minister are hired by the government just as much as are the factory workers. Moreover, unlike American officers of large corporations, their incomes come almost entirely from salary and bonus rather than from earnings on investments.

The concept of "managerial class" stems from a different definition. In this sociological usage of the term, "class" refers to a set of people who *consider* themselves to be distinct from other groups in society. This feeling of similarity among the members of the class is caused by the fact that they share certain things in common. It may be that what they have in common is a similar annual income or the means by which they earn this income; but the feeling of similarity may also be based on the sort of neighborhood in which people live, the type of education they have been given, the style of furniture they own, or even their politics. In England, it is commonly claimed, the truly distinguishing mark of class is the accent with which a person speaks his native tongue. It has been found, at least in Western societies, that all of these various marks of a distinctive social grouping are rather closely related to one another. When this is so, we can call the grouping a social class. This concept of social class obviously bears some relation to the Marxist definition of economic class, but it differs from the Marxist definition in that it rests upon persons' beliefs as to their place in society rather than on an objective measure of this place.

The sociological concept of class has still another aspect. If classes are to exist, then there must be reasonably sharp boundaries between these classes; people cannot move too readily from one class to another, nor can there customarily be rapid class movement between the generations. For, if there is very high mobility between classes, then the feeling of unity within a class and of its separateness from other classes breaks down.

Using this sociological concept of class, we can distinguish sharply between Soviet industrial managers and run-of-the-mill Soviet workers.

Soviet managers receive incomes which are many times that of an ordinary Soviet worker. The director of a plant with a labor force of one thousand employees may earn five to six times as much as the average Soviet worker. In the steel industry, where workers are highly paid compared to those in other industries, the director of a very large plant earns five times as much as a semiskilled worker under him. Certainly, an income differential of this size must lead to sharp differences in consumption patterns.

The Soviet educational differential is no less sharp. Present-day medium and top industrial management share in common the fact that most have completed college training. Moreover, the great majority of these have had an education in straight engineering, with a second group which is substantially smaller having gone through a business-engineering program. Contrasting Soviet with American backgrounds, we find that a considerably larger proportion of Soviet than of American industrial managers are college-educated. In addition, American managers have graduated from widely diverse types of college programs, while Soviet managers share what was a more similar experience in their college years. Finally, the proportion of the nation's adults who have a college background is much larger in America than it is in the Soviet Union. All in all, it is much more true in Russia than in the United States that the manager is set off from the mass of the population by the amount and type of education which he has had.

When we turn to political activity, the same phenomenon is noted. Virtually all top managers are members of the Communist Party. Data of 1936 showed that 98 per cent of all factory directors in heavy industry were Communist Party members. The proportion for responsible management above the factory level ran between 97 and 100 per cent in the various major industries. It would be a fair presumption that much the same proportions still hold today. Communist Party membership is a virtual requirement for a top-management job. Men who are not Party members do hold key management posts —for example, the assistant head of construction activities in Moscow is not a Party member—but such people are rare.

While management is recruited almost completely from Party ranks, only some 4 per cent of the total population are Party members. Even among industrial workers, the proportion is probably close to the range of 14 to 19 per cent which I observed in two factories. Soviet managers share in common Communist Party membership and activity, and in this respect —just as in income and in education—they are distinct from the masses of the Russian people.

Finally, it seems reasonable to expect that, as between the managerial group and the population as a whole, there is a pattern of youths being more likely to remain in their parents' class, whatever that may be, than to move out of it. Soviet data of the 1930's showed that much of such social stability had developed even then; in all probability, this stability of social-class structure has since further increased. For the reasons discussed in Chapter Three, primarily those of training and motivating children within the family, the Soviet Union seems no exception to the generalization that the son of a professional man or manager is himself much more likely to become a manager than is the son of a worker.

There can be no question that managers comprise a group

which is both highly differentiated from the general Russian population and is recruited very unevenly from among the different occupational levels of Soviet society. Are these characteristics sufficient to permit us to speak meaningfully of a "managerial class"?

The answer, in my opinion, is no. The concept of "managerial class" is intended not just to differentiate managers from ordinary workers and peasants, but more particularly to distinguish them from Communist Party officials and other subgroups within the stratum at the top of the Soviet ladder of power, prestige, and income. The real question is not whether we can differentiate Soviet managers from the base of the Soviet population, but rather whether the managers comprise a group quite separate from the full-time Party functionaries.

Party functionaries would seem to have incomes reasonably in line with those of management personnel. As to education, although that of the full-time Party official is certainly somewhat less on the average than that of industrial managers, it is still vastly more than the norm for the population. Already in 1939, 59 per cent of the heads of all regional Communist Party bodies in the country had at a minimum completed high school. Moreover, this figure seems to have been growing rapidly. In the Ukraine, the proportion of regional Party heads with a minimum of a high-school education was 63 per cent in early 1938, and had risen to 81 per cent by early 1940. In all probability, most of these Party secretaries had graduated not only from high school but also from college. It seems a fair guess that, in 1959, a substantial majority of high-ranking full-time Party officials in the Soviet Union are college graduates. Moreover, for most of the college-trained group of Party officials, college has meant the same five-year engineering school to which the managers have gone.

To a considerable extent, therefore, industrial managers and full-time Communist Party officials are the same type of people. Members of both groups must normally be trusted Party members, active politically; their incomes are similar; even their education is not too different.

To push the matter even further, they are frequently not only much the same type of people, but are identical individuals

PAST AND PRESENT FULL-TIME POSTS HELD BY MEMBERS OF THE CENTRAL COMMITTEE, SOVIET COMMUNIST PARTY

ALL RECORDED POSTS / PRESENT FULL-TIME POSITION	MEMBERS CENTRAL COMMITTEE ELECTED FEB. 1956			NUMBER OF POSTS IN DIFFERENT CATEGORIES HELD BY THOSE FOR WHOM THERE IS PRE-1950 BIBLIOGRAPHICAL DATA								
				PARTY OFFICIALS			INDUSTRY OFFICIALS			ALL OTHERS		
	TOTAL NO.	NO. FOR WHOM THERE IS DATA AS TO PRESENT POSITION	NO. FOR WHOM BIBLIOGRAPHICAL DATA EXISTS PRE-1950	NO. OF POSTS	POSTS HELD BY THOSE WITHOUT CAREERS IN OTHER LINES NO.	%	NO. OF POSTS	POSTS HELD BY THOSE WITHOUT CAREERS IN OTHER LINES NO.	%	NO. OF POSTS	POSTS HELD BY THOSE WITHOUT CAREERS IN OTHER LINES NO.	%
PARTY OFFICIAL	—	62	42	42	20	48%	1	—	—	22	—	—
INDUSTRY OFFICIAL	—	7	7	2	—	—	7	3	43%	4	—	—
ALL OTHERS	—	48	39	20	—	—	10	—	—	39	14	36%
TOTALS	133	117	88	64	20	31%	18	3	17%	65	14	22%

TWO OR MORE POSTS HELD IN ONE CATEGORY AT DIFFERENT TIMES BY A SINGLE MAN ARE COUNTED AS ONLY ONE POST. BIBLIOGRAPHICAL DATA END BETWEEN LATE 1957 AND EARLY 1958.

at different stages of their career. Remember the director of the major steel plant in Chelyabinsk, mentioned in Chapter Two, who a few years earlier had been the full-time Party leader of that area! Remember the tendency to recruit Party secretaries of factories from practicing engineers!

An interesting illustration both of the extent to which Soviet upper-class individuals alternate hats, changing from one type of job to another, and of the major role within the Party of those who are not themselves full-time Party officials, is given in the table (opposite page). This table summarizes the available biographical information as to the backgrounds of full members of the Central Committee of the Soviet Communist Party elected at the national Party Congress in 1956. These 133 people stand at the head of the Communist Party and of Soviet society; they comprise the group which made the decision between Khrushchev on one side and Malenkov, Molotov, and Kaganovich on the other.

It is noteworthy that, of these Central Committee members, only 53 per cent have full-time Party jobs. Of those Central Committee members who are full-time Party officials, the careers of no more than half have been exclusively within the Party. In short, at least three quarters of the Central Committee members have, either now or in the past, held major career positions outside of the Party itself.

However, it is also quite clear from our table that only 20 per cent of the Central Committee members have ever engaged in industrial careers. This fact would seem to indicate that, by and large, industrial management is at the moment a relatively poor road to the heights of Soviet power. But doubtless, if we were to consider a Communist Party group at a lower level of influence than the Central Committee, we would find that industry makes a more substantial contribution to the total membership.

Another Party group worth examining is the Praesidium of the Central Committee of the Communist Party, the peak group chosen out of the Central Committee. In view of the transformation of the membership of this body between the 1956 and 1959 national Communist Party Congresses, let us consider separately the backgrounds of those men who remained in the Praesidium, those who were dropped, and those who were added during these years of internal Party strife.

MEMBERS OF THE PRAESIDIUM
OF THE CENTRAL COMMITTEE

PREVIOUS FULL-TIME OCCUPATIONS	MEMBERS FEB. 1956 AND NOT FEB. 1959		MEMBERS FEB. 1956 AND ALSO FEB. 1959		MEMBERS FEB. 1959 AND NOT FEB. 1956	
	No.	%	No.	%	No.	%
Party official only	0	0	0	0	3	33
Never a Party official	3	50	1	20	0	0
Party official as well as holder of other posts	3	50	4	80	6	67
Industry official as well as holder of other posts	5	83	0	0	1	11
TOTAL	6		5		9	

Looking at these statistics, we can readily see that the Party strife of 1957–58 enlarged the proportion of Praesidium members whose known careers have been entirely within the Party bureaucracy. Moreover, it reduced from five to one the number who had had careers within industry. In this sense, the changing membership of the Praesidium might be interpreted as a defeat for the industrial managers of the Soviet Union.

On the other hand, it would be very wrong to draw strong conclusions from a shift in the membership of such a small body as the Praesidium. With only tiny numbers of individuals involved, it may easily have been coincidence that the new and old members should have such differing backgrounds.

What strikes me as more impressive and meaningful than the change in industrial backgrounds is the fact that the Praesidium has not, either now or earlier, been dominated by men whose careers were solely inside the Party. In 1956, there were no such men. Today, there are still only three out of fourteen.

Considering all the evidence together, there seems to be no sound basis for differentiating between a "management class" and a class of "full-time Communist Party officials." The two groups are highly similar in income, education, political activity, and even in the fact of having as members the same individuals at different stages of their career.

Moreover, there seems no reason to categorize the Party official as the fire-eating ideological fanatic, thus contrasting him with the businesslike manager who has strong vested interests in existing society. The Party official, after all, is also primarily an administrator—normally concerned with all the problems of his specific geographic region. He can perform this function quite well even if he is not particularly acquainted with or interested in the fine points of Marxist ideology, world revolution, or foreign policy. He may indeed have such special intellectual interests, as may the manager of a factory or the head of an industry; for both, however, such interests are essentially extracurricular.

It may well be that the present-day Soviet leadership has more of a desire to preserve the *status quo* and to build further upon it than was the case in earlier periods of Soviet history. It may be, as is often argued, that the Soviet Union can be expected to move even further in the direction of "settling down." But if these theories should in fact turn out to be correct, it will not be due to the rise of a Soviet "managerial class." Instead, it will be a result of influences which affect all of the Soviet upper class—Party as well as industrial.

If we turn our glance to American business, much the same conclusions would seem to hold. It is difficult to delimit a specifically "business" class whose members have far more in common with one another than with other upper-class individuals in our culture. A specifically "business" ideology—particularly as it relates to foreign affairs—would be even harder to identify.

As to the strength of American business in dominating American politics, it is true that businessmen have lately shown increasing political appeal. The 1958 nomination of the scions of two of America's great fortunes as candidates for governor of our most populous state is a political phenomenon which would hardly have seemed possible twenty-five years earlier. Yet the great changes in government which were heralded as the expected fruits of the Eisenhower "businessman's government" have failed to materialize. This is particularly the case in the area of foreign affairs. Businessmen have, in fact, shown increasing reluctance to take up government posts. The glorious days of 1952, with the expectation of major change now that business at last was in the saddle, are long past.

Thus, both in Russia and the United States, the dream that businessmen comprise a very special and powerful force for peace seems to remain only a dream. Moreover, in neither country is there a noticeable tendency for business interests to grow markedly in their political power. In neither country is there reason to believe that business groups respond to international politics and crises in ways which are peculiar to themselves, and different from those of other members of the upper class of their society. In short, it seems to me that business plays no special role in either soothing or exciting the waves of emotion and national interest which disturb the peace of the world.

EPILOGUE

The Red Executive has come far since the days of the Revolution. Today he is a college-educated engineer with a sound technical and administrative background, and he bears little resemblance to the flamboyant Party director of the early days whose credentials were years in Tsarist prisons, escapes from exile, and oratory exercised in stirring the masses. But the present-day Red Executive is also no throwback to the bourgeois plant manager of the late twenties and early thirties who, for all his education, was distrusted as an enemy of the Revolution and a potential saboteur. Today's executive combines sound training with the political assurance and power which permit him the freedom to make creative use of this training.

The Soviet manager may not live well when judged by the standards of his American counterpart, but he does quite satisfactorily compared to the ordinary Soviet citizen. He is given powerful monetary incentives to turn in a first-rate job. Yet never in his life will he have any certainty of tenure in his post. No civil service rules or old-school tie protect him; his superiors show a marked impatience with failure. This impatience, it is true, is now tempered more with common sense than was the case in the past. No longer, as often occurred during the mid-1930's, do production lapses lead swiftly to charges of sabotage and to a forced-labor camp. Nevertheless, blunders can result in swift demotion. The executive ulcer rate is high.

The Russian manager is a man with power, but he is no independent decision-maker. He is an organization man, filling a slot in an industrial bureaucracy which has lines reaching to the very heights of Soviet power. His production goals, his costs, and even his industrial research objectives are set for him.

Moreover, he must establish and maintain successful contact with the members of other powerful bureaucracies—and in particular with that of the Communist Party.

But if the manager's goals are established for him, their achievement is his personal responsibility. No excuse exists for failure. Often, the drive to meet quotas will force him into illegal activities; this cannot be helped. It is a basic part of his task to determine what is necessary in order to "succeed"; in this sense, the Red Executive is very much an independent businessman.

The Soviet manager is oriented to production. Volume of output is the acid test of his work. Marketing is no problem; finance is a trivial concern. But the purchasing department is the rock on which the factory organization stands, for supply shortages lead to production shortages. A good procurement man is above price.

Although the situation is now in the process of change, raw materials and machinery are still the items of greatest scarcity to the Russian manager. It is these which are his bottlenecks. Labor, of course, is also a problem—but a labor-saving device is not nearly as valuable to him as is one which saves materials or which permits more production from a machine. Thus, the Soviet manager tends to emphasize in his daily work different problems and different shortages than does the American company president or even the plant superintendent.

Well trained, well disciplined, politically conscious and active, the Red Executive seems a figure permanently established in the seats of the mighty. There is no justification for picturing him as a man in conflict with the Communist Party official, the two uneasily sharing power for the moment. Rather, the industrial manager and the Party secretary are old classmates, neighbors, and colleagues, seeing the world from the same perspective.

Neither the Red Executive nor his Party-official colleague is any longer the revolutionary of the 1920's to whom ideology was everything. Both are men well established in the second most powerful country in the world, with enormous personal stakes in world stability and in peace. When Marx in the *Communist Manifesto* appealed for world revolution, he addressed himself to the worker who had "nothing to lose but his chains." The Red Executive and the Party administrator have a great deal more to lose—and they know it well. Their attitude toward world revolution and other threats to peace must inevitably bear the imprint of this knowledge.

SOURCES

My background for writing this book is that of an eleven-year professional interest in problems of Soviet economics and management. This interest has led me into the use of a wide variety of Soviet sources, from official statistical tabulations to newspapers and technical journals.

During the summer of 1958 I spent a month in the Soviet Union. This trip is the source of many of the anecdotes, descriptions of particular factories, and analyses of educational facilities and methods which have been presented in this book. Any such firsthand experience, however, is likely to give rise to highly misleading conclusions. This danger is a result of the limitations of time and spatial coverage which are inherent in the process of one person's trying to observe everything himself. I have done my best to guard against the error of misinterpretation by being careful to evaluate my own experience against the accounts of other visitors to the Soviet Union and of Russian émigrés, as well as against the background of a personal knowledge of the Soviet Union acquired from secondary sources over the years.

Finally, some intensive work has been done in accumulating data about American industry. Here, as in the Russian case, I have relied mainly upon the printed word. But I have also leaned on a series of brief studies of American factories which I carried on during 1957, and on the impressions gained firsthand by some of my colleagues at the Graduate School of Industrial Administration, Carnegie Institute of Technology.

Figures as to both Russia and the United States are mostly taken from official statistical collections. The general view of American experts is that the use of Russian statistics is no task for the novice; such statistics are often incomplete or deliberately misleading, and not infrequently they are based upon curious and unexpected definitions which are not carefully spelled out. Nevertheless, given an awareness by the user of the problems involved, the statistics are considered by most authorities as reasonably reliable.

It is quite impossible to list all of the sources used in this book. Most are books, magazines, and newspapers written in the Russian language, and thus of no interest to the general reader. However, the following short list of English-language works may be useful for some readers:

I. WORKS ON THE SOVIET ECONOMY:

a. Soviet industrial management

David Granick, *Management of the Industrial Firm in the USSR* (Columbia University Press, New York, 1954)

Joseph S. Berliner, *Factory and Manager in the USSR* (Harvard University Press, Cambridge, 1957)

b. Other aspects of Soviet industry

Steel in the Soviet Union (American Iron and Steel Institute, New York, 1958). Report of visit to the U.S.S.R. of May 21–June 21, 1958.
 (for Chapters Two, Seven, Fifteen)

Michael Kaser, "The Reorganization of Soviet Industry and Its Effects on Decision-Making"; Gregory Grossman, ed., *Symposium on Economic Calculation and Organization in Eastern Europe* (University of California Press, Berkeley, forthcoming)
 (for Chapter Eleven)

Walter Galenson, *Labor Productivity in Soviet and American Industry* (Columbia University Press, New York, 1955)
 (for Chapter Fifteen)

c. Soviet labor

Emily Clark Brown, "Labor Relations in Soviet Factories,"

Industrial and Labor Relations Review, January 1958.
(for Chapter Thirteen)

d. Soviet foreign aid and trade

Joseph S. Berliner, *Soviet Economic Aid* (Frederick A. Praeger, Inc., New York, 1958)
(for Chapter Eighteen)

e. Soviet biographies

Institute for the Study of the USSR, Munich, *Biographic Directory of the USSR* (Scarecrow Press, Inc., New York, 1958)
(for Chapters Eight and Eighteen)

II. WORKS ON THE AMERICAN ECONOMY:

a. Management compensation and functions

Bureau of National Affairs, *Personnel Policies Forum*.
(for Chapters Two and Sixteen)

b. Business and legal violations

Edwin H. Sutherland, *White Collar Crime* (The Dryden Press, New York, 1949)
(for Chapter Two)

c. Business recruitment and education

W. Lloyd Warner and James C. Abegglen, *Occupational Mobility in American Business and Industry 1928–1952* (University of Minnesota Press, Minneapolis, 1955)
(for Chapters Three to Six, Eight)

Mabel Newcomer, *The Big Business Executive* (Columbia University Press, New York, 1955)
(for Chapter Three)

d. Consumption patterns of the upper-income group

Study of Consumer Expenditures, Incomes and Savings. Statistical Tables, Urban U.S.—1950. Tabulated by the Bureau of Labor Statistics, U.S. Department of Labor for the Wharton School of Finance and Commerce, Univer-

sity of Pennsylvania (University of Pennsylvania, 1956)
(for Chapter Seven)

e. White-collar personnel; materials handling

Seymour Melman, *Dynamic Factors in Industrial Productivity* (John Wiley and Sons, Inc., New York, 1956)
(for Chapters Eleven and Fifteen)

f. General Motors and decentralization

Peter F. Drucker, *Concept of the Corporation* (The John Day Company, New York, 1946)
(for Chapter Eleven)

g. Shareholders and managers

Robert Aaron Gordon, *Business Leadership in the Large Corporation* (The Brookings Institution, Washington, D.C., 1945)
(for Chapter Twelve)

Lewis H. Kimmel, *Share Ownership in the U.S.* (The Brookings Institution, Washington, D.C., 1952)
(for Chapter Twelve)

h. Time study

Adam Abruzzi, "The Quest for Certainty," *The Journal of Industrial Engineering,* September–October 1958.
(for Chapter Thirteen)

III. WORKS ON THE ECONOMIES OF OTHER COUNTRIES:

David S. Landes, "French Business and the Businessman: A Social and Cultural Analysis"; Edward M. Earle, ed., *Modern France* (Princeton University Press, New York, 1951)
(for Chapter Three)

Richard A. Lester, "Reflections on Collective Bargaining in Britain and Sweden," *Industrial and Labor Relations Review,* April 1957.
(for Chapter Thirteen)

INDEX

Abegglen, James C., 36, 46, 48, 74, 82–83, 115, 147

Abruzzi, Adam, 179

Accidents, industrial, 18–19

Administrators, growing number, 140–44

Afghanistan, 259

Aid program, underdeveloped countries, 258–65

American Management Association, 107, 131, 180

Ancestors, importance, 35–45

Apartments, 16–18, 92–94. *See also* Housing conditions

Appeals, 176–77

Argentina, 259

Authority, managerial, 12–15

Automation, 201, 207

Automobiles, 97, 216

Bank, State, 203–4

Bennett, Harry, 127

Beria, 167, 169

Berliner, Joseph, 133

Birth control, 90

Blaw-Knox Company, 130

Board of directors, 161–62, 169–70, 174, 177

Bolsheviks, 84

Bonus system, 4, 108–11. *See also* Incentives

Boss-dominated business, 196–97

Bottlenecks, 151–52

Brick production, 135

British trade unions, 192–93

Brown, Emily Clark, 195

Budgeting, 229–30

Bulganin, 113, 187

Bureaucracy, breaking up the, 117–56; how to live with, 127–40; nature of, 119–28; size of the, 141–56

Burma, 259

Business administration schools, 52–54

Business-school graduates, first job, 78–79

Business Week, 83

California, University of, 161

Cambodia, 259

Camps for children, 17–18, 98

Capital gains, 173, 253

Carnegie Institute of Technology, 52, 60, 62

Catherine the Great, 125

Central authority, 135

Central Committee, Communist Party, 165, 176–77, 193, 203, 275

Central planning for industry, 121

Centralization, 123, 136, 234, 238

Ceylon, 259

Changeovers, plant, 216–20
Chelyabinsk, 27
Children, 17–18, 98
China, 8, 262
Chinoy, Ely, 244
Class stability, 39
Clemenceau, Georges, 201
Clothing expenditures, 95–96
College education, 4–5, 8
Columbia University, 52
Commissar, clash with Party Secretary, 165–77
Communication upward, 148–50
Communist Manifesto, 60, 280–81
Communist Party, 7, 9, 16, 23–27, 30, 40, 54, 61, 92, 101, 121, 124–25, 137, 145–47, 160, 165–69, 171–77, 183, 193–94, 196, 199–200, 202–4, 272–73, 275–76, 280–81
Company training program, 56–57. *See also* On-the-job training
Competition, economic, 251–65; managerial, with Party officials, 12–15
Compromise, 159, 175
Comptroller, factory, 128, 150
Comsomol. *See* Young Communist League
Congressional committees, 201–2
Conspicuous consumption, 105
Constitution, Soviet, 6
Consumer-be-damned attitude, 216
Consumer spending, 99, 101
Contracts, union, 189–90, 195–96
Control, circle of, 200–4
Co-ordination, problems of, 152

Council of Ministers, 25, 125, 165–66, 176, 202, 245
Creative-problem solving, 65
Criminal responsibility, managerial, 30–31
Custom-made clothing, 96–97
Cut-and-try research methods, 57–58

Decentralization, 120, 129–31, 140, 153
Decision-making, 122–23, 132–33, 136, 160, 202, 204
Democracy, Communist Party, 166–69
Depression of 1930's, 46, 68
Design, 223–26; research, 57–58
Detroit, 220
Development, 223–26; economic, planning, 121–22
Diesel motors, 219
Diploma defense, 65–67
Directives, Communist Party, 25
Discrimination, class, 44–45
Dispatchers, shop, 77–78
Divorce, 171–72
Dnieper River, 99
Doctors, 98, 222
Drop-out rate, educational, 68–69
Drucker, Peter F., 146–47
Dues, Communist Party, 171; trade union, 92

Earnings per capita, 105
Economic competition, 251–65
Economic development, planning, 121–22
Economic growth, 246–47
Economic pressures in Soviet plant, 246–47
Economists, shop, 78

Education, business administration, 52–54; college, 49–50; diploma defense, 65–67; dropout rate, 68–69; engineering, 51–52; evening classes, 72–73; examinations, 61, 63–64; extension courses, 72; financial institutes, 53; general, 48–50; high school, 78–79; managerial, 55–56; marketing institutes, 53; night school, 72–73; professional, 48–51; research institutes, 217–18, 226; specialized, 55–56; utilitarian, 50–51. *See also* Training

Egypt, 259

Eisenhower, Dwight D., 277

Electric Meter Plant, Moscow, 7, 23

Employment, full, 256

Enforcement organs, 203–4

Engineering-Economic Institute, Leningrad, 5, 53–54, 66, 71, 78

Engineers, 223; graduate, first job, 78, 83, 85

Entertainment expenditures, 98–99

Espionage system, 150; organizational rivalry and, 127–28

Evening classes, 72–73

Evening Moscow, 24

Examinations, 61, 63–64

Expenditures, clothing, 95–96; consumer spending, 98–99; entertainment, 98–99; food, 95–96; living expenses, student, 98; medical care, 98; rent, 95; transportation, 97; vacation, 98

Extension courses, 72

Factories, 207–26; running, 227–47

Factory housing, 94–95

"Family atmosphere," creation, 149–50

Family business, 35

Family origin, 35–45

Family patterns, 90

Family unit, 90

Favors, personal, 29

Federal Trade Commission, 159, 201

Financial incentives, 28–29, 43

Financial institutes, 53

Five-Year Plan, first, 121, 148

Flexibility, size of factory and, 238–40

Food expenditures, 95–96

Ford, Henry, 216

Foreign aid program, 258–65

Foreman, the, 240–45

Foreman's Association of America, 242

Fork trucks, 211–12

Formative years, managers in, 35–85

Fortune, 243

Free enterprise, 27–30

Freight handlers, 211–12

Gary, Judge, 131

General education, 48–50

General Motors Corporation, 130–31, 146–47, 154, 189–90, 201

Germany, 267

Gordon, Robert A., 161

Gorky automobile plant, 216

Government-owned industry, 121

Grades, students', 67–71

Grievances, 194–95

Growth, economic, 251–58

"Hammer and Sickle" Plant, 19, 218
Hat and Cap union, 191
Heroes, national, 166, 183–84
Hierarchy, Communist Party, 165–67, 204
High-pressure system, 151
High school graduates, 78, 223
Highways, 255
Hours of work, 107–8, 255
Housing conditions, 16–18, 27–28, 93–94, 102, 106, 255
Human relations, training in, 81, 85

Incentive system, 27–30, 108–11, 178–79, 185–86, 253
Income, family, 92–94, 100, 106
India, 259
Indoctrination, 9–10, 144–48
Indonesia, 259
Industrial relations, 145, 154–55
Inflation, 101, 188
Informal groups at work, 178–89
Internal Revenue Department, 201
Information, upward flow, 126–28
Innovations, technical, 83
Inspection, 212–14, 237–38
Installment buying, 99
Internal-combustion motors, 219
International trade, 266–69
Intourist agency, 13, 207
Investment control, 140
Investment funds, 214
Investment programs, 20–22

Japan, 260, 267
Job experience, early, 74–79, 85

Job security, 112–14
Joslyn, 114
Justice Department, 201
Juvenile delinquency, 104–5

Kaganovich, 169, 275
Keynes, Lord, 71
Kharkov, 18–19, 207–8, 211, 218–19
Khrushchev, 45, 62, 90, 137, 165–67, 169, 176, 252, 275
Kiev, 15–16, 93, 232
Kiev University, 15
Kirov, 166
Kogovt, Pavel, 172

Labor, 6
Labor camps, 6
Labor Party, British, 192
Landes, David, 35
Lapointe Machine Tool Company, 180
Leadership training, 55, 81
Learning curve, 182–83
Lebanon, 259
Legitimacy, sources of, Communist Party, 166
Leibnitz, 51
Leisure-time activities, 100–1
Lenin, Nikolai, 59, 84, 166
Leningrad, 15, 19, 28–29, 67, 78, 92, 97, 109, 139, 166, 217–18
Leningrad Economic Council, 78
Leningrad University, 60, 72
Life expectancy, managerial, 30–31
Living expenses, student, 29
Loose standards, 186–87

Magnotogorsk steel works, 19

Maintenance, 214–16, 221

Maintenance organization, 234–37

Malenkov, 275

Malenkov-Molotov-Kaganovich coalition, 167

Management, 12, 20; middle, 132, 154–55; shop, 227–29; top, 148, 155, 161–62; worker, 181; worker participation in, 197

Management-governed corporations, 162–64

Managerial, authority, 12–15; class, 269–78; education, subject matter, 55–57; game, the, 107–15; life expectancy, 30–31; recruitment, 22–24; revolution, American, 160–64

Manual workers, 72

Market, role of the, 150–56. *See also* Sellers' market

Marketing, 8; institutes, 53

Martyrs, Russian, 166

Marx, Karl, 84, 280–81

Marxism, 12, 58, 84, 166

Masters, Edgar Lee, 35

Materials handling, 211–12

Means, 162

Medical care expenditures, 98

Membership, Communist Party, 168–69, 171–73, 273

Middle management, 132, 154–55

Mikoyan, Anastas, 3, 266, 269

Ministry of Agriculture, 213

Ministry of Higher Education, 66, 71–72

Ministry of Heavy Machine-building, 47

Ministry of Light Industry, 47

Molotov, V. M., 132, 169, 275

Moscow, 13, 15, 18, 28, 76–77, 89, 92–94, 97–98, 107, 121–22, 124, 132–33, 135, 138, 167, 174, 186, 198, 209, 223, 272

Moscow City Council, 14–15, 20, 23–24, 28, 77, 92, 94, 109

Moscow News, 19

Moscow Public Library, 231

Moscow State Economic Institute, 53, 70, 72, 78

National Labor-Management Conference, 189

National Plan of 1956, 124–25, 159–60

National War Labor Board, 242

Natural resources, depletion, 253–54

Nepal, 259

Newcomer, Mabel, 36

New Economic Policy, 120

New Moscow University, 15

New York City, 220

Nicholas I, 127

Night routine, 107–8

Night school, 72–73

Nobel prize, 165

Occupational mobility, 41

O'Neill, Eugene, 103

On-the-job training, 56–57, 72–79, 85

Opportunity, equality of, 42–43

Organization, maintenance, 234–37; quality-control, 237–38

Organization chart, new Russian, 137–40

"Organization man," 44–45, 80–81

Organizational centralization, 122–23

Organizational personality, 144–48

Organizational pressures in Soviet plant, 246–47

Organizational rivalry and espionage, 127–28

Owner-manager, 163

Output restriction, 178, 181–82, 188, 197–98

Paraguay, 259

Penalties for failure, 113

Pension system, 101

Peter the Great, 166

Physical sciences, 59

Physical training, 19

Piece-rate payment system, 109, 178–80, 182–84, 186

Planning system, 20–22

Plant changeovers, 216–20

Plant committee, Communist Party, 25

Plant quotas, 184–85

Polish industries, 111

Polish Planning Commission, 263

Political prisoners, 30–31

Potemkin, 125

"Potemkin villages," 125

Praesidium of the Communist Party, 6, 25, 124–25, 160, 165–66, 169, 175–77, 202–4, 275–76

Pre-Khrushchev Russia, 131–37

Pressures, economic, 246–47; high-pressure system, 151; reorganizational, 246–47

Price-fixing, 159

Product, the, 216–20

Production Handbook, 214

Production meeting, 198–99

Production scheduling, 180

Production targets, 229–30

Professional education, 48–51

Profitability, 154–56

Profit incentive, 27–28

"Proletariat," the, 44–45

Propaganda, political, 194

Public service, 164

Pugachev, 166

Purges, 30, 40, 135, 166

Quality control, 212–14; organization, 237–38

Quit rate, 185–86

Railroads, 255

Reading, 103–4

Ready-made clothing, 96

Recruitment, managerial, 22–24

Regional councils, 137–38

Regional Economic Council, Leningrad, 14, 46

Rent expenditure, 92

Research, 223–26

Research design, 57

Research institutes, 217–18, 225

Revision of standards, 187

Revolution of 1917, 39, 41

Running the factory, 227–47

Safety, industrial, 18–20

Savings, 99–100

Scanlon Plan, 197

Scarcity of materials, 217

Second Socialist International, 266

Secrecy, 15–16

Secret Police, 204

Secretary, Communist Party, 25–27, 149, 165–77

Sector for Foreign Relations, 14

Securities and Exchange Commission, 164

Security, job, 112–14
Security-consciousness, 15–16
Sellers' Market, 21–22, 217, 246
Shift work, 220–21
Shop dispatchers, 78
Shop economists, 78
Shop management, 227–29
Shop stewards, 181–82, 191–92
Shvernik, 193
Silberstein, Leopold, 162
Size of factories, 209–11; flexibility and, 238–40
Smith, Adam, 119, 163–64
Social classes, 80, 82
Social mobility, 41–43
Social origin, 36, 39
Social sciences, 59–60
Specialized education, 55–56
Staff groups, 150
Stakhanovite movement, 183–84
Stalin, Joseph, 6, 25, 30, 59, 89, 107, 113, 167, 169, 194, 252
Standardization, 256–57
State Planning Commission, 11, 20, 140, 262
Stewards, shop, 181–82, 191–92
Stipends, cash, 29–30, 70–71
Stockholders, 159–77
Storming, 230–34
Streetcars, 97–98
Strikes, 6, 183, 190–92
Student, the Russian, 4–5, 67–68
Style obsolescence, 257
Subcontractors, 152
Subway, 97–98
Such a Love, 172
Sudan, 259
Suggestion system, 196–200
Summer homes, 99
Supreme Soviet, 165
Sutherland, Edwin H., 31
Suvorov, General, 166

Syria, 259

Taft-Hartley Law, 242
Taussig, 114
Taxes, 29, 92
Teachers, 222
Technological ideas, receptivity to, 83
Tennessee Valley Authority, 144
"Test of the market," evaluation method, 153
Theses, individual, 65–67, 231–32
Three-shift program, 221
Threshing machines, 218–19
"Ticket" system, 61–62
Time-and-motion study, 178
Top management, 148, 155, 161–62
Tractor Plant, Kharkov, 18
Trade. See International trade
Trade unions, 189–96. See also British trade unions
Training, company program, 56–57; leadership, 55; on-the-job, 56–57, 74–79, 80–81; physical, 19; within industry, 56–57, 74–79
Train travel, 97–98
Transfers in business posts, 203–4
Transportation expenditures, 97–98
Trucks, fork, 211–12
Truman, Harry S., 189
Turkey, 259
Turnover, executive, 112–14, 186
Two-shift program, 220

Ulcers, 107–8

Underdeveloped countries, 258–65

Unemployment, 256

Union of Soviet Writers, 165

Unions. *See* Trade unions

United Arab Republic, 260

United Automobile Workers, 190

United Nations, 260

United States Steel Company, 131, 159

Upward mobility, 114–15

Urals Machinebuilding Plant, 136, 244

Utilitarian education, 50–51

Vassar College, 195

Vacation expenditures, 98

Veblen, Thorstein, 84, 105

Wage minimum, 92

Wallace, Henry, 260

Warner, W. Lloyd, 36, 46, 48, 74, 82–83, 115, 147

War Production Board, 197

Watchfulness, 15–16

Way of Life, Russian executive's, 89–106

White Collar Crime, 31

Wilson, Charles E., 189

Women workers, 221–22

Worker management, 181

Worker participation in management, 197

Working conditions, 18–20

Working students, 68

Yemen, 259

Young Communist League (Comsomol), 54

Yugoslavia, 259

ANCHOR BOOKS

ADAMS, HENRY Democracy *and* Esther A243
——————— A Henry Adams Reader A177
——————— Mont-Saint-Michel and Chartres A166
ALAIN-FOURNIER, HENRI The Wanderer A14
ALBRIGHT, W. F. From the Stone Age to Christianity A100
ALLPORT, GORDON W. The Nature of Prejudice A149
ANDRADE, E. N. DA C. An Approach to Modern Physics A111
——————— Sir Isaac Newton A151
ARENDT, HANNAH The Human Condition A182
ARISTOPHANES Five Comedies A57
ARON, RAYMOND On War A171
AUDEN, W. H.; GREENBERG, NOAH; KALLMAN, CHESTER An Elizabethan Song Book A56
AUERBACH, ERICH Mimesis A107
BARK, WILLIAM CARROLL Origins of the Medieval World A190
BARTH, KARL Community, State and Church A221
BARZUN, JACQUES Classic, Romantic and Modern A255
——————— Darwin, Marx, Wagner A127
——————— Teacher in America A25
BATE, WALTER JACKSON Prefaces to Criticism A165
BAUDELAIRE, CHARLES The Mirror of Art A84
BEDIER, JOSEPH The Romance of Tristan and Iseult A2
BEERBOHM, MAX A Selection from "Around Theatres" A226
BEETHOVEN Letters, Journals and Conversations A206
BENTLEY, ERIC (Ed.) The Classic Theatre I: Six Italian Plays A155a
——————— The Classic Theatre II: Five German Plays A155b
——————— The Classic Theatre III: Six Spanish Plays A155c
BENTLEY, ERIC (Ed.) The Modern Theatre I, II, III, IV, V, VI A48a, A48b, A48c, A48d, A48e, A48f
——————— From the American Drama (The Modern Theatre IV) A48d
BERENSON, BERNARD Aesthetics and History A36
BERGSON, HENRI "Laughter" in Comedy A87
——————— Matter and Memory A172
——————— The Two Sources of Morality and Religion A28
BETTELHEIM, BRUNO Paul and Mary: Two Case Histories from *Truants from Life* A237
BISHOP, AMASA Project Sherwood, A202
BLACKMUR, R. P. Form and Value in Modern Poetry A96
BRENNER, CHARLES An Elementary Textbook of Psychoanalysis A102
BROGAN, D. W. Politics in America, A198
BROOKS, VAN WYCK America's Coming of Age A129
BROWN, ROBERT McAFEE and GUSTAVE WEIGEL, S.J.
    An American Dialogue A257
BURCKHARDT, JACOB The Age of Constantine the Great A65
BURTT, EDWIN ARTHUR The Metaphysical Foundations of Modern Science A41
BUTTERFIELD, HERBERT and OTHERS A Short History of Science A180
CABLE, GEORGE W. Creoles and Cajuns A179
——————— The Negro Question A144
CARY, JOYCE A Fearful Joy A242
CASSIRER, ERNST An Essay on Man A3
CASTIGLIONE, BALDESAR The Book of the Courtier A186
CHAPMAN, JOHN JAY The Selected Writings of John Jay Chapman A161
CHASE, RICHARD The American Novel and Its Tradition A116
CHEKHOV, ANTON Peasants and Other Stories A66
CLARK, KENNETH The Nude A168

COLETTE   My Mother's House and The Vagabond A62
CONANT, JAMES B.   Modern Science and Modern Man A10
CONNOLLY, CYRIL   Enemies of Promise and Other Essays, A194
CONRAD, JOSEPH   Chance A113
————————   A Mirror of the Sea and A Personal Record A207
————————   The Rescue, A199
————————   The Rover A240
————————   The Secret Agent A8
————————   The Shadow-Line and Two Other Tales A178
————————   Tales of Heroes and History A228
————————   Victory A106
————————   Youth: A Narrative and Two Other Stories A173
COULANGES, FUSTEL DE   The Ancient City A76
CRANE, HART   The Complete Poems of Hart Crane A128
CROMBIE, A. C.   Medieval and Early Modern Science: I, II A167a, A167b
DANTZIG, TOBIAS   Number, the Language of Science A67
DICKINSON, EMILY   Selected Poems and Letters A192
DIDEROT, DENIS   Rameau's Nephew and Other Works A61
DOLLARD, JOHN   Caste and Class in a Southern Town A95
DOSTOEVSKY, FYODOR   Three Short Novels A193
DOUGHTY, C. M.   Travels in Arabia Deserta A50
DUBOS, RENE   Mirage of Health A258
DUMAS, ALEXANDRE   Adventures in Spain A211
DUPEE, F. W.   Henry James A68
EDEL, LEON   Literary Biography A188
ESSLIN, MARTIN   Brecht: The Man and His Work A245
FERGUSSON, FRANCIS   The Human Image in Dramatic Literature A124
————————   The Idea of a Theatre A4
FINCH, JAMES K.   The Story of Engineering A214
FLORES, ANGEL (Ed.)   An Anthology of French Poetry A134
————————   An Anthology of German Poetry A197
————————   Nineteenth Century French Tales A217
————————   Nineteenth Century German Tales A184
FLORNOY, BERTRAND   The World of the Inca A137
FORSTER, E. M.   Alexandria: A History and a Guide A231
FORTUNE, EDITORS OF   The Exploding Metropolis A146
FRANKFORT, HENRI   The Birth of Civilization in the Near East A89
FREUD, SIGMUND   Civilization and Its Discontents A130
————————   The Future of an Illusion A99
————————   A General Selection from the Works of A115
————————   The Origins of Psychoanalysis A112
FRY, ROGER   Transformations A77
GALILEO   Discoveries and Opinions A94
GARNETT, DAVID   Pocahontas A157
GASTER, T. H.   The Dead Sea Scriptures in English Translation A92
GEIRINGER, KARL   Brahms A248
GOFFMAN, ERVING   The Presentation of Self in Everyday Life A174
GOGOL, NICOLAI   Tales of Good and Evil A120
GONCOURT, EDMOND and JULES DE   The Goncourt Journals A158
GOYA, FRANCISCO DE   The Disasters of War AA1
GRANICK, DAVID   The Red Executive A246
GRANVILLE-BARKER, H. and HARRISON, G. B.   A Companion to
   Shakespeare Studies, A191
GRAVES, ROBERT   Good-Bye to All That A123
————————   The Poems of Robert Graves—Chosen by Himself A139
GREEN, HENRY   Loving A18
HADAS, MOSES (Ed.)   A History of Rome A78
————————(Ed)   The Stoic Philosophy of Seneca A148
————————(Trans.)   Three Greek Romances A21
HAGGIN, B. H.   The Listener's Musical Companion A183

HAHN, WALTER F. and NEFF, JOHN C. American Strategy for the Nuclear Age A224
HALL, ROBERT A. JR. Linguistics and Your Language A201
HAMILTON, ALEXANDER, MADISON, JAMES, and JAY, JOHN The Federalist Papers (Edited by Roy P. Fairfield) A239
HANDLIN, OSCAR Race and Nationality in American Life A110
HENDERSON, HAROLD An Introduction to Haiku A150
HERBERG, WILL Four Existentialist Theologians A141
————— Protestant, Catholic, Jew A195
HINDEMITH, PAUL A Composer's World A235
HOLT, ELIZABETH GILMORE A Documentary History of Art: I, II A114a, A114b
HOOVER, CALVIN B. The Economy, Liberty and the State A241
HUIZINGA, J. The Waning of the Middle Ages A42
IBSEN, HENRIK Brand A215
————— When We Dead Awaken and Three Other Plays A215b
JAMES, HENRY The Ambassadors A154
————— The Awkward Age A138
————— In the Cage and Other Tales A131
————— Selected Letters, A204
————— What Maisie Knew A43
JARRELL, RANDALL (Ed.) The Anchor Book of Stories A145
JASPERS, KARL Man in the Modern Age A101
JESPERSEN, OTTO Growth and Structure of the English Language A46
JEWETT, SARAH ORNE The Country of the Pointed Firs A26
JONES, ERNEST Hamlet and Oedipus A31
JUNG, C. G. Psyche and Symbol A136
KAFKA, FRANZ Amerika A49
KAUFMANN, WALTER Critique of Religion and Philosophy A252
————— From Shakespeare to Existentialism A213
KAZIN, ALFRED On Native Grounds A69
KEATS, JOHN Selected Letters A70
KIERKEGAARD, SOREN Either/Or, I, II A181a, A181b
————— Fear and Trembling and The Sickness Unto Death A30
————— Selections from the Writings of Kierkegaard A210
KISSINGER, HENRY Nuclear Weapons and Foreign Policy A152
KITTO, H. D. F. Greek Tragedy A38
KRAMER, SAMUEL NOAH History Begins at Sumer A175
————— (Ed.) Mythologies of the Ancient World A229
LASKY, MELVIN J. (Ed.) The Anchor Review: Number One A64, Number Two A109
LAWFORD, GIOVANNA The Human Frame A234
LAWRENCE, D. H. Sea and Sardinia and Selections from Twilight in Italy A39
————— Selected Letters of D. H. Lawrence (Edited by Diana Trilling) A236
————— Studies in Classic American Literature A5
LEAVIS, F. R. The Great Tradition A40
LERMONTOV, MIHAIL A Hero of Our Time A133
LEWIS, D. B. WYNDHAM François Villon A147
LEWIS, W. H. The Splendid Century A122
LUBELL, SAMUEL The Future of American Politics A71
LYNN, Kenneth S. The Comic Tradition in America A187
MALINOWSKI, BRONISLAW Magic, Science and Religion A23
MARX, KARL and ENGELS, FRIEDRICH Basic Writings on Politics and Philosophy A185
MATTINGLY, HAROLD Roman Imperial Civilisation A160
MAURIAC, FRANCOIS Thérèse A79
MELVILLE, HERMAN Redburn: His First Voyage A118
MEREDITH, GEORGE "An Essay on Comedy" in Comedy A87
MERWIN, W. S. Spanish Ballads A253

MEYERHOFF, HANS (Ed.) The Philosophy of History in Our Time A164

MILLER, PERRY (Ed.) The American Puritans: Their Prose and Poetry A80

———(Ed.) The American Transcendentalists: Their Prose and Poetry A119

MONTAIGNE, MICHEL DE The Complete Essays, Vols. I, II, III A227a, A227b, A227c

MURASAKI, LADY The Tale of Genji A55

——— The Tale of Genji, Part II A176

MURRAY, GILBERT Five Stages of Greek Religion A51

MURRAY, MARGARET The God of the Witches A212

NEALE, J. E. Queen Elizabeth I A105

NEHRU, JAWAHARLAL Discovery of India, A200

NIETZSCHE, FRIEDRICH The Birth of Tragedy and The Genealogy of Morals A81

ORTEGA Y GASSET, JOSE The Dehumanization of Art A72

ORWELL, GEORGE A Collection of Essays A29

PANOFSKY, ERWIN Meaning in the Visual Arts A59

PEIRCE, CHARLES S. Values in a Universe of Chance A126

PETERSEN, WILLIAM (Ed.) American Social Patterns A86

PETERSON, SPIRO (Ed.) The Counterfeit Lady Unveiled and Other Criminal Fiction of Seventeenth-Century England A232

PIERSON, GEORGE W. and LUNT, DUDLEY C. Tocqueville in America A189

PIRENNE, HENRI A History of Europe: I, II A156a, A156b

——— Medieval Cities A82

POLYA, G. How to Solve It A93

POWER, EILEEN Medieval People A32

PRAZ, MARIO The Flaming Heart A132

PROUST, MARCEL Pleasures and Days and Other Writings A97

RAHV, PHILIP Discovery of Europe A208

REPS, PAUL (Ed.) Zen Flesh, Zen Bones A233

RIESMAN, DAVID Constraint and Variety in American Education A135

——— The Lonely Crowd A16

——— Selected Essays from Individualism Reconsidered A58

RILKE, RAINER MARIA Selected Letters A223

ROUGEMONT, DENIS DE Love in the Western World A121

ROURKE, CONSTANCE American Humor A12

RUSSELL, BERTRAND Mysticism and Logic A104

SANTAYANA, GEORGE Character and Opinion in the United States A73

——— Three Philosophical Poets A17

SCHRODINGER, ERWIN What Is Life? A88

SCIAMA, D. W. The Unity of the Universe A247

SCOTT, GEOFFREY The Architecture of Humanism A33

SHATTUCK, ROGER The Banquet Years A238

SHAW, BERNARD Shaw on Music A53

SHERRINGTON, SIR CHARLES Man on His Nature A15

SIGERIST, HENRY E. The Great Doctors A140

SNOW, C. P. The Masters: A Novel A162

STEEGMULLER, FRANCIS The Grand Mademoiselle A205

STENDHAL The Charterhouse of Parma A1

——— Five Short Novels of Stendhal A153

——— On Love A103

STRINDBERG, AUGUST Six Plays A54

——— Five Plays A219

SUZUKI, D. T. Zen Buddhism A90

SYPHER, WYLIE (Ed.) Comedy A87

——— Four Stages of Renaissance Style A45

TAYLOR, A. E. Socrates A9

TITCHMARSH, E. C. Mathematics for the General Reader A169

TOCQUEVILLE, ALEXIS DE The European Revolution and the Correspondence with Gobineau A163
———————— The Old Regime and the French Revolution A60
TOKLAS, ALICE B. The Alice B. Toklas Cook Book A196
TRAVERSI, D. A. An Approach to Shakespeare A74
TRELAWNEY, E. J. The Last Days of Shelley and Byron A225
TREVELYAN, G. M. History of England I, II, III A22a, A22b, A22c
TRILLING, LIONEL The Liberal Imagination A13
———————— The Middle of the Journey A98
TROTSKY, LEON The Russian Revolution A170
TSAO HSUEH-CHIN Dream of the Red Chamber A159
TURGENEV, IVAN Selected Tales A203
TURNER, W. J. Mozart: The Man and His Works A24
VAN DOREN, MARK Shakespeare A11
VERGA, GIOVANNI The House by the Medlar Tree A47
VIDICH, ARTHUR J. and BENSMAN, JOSEPH Small Town in Mass Society A216
VIRGIL The Aeneid A20
WADDELL, HELEN The Wandering Scholars A63
WALEY, ARTHUR Three Ways of Thought in Ancient China A75
WEDGWOOD, C. V. The Thirty Years War A249
WESTON, JESSIE From Ritual to Romance A125
WHYTE, WILLIAM H., JR. The Organization Man A117
WIENER, NORBERT The Human Use of Human Beings A34
WILDER, THORNTON Heaven's My Destination A209
WILLEY, BASIL The Seventeenth Century Background A19
WILLIAMS, RAYMOND Culture and Society 1780–1950 A220
WILSON, EDMUND Eight Essays A37
———————— A Literary Chronicle: 1920–1950 A85
———————— A Piece of My Mind A143
———————— To the Finland Station A6
WOODWARD C. VANN Reunion and Reaction A83
WRIGHT, G. ERNEST and DAVID NOEL FREEDMAN, eds. The Biblical Archaeologist Reader A250
WRIGHT, G. ERNEST and FULLER, REGINALD H. The Book of the Acts of God A222
YEATS, WILLIAM BUTLER The Autobiography of William Butler Yeats A142
YARMOLINSKY, AVRAHM (Ed.) Soviet Short Stories A218
YOURCENAR, MARGUERITE Hadrian's Memoirs A108

DOLPHIN BOOKS AND DOLPHIN MASTERS

The bold face **M** indicates a Dolphin Master. Dolphin Masters are Dolphin Books in the editions of greatest importance to the teacher and student. In selecting the Dolphin Masters, the editors have taken particular pains to choose copies of the most significant edition (usually the first) by obtaining original books or their facsimiles or by having reproductions made of library copies of particularly rare editions. Facsimiles of original title pages and other appropriate material from the first edition are included in many Masters.

FICTION

JANE EYRE Charlotte Brontë	C5
THE SCARLET LETTER Nathaniel Hawthorne	C7
KIDNAPPED Robert Louis Stevenson	C8
THE RISE OF SILAS LAPHAM William Dean Howells	C9
UNCLE TOM'S CABIN Harriet Beecher Stowe **M**	C13
THE PRAIRIE James Fenimore Cooper	C14
THE PICTURE OF DORIAN GRAY Oscar Wilde	C15
THE WAY OF ALL FLESH Samuel Butler	C16
THE RED AND THE BLACK Stendhal	C17
PERE GORIOT Honoré de Balzac	C18
MADAME BOVARY Gustave Flaubert	C19
THE VICAR OF WAKEFIELD Oliver Goldsmith	C20
THE MILL ON THE FLOSS George Eliot	C21
JUDE THE OBSCURE Thomas Hardy	C22
MANON LESCAUT Abbé Prévost	C29
IVANHOE Sir Walter Scott	C31
A TALE OF TWO CITIES Charles Dickens	C32
NORTHANGER ABBEY and PERSUASION Jane Austen **M**	C34
THE MOONSTONE Wilkie Collins	C35
FRANKENSTEIN Mary Shelley	C44
THREE MEN IN A BOAT Jerome K. Jerome	C46
TALES OF THE GROTESQUE AND ARABESQUE Edgar Allan Poe **M**	C50
HIS MONKEY WIFE John Collier	C53
LOOKING BACKWARD (2000–1887) Edward Bellamy	C55
MOLL FLANDERS Daniel Defoe	C56
BARCHESTER TOWERS Anthony Trollope	C57
CRANFORD E. C. Gaskell	C60
THE RED BADGE OF COURAGE Stephen Crane	C61
ADAM BEDE George Eliot	C62
JOSEPH ANDREWS Henry Fielding	C63
A CHRISTMAS CAROL Charles Dickens	C65
VILLETTE Charlotte Brontë	C66
MOBY DICK Herman Melville	C70
TREASURE ISLAND Robert Louis Stevenson	C72
PRIDE AND PREJUDICE Jane Austen	C74
FAR FROM THE MADDING CROWD Thomas Hardy	C75
THE LOG OF A COWBOY Andy Adams	C77
BLACK BEAUTY Anna Sewell	C78
GULLIVER'S TRAVELS Jonathan Swift	C86

A HAZARD OF NEW FORTUNES William Dean Howells C88
QUENTIN DURWARD Sir Walter Scott C89
ALICE'S ADVENTURES UNDERGROUND and ALICE'S
     ADVENTURES IN WONDERLAND Lewis Carroll M C94
THE ADVENTURES OF HUCKLEBERRY FINN Mark Twain C98
ROBINSON CRUSOE Daniel Defoe C103
TRISTRAM SHANDY Laurence Sterne C104
BURIED ALIVE Arnold Bennett C105
WUTHERING HEIGHTS Emily Brontë C107
PORTRAIT OF A MAN WITH RED HAIR Hugh Walpole C108
THE MARBLE FAUN Nathaniel Hawthorne C110
AUTOCRAT OF THE BREAKFAST TABLE
     Oliver Wendell Holmes C111
MANSFIELD PARK Jane Austen C113
HARD TIMES Charles Dickens C114
THE DAMNATION OF THERON WARE Harold Frederic C116
THE RETURN OF THE NATIVE Thomas Hardy C119
THE EXPEDITION OF HUMPHRY CLINKER Tobias Smollett C120
THE HISTORY OF HENRY ESMOND, ESQ.
     William Makepeace Thackeray C121
EVELINA Fanny Burney C123
THE DAY OF THE TRIFFIDS John Wyndham C130
THE PRIVATE PAPERS OF HENRY RYECROFT
     George Gissing C131
THE ADVENTURES OF TOM SAWYER Mark Twain C133
THE WARDEN Anthony Trollope C134
TRILBY George du Maurier C135
TESS OF THE D'URBERVILLES Thomas Hardy C138
NEW GRUB STREET George Gissing C139
RODERICK RANDOM Tobias Smollett C140
DAVID HARUM Edward Noyes Westcott C146
EUGENIE GRANDET Honoré de Balzac C147
THE HOUSE OF THE SEVEN GABLES Nathaniel Hawthorne C148
EMMA Jane Austen C149
SILAS MARNER George Eliot C151
RESURRECTION Leo Tolstoy C152
THE MAYOR OF CASTERBRIDGE Thomas Hardy C153
ELSIE VENNER Oliver Wendell Holmes C154
SISTER CARRIE Theodore Dreiser C160
TWENTY THOUSAND LEAGUES UNDER THE SEA Jules Verne C167
AROUND THE WORLD IN EIGHTY DAYS Jules Verne C168
THE PATHFINDER James Fenimore Cooper C173
SENSE AND SENSIBILITY Jane Austen C174
BEN-HUR Lew Wallace C175
GREAT EXPECTATIONS Charles Dickens C181
OLIVER TWIST Charles Dickens C182
OMOO Herman Melville C183
KING SOLOMON'S MINES H. Rider Haggard C188
THE FANCHER TRAIN Amelia Bean C197
THE DEERSLAYER James Fenimore Cooper C199
THE SKETCHBOOK OF GEOFFREY CRAYON, GENT.
     Washington Irving M C206
THE SPY James Fenimore Cooper C207
NANA Emile Zola C208
SHE H. Rider Haggard C210
THE LAST OF THE MOHICANS James Fenimore Cooper C211
EREWHON Samuel Butler C212
THE EGOIST George Meredith C223
THE LUCK OF ROARING CAMP, AND OTHER SKETCHES
     Francis Bret Harte C226

LETTERS FROM MY MILL Alphonse Daudet   C232
AMELIA Henry Fielding   C233
BLACK GODS, GREEN ISLANDS
    Geoffrey Holder with Tom Harshman   C235
LITTLE WOMEN Louisa M. Alcott   C237
LITTLE MEN Louisa M. Alcott   C238
JO'S BOYS Louisa M. Alcott   C239
THE CHRONICLE OF THE CID The Southey Translation   C243
HANS BRINKER or THE SILVER SKATES Mary Mapes Dodge   C244
A WONDER-BOOK and TANGLEWOOD TALES
    Nathaniel Hawthorne   C245
THE PIONEERS James Fenimore Cooper   C247
THE SECRET OF LUCA Ignazio Silone
    Translated by Darina Silone   C251
THE PRINCE AND THE PAUPER Mark Twain   C254
THE SWISS FAMILY ROBINSON Johann Wyss   C255
TOM SAWYER ABROAD and TOM SAWYER, DETECTIVE
    Mark Twain   C256
THE SHELTERED LIFE Ellen Glasgow   C257
TOBY TYLER or TEN WEEKS WITH A CIRCUS James Otis   C258
DOCTOR THORNE Anthony Trollope   C259
THE BLITHEDALE ROMANCE Nathaniel Hawthorne   C260
THE PRISONER OF ZENDA Anthony Hope   C261
SYBIL, or THE TWO NATIONS Benjamin Disraeli   C262
THE SCARLET PIMPERNEL Baroness Orczy   C269
NEW ARABIAN NIGHTS Robert Louis Stevenson   C270
THE MYSTERY OF EDWIN DROOD Charles Dickens   C275
RAFFLES E. W. Hornung   C276
THE LAST DAYS OF POMPEII Edward Bulwer-Lytton   C277
THE BRONC PEOPLE William Eastlake   C282
THE LADY OF THE CAMELLIAS Alexandre Dumas, fils   C283
KENILWORTH Sir Walter Scott   C284
GALLEGHER AND OTHER STORIES Richard Harding Davis   C285
HEIDI Johanna Spyri   C286
TYPEE: A PEEP AT POLYNESIAN LIFE Herman Melville   C291
THE MYSTERIOUS ISLAND Jules Verne   C292
ALTON LOCKE Charles Kingsley   C295
ISRAEL POTTER: HIS FIFTY YEARS OF EXILE
    Herman Melville   C296
GERMINAL Emile Zola   C297
FICTION OF THE FIFTIES Herbert Gold, ed.   C299
THROUGH THE LOOKING-GLASS and THE HUNTING OF
    THE SNARK Lewis Carroll   C300
THE WAR OF THE WORLDS and THE TIME MACHINE
    H. G. Wells C304
BILLY BUDD and THE PIAZZA TALES Herman Melville   C307

POETRY AND DRAMA

THE DIVINE COMEDY OF DANTE ALIGHIERI: THE INFERNO
    Translated by Henry Wadsworth Longfellow M   C1
LEAVES OF GRASS Walt Whitman M   C3
LYRICAL BALLADS William Wordsworth and
    Samuel Taylor Coleridge M   C4
POEMS OF KEATS AND SHELLEY (1820) M   C11
INVITATION TO POETRY Lloyd Frankenberg   C24
archy and mehitabel don marquis   C26
RUBAIYAT OF OMAR KHAYYAM Edward FitzGerald, translator C28

SHAKESPEARE'S SONNETS M C33
THE GOLDEN TREASURY OF ENGLISH SONGS AND LYRICS
    Francis Turner Palgrave M C45
THE DRAMATIC WORKS OF SHERIDAN
    Richard Brinsley Sheridan M C47
THE DIVINE COMEDY OF DANTE ALIGHIERI: PURGATORIO
    Translated by Henry Wadsworth Longfellow M C51
THE DIVINE COMEDY OF DANTE ALIGHIERI: PARADISO
    Translated by Henry Wadsworth Longfellow M C52
DON JUAN Lord Byron C64
PARADISE LOST John Milton C73
MEN AND WOMEN Robert Browning C136
THE PLAYS OF OSCAR WILDE Oscar Wilde C137
H. M. S. PINAFORE, AND SIX OTHER SAVOY OPERAS
    W. S. Gilbert C155
THE MIKADO, AND FIVE OTHER SAVOY OPERAS
    W. S. Gilbert C158
IDYLLS OF THE KING Alfred, Lord Tennyson C165
EIGHT DRAMAS OF CALDERON
    Edward FitzGerald, translator M C169
PLEASURE DOME Lloyd Frankenberg C190
SIBYLLINE LEAVES Samuel Taylor Coleridge M C195
SONNETS FROM THE PORTUGUESE AND OTHER POEMS
    Elizabeth Barrett Browning C209
A NONSENSE ANTHOLOGY Collected by Caroline Wells C224
NEW POEMS (1867) Matthew Arnold M C252

HISTORY AND BIOGRAPHY

THE BERNAL DIAZ CHRONICLES
    Albert Idell, editor and translator C25
OUR FRIEND JAMES JOYCE Mary and Padraic Colum C27
GIANTS OF GEOLOGY Carroll Lane and Mildred Adams Fenton C36
MR. LINCOLN'S ARMY Bruce Catton C37
BATTLES THAT CHANGED HISTORY Fletcher Pratt C38
TEACHER Helen Keller C39
THE LIFE OF CHARLOTTE BRONTE E. C. Gaskell M C48
COMMON SENSE and THE CRISIS Thomas Paine M C49
THE FOUR GEORGES William Makepeace Thackeray C54
TWO YEARS BEFORE THE MAST R. H. Dana C76
SEA FIGHTS AND SHIPWRECKS Hanson W. Baldwin C84
THE AUTOBIOGRAPHY OF BENJAMIN FRANKLIN M C87
LIVES OF THE POETS [Cowley to Prior] Samuel Johnson C91
LIVES OF THE POETS [Congreve to Gray] Samuel Johnson C92
THE MAN WHO KILLED LINCOLN Philip Van Doren Stern C101
LIFE OF NELSON Robert Southey C112
THE LIFE OF SIR ARTHUR CONAN DOYLE John Dickson Carr C117
TONGUE OF THE PROPHETS Robert St. John C118
AN AUTOBIOGRAPHY Anthony Trollope C128
AUTOBIOGRAPHY OF BENVENUTO CELLINI Benvenuto Cellini C129
THE PELOPONNESIAN WAR Thucydides C150
VENERABLE ANCESTOR Harry Hussey C157
BENT'S FORT David Lavender C159
BALBOA OF DARIEN Kathleen Romoli C162
THE CONQUEST OF PERU William H. Prescott C166
EXPERIMENT IN REBELLION Clifford Dowdey C171
THE AUTOBIOGRAPHY OF JOHN STUART MILL
    John Stuart Mill C179
BLACK MAJESTY John W. Vandercook C219

THE LONESOME ROAD Saunders Redding   C234
GLORY ROAD Bruce Catton   C236
REFLECTIONS ON THE REVOLUTION IN FRANCE and
    THE RIGHTS OF MAN Edmund Burke and Thomas Paine C246
BOUND FOR GLORY Woody Guthrie   C248
THIS I REMEMBER Eleanor Roosevelt   C263
THIS IS MY STORY Eleanor Roosevelt   C264
CRUSADE IN EUROPE Dwight D. Eisenhower   C267
PERIOD PIECE Gwen Raverat   C273
PIRATE: RASCALS OF THE SPANISH MAIN A. B. C. Whipple   C278
THE TRAMPLING HERD Paul I. Wellman   C287
FIVE YEARS IN THE WARSAW GHETTO Bernard Goldstein   C294

PHILOSOPHY AND RELIGION

WALDEN Henry David Thoreau   C10
THE REPUBLIC AND OTHER WORKS Plato   C12
THE LIFE OF JESUS Ernest Renan   C59
THE MEDITATIONS OF MARCUS AURELIUS
    Translated by George Long   C68
THE VARIETIES OF RELIGIOUS EXPERIENCE William James   C71
ON THE NATURE OF THINGS Lucretius
    Translated by H. A. J. Munro   C80
THE RATIONALISTS Descartes, Spinoza, Leibniz   C82
THE EMPIRICISTS Locke, Berkeley, Hume   C109
THE SECRET SAYINGS OF JESUS
    Robert M. Grant with David Noel Freedman   C163
THE THOUGHTS OF BLAISE PASCAL Blaise Pascal   C231
THE UTILITARIANS Jeremy Bentham and John Stuart Mill   C265
THE LIGHT OF ASIA: THE LIFE AND TEACHING OF
    GAUTAMA Edwin Arnold   C289
A TREATISE OF HUMAN NATURE David Hume   C305

ESSAYS AND LETTERS

THE CONDUCT OF LIFE Ralph Waldo Emerson M   C2
THE ESSAYS OF ELIA and THE LAST ESSAYS OF ELIA
    Charles Lamb M   C6
LECTURES ON THE ENGLISH COMIC WRITERS
    William Hazlitt M   C30
HAWTHORNE Henry James   C58
THE ESSAYS OF FRANCIS BACON   C67
THE SPIRIT OF THE AGE William Hazlitt   C79
ON HEROES AND HERO-WORSHIP and REPRESENTATIVE MEN
    Thomas Carlyle and Ralph Waldo Emerson   C83
LIFE IN MEXICO Frances Calderón de la Barca   C93
THE NATURAL HISTORY OF SELBORNE Gilbert White   C96
CONFESSIONS OF AN ENGLISH OPIUM-EATER and SUSPIRIA
    DE PROFUNDIS Thomas De Quincey M   C97
THE COMPLETE ANGLER Izaak Walton   C102
THE NEXT MILLION YEARS C. G. Darwin   C106
AN ALMANAC OF LIBERTY William O. Douglas   C115
LETTERS FROM AN AMERICAN FARMER
    J. H. St. John Crèvecoeur   C164
FABIAN ESSAYS IN SOCIALISM Edited by G. B. Shaw   C170
INTENTIONS AND OTHER WRITINGS Oscar Wilde   C249
THE BOOK OF SNOBS William Makepeace Thackeray   C268
MURDER FOR PROFIT William Bolitho   C302

MYSTERY

BLACK PLUMES Margery Allingham   C41
THE MAN IN THE GREEN HAT Manning Coles   C42
THE BELL IN THE FOG John Stephen Strange   C43
THE PEOPLE AGAINST O'HARA Eleazar Lipsky   C122
A STUDY IN SCARLET & THE SIGN OF FOUR
    Sir Arthur Conan Doyle   C124
ADVENTURES OF SHERLOCK HOLMES
    Sir Arthur Conan Doyle   C125
MEMOIRS OF SHERLOCK HOLMES Sir Arthur Conan Doyle   C126
THE HOUND OF THE BASKERVILLES
    Sir Arthur Conan Doyle   C127
POOR HARRIET Elizabeth Fenwick   C185
THE WHISPER IN THE GLOOM Nicholas Blake   C186
THE LADY AND HER DOCTOR Evelyn Piper   C187
A HERO FOR LEANDA Andrew Garve   C189
THE GOLDEN DEED Andrew Garve   C216
BLUE HARPSICHORD Francis Steegmuller   C217
THE BROKEN PENNY Julian Symons   C227
END OF CHAPTER Nicholas Blake   C228
BE SHOT FOR SIXPENCE Michael Gilbert   C229
BLOOD AND JUDGMENT Michael Gilbert   C230
MURDER THROUGH THE LOOKING GLASS Andrew Garve   C250
A CAPITOL OFFENSE Jocelyn Davey   C281
THE NAKED VILLANY Jocelyn Davey   C288
BOGUE'S FORTUNE Julian Symons   C290
GREEN HAZARD Manning Coles   C293
THE DEVIL'S OWN Peter Curtis   C301
THE WOMAN IN WHITE Wilkie Collins   C303
THE PAPER THUNDERBOLT Michael Innes   C306

MISCELLANEOUS

A HANDBOOK TO MARRIAGE Theodor Bovet   C23
SEX AND FAMILY IN THE BIBLE AND THE MIDDLE EAST
    Raphael Patai   C40
THE EXECUTIVE LIFE Editors of FORTUNE   C69
ZAPOTEC Helen Augur   C81
CONVERSATIONS WITH TOSCANINI B. H. Haggin   C85
AMERICAN WAYS OF LIFE George R. Stewart   C90
THE ABC OF CHILD CARE Allan Fromme, Ph.D.   C95
THE AGE OF FABLE Thomas Bulfinch   C132
THE LIFE AND DEATH OF CELLS Joseph G. Hoffman   C156
MARRIAGE EAST AND WEST David and Vera Mace   C161
THE ORIGIN OF SPECIES Charles Darwin   C172
PRIMITIVE PEOPLES TODAY Edward Weyer, Jr.   C200
A JOY OF GARDENING V. Sackville-West   C220
THE DEVIL'S DICTIONARY Ambrose Bierce   C225
SONGS OF WORK AND FREEDOM Edith Fowke and Joe Glazer   C240
THE ENGLISH CONSTITUTION Walter Bagehot   C241
THE CHANGING YEARS Madeline Gray   C242
HERBS AND THE EARTH Henry Beston   C271
THE NEXT DAY James A. Pike   C272
LOVE AND CONFLICT Gibson Winter   C279

DOLPHIN REFERENCE SERIES

POEMS TO REMEMBER John Kieran, editor C99
100 GREAT OPERAS AND THEIR STORIES Henry W. Simon C100
THE FAMILY HANDBOOK OF HOME NURSING AND MEDICAL
    CARE I. J. Rossman, M.D. and Doris R. Schwartz, R.N. C141
THE COMPLETE BOOK OF CHESS TACTICS Fred Reinfeld C143
THESAURUS OF ANECDOTES Edmund Fuller C191
POPULAR QUOTATIONS FOR ALL USES Lewis Copeland, editor C201

DOLPHIN HANDBOOK SERIES

THE FINE ART OF MIXING DRINKS David A. Embury C177
HOW TO SAY A FEW WORDS David Guy Powers C178
HOW TO BE A CONSISTENT WINNER IN THE MOST POPULAR
    CARD GAMES John R. Crawford C180
COOKING WITH A FRENCH TOUCH Gerald Maurois C184
BEER AND GOOD FOOD Myra Waldo C196
THE GOLD COOK BOOK Louis De Gouy C202
PATTERN WISE: HOW TO MAKE AND USE A BASIC PATTERN
    Adele P. Margolis C203
CREATIVE COOKING Nicholas Roosevelt C213
A NEW WAY TO BETTER ENGLISH Rudolf Flesch C214
IT'S EASY TO INCREASE YOUR VOCABULARY William Morris C215
A TRAVELER'S GUIDE TO GOOD HEALTH Colter Rule, M.D. C218
SALADS FOR THE GOURMET Gillian Sandlands C253
FOOD BECOMES YOU Ruth M. Leverton C266
OLD WORLD FOODS FOR NEW WORLD FAMILIES
    Lelia McGuire C280
AROUND THE WORLD IN EIGHTY DISHES Lesley Blanch C298